FRANK SINATRA

FRANK SINATRA

JOHN FRAYN TURNER

TAYLOR TRADE PUBLISHING
Dallas • Lanham • Boulder • New York • Toronto • Oxford

Published by Taylor Trade Publishing
An imprint of The Rowman & Littlefield Publishing Group, Inc.
4501 Forbes Boulevard, Suite 200
Lanham, MD 20706

Distributed by NATIONAL BOOK NETWORK

Library of Congress Cataloging-in-Publication Data

Turner, John Frayn.
    Frank Sinatra / John Frayn Turner.—1st Taylor Trade Pub. ed.
        p. cm.
    Includes index.
    ISBN 1-58979-145-2 (cloth : alk. paper)
    1. Sinatra, Frank, 1915– 2. Singers—United States—Biography. 3. Motion picture actors and actresses—United States—Biography. I. Title.

ML420. S565T87 2004

782.42164'092—dc22

To Joyce

CONTENTS

ACKNOWLEDGMENTS

W hether they are conscious of it or not, the following helped me with this book: Nancy Sinatra, Top Billing Ltd., Reprise Records, Warner Communications, the Sinatra Musical Society, the Frank Sinatra Discography, *The Stage Newspaper,* Theatregraphics, Benny Green, George T. Simon, Stan Cornyn, Ian Morley-Clarke, Peter Hepple, Mike Butcher, Lee J. Cobb, Hal Halverstadt, James Green, Frankie Valli, Nelson Riddle, Count Basie, Harold Davison, Frank Warren, and Jimmy Carter.

CHAPTER ONE

HOBOKEN, NANCY, AND
THE RUSTIC CABIN
1915-1939

The last time I saw Sinatra was in Dortmund on 31 May 1993. I was covering the concert for *The Stage Newspaper* (London). As far as I know, it was the last review in English of any Sinatra show in Europe. After that week, he never appeared again on the Continent. For this reason, I think it is worth quoting the review in full:

A morning on the Rhine, an afternoon in Cologne Cathedral, and an evening with Frank Sinatra at Dortmund. The perfect day? Well, nearly but not quite . . . for the 77 years are beginning to show. Yet the wonder must be that he is still singing at all.

Sinatra gave the first of his five-venue German concerts at the famous Westfalenhalle—followed by Hamburg, Berlin, Stuttgart and Cologne. At last the years are catching up with him—he cannot defy them forever. He had trouble with lyrics several times and the [mellifluousness] of the voice now reveals raw edges.

And yet, and yet. Having said all that, Sinatra is still supreme and subconsciously turns his very age to advantage with an audience. His whole life appears exposed for us to witness with poignancy. He is putting over a song with greater effect than at any time in his past half-century, and the fallibility of his age actually creates an empathy between audience and star, as singer, actor and man.

So the singer is now increasingly augmented, supplanted, by the actor. Perhaps the more profound numbers come across best—"For Once in My Life," "What Now My Love," "My Heart Stood Still," "Summer Wind."

Followed by those always associated with phases in his long career: "All or Nothing at All," "Strangers in the Night," "Mack the Knife." Plus the obligatory "New York, New York" and "My Way," which the Germans loved.

Despite the lyric lapses, he still found time to change lines on purpose, as in "A Foggy Day": "The British Museum it blew its charm . . ."

Conductor Frank Sinatra Jr. steered father and band through any audience-worrying patches to produce an evening memorable in a manner different from all previous performances I can recall. Sinatra is still marvelously moving, and it saddens me to say so—but soon he may have to stop. Meanwhile, the man and the legend live on.

The charismatic magic of Sinatra made him the entertainer supreme on any stage. What made the magic? It was an inner incandescence that could glow or blaze. He actually became each song he sang. He assembled his whole being and projected it to us complete. He articulated our aspirations and defined our emotions. Even in 1993 an incredible quality was there—the phrasing, timing, inflection, control, and sheer living spirit.

Sinatra synthesized the whole of humanity, its hopes, its hates. We recognized sides of ourselves that were hidden or unexplored. His whole emotional fiber lay forever exposed, exhausted, renewed. So no wonder we saw him in a mixture of moods. From sensitive to steel-hard. Comic to tragic. From tolerant to short tempered. Sociable yet lonely. Haughty and haunted. Unconventional yet well mannered. Fastidious and casual. Modest but brash. Polite or rude. Assured and restive. Faithful and flippant. And always generous—of himself and his wealth. Sinatra was a perfectionist. Creator of hundreds of records, of over fifty films, of thousands of personal appearances, doing what he did best: singing.

Throughout his life, he always remembered people. He never forgot that he was once one of those anonymous millions whose families formed part of the great American epic of immigration. People from older countries looking for fresh faith in a newer world. Many colors, creeds, and tongues, all with the same aim: a better life in a better land. The only thing they had in common was that they were all poor. Sinatra always sided with the poor and the victims of circumstance, discrimination, and racialism. And he used his power on their behalf.

Over in Europe, the former home of so many immigrants to the United States, World War I was in its eighth month when Frank Sinatra was conceived. America had not yet become actively involved in the war, which still seemed far off as Christmas 1915 approached. The more immediate problem for the immigrants living in Hoboken, New Jersey, was how to keep warm in that icy, snow-swept month.

Europeans from countries on both sides of the war were living alongside each other in the melting-pot congestion of Hoboken. Not that immigrants were anything new to the area. Eleven years before the Pilgrim fathers sailed from Plymouth, England, and landed at Plymouth, North America, the history of Hoboken began with a footing there by Henry Hudson in 1609. Hence the Hudson River running alongside Hoboken.

Then in 1630 the new Dutch discoverers bought the area from the American Indians living there at the time. It was the American Indian word *hobocan*, meaning "tobacco pipe," that gave the township its name. The town itself was planned much later, in the early nineteenth century, in fact—and it graduated to city status in 1855. The mass of close-built three- and four-story houses was the legacy of Hoboken's growth throughout that century.

Hoboken lies between Union City and Jersey City, on the waterfront near the mouth of the Hudson. It also stands right opposite downtown New York City, toward the Battery end of Manhattan Island. The main street of Hoboken runs north and south, roughly parallel to the Hudson. This long frontage to the river, coupled with its proximity to New York, meant that it was ideal for shipping on the rapidly burgeoning U.S. eastern seaboard.

Piers for ocean liners began to be built into the Hudson, and in those early days of the nineteenth century both European and South American steamship lines used it as their port for New York and for the eastern states. Inevitably, too, many of the variegated vessels carrying the European immigrants also berthed at Hoboken—and both this town and Jersey City found their popularity leaping. Indeed, because many boats landed there, Hoboken became one of the most crowded cities in America at that time, with all nationalities flocking into its small area of only 1.4 square miles.

Germans, Dutch, Russians, and Italians all settled in this cosmo-
politan, colorless place and went to work at equally drab factories
producing everything from foodstuffs to furniture. And against the
verbal cacophony of a half-dozen different languages came the continuing background of muffled hoots from the ferryboats chugging
across the water to New York or from the tugs towing in the liners
large and small.

That December 1915, though, the snow deadened the waterfront
and city sounds—and underlined by contrast the bleakness of the
brown-grey buildings. Many of these were split up into apartments.
It was on 12 December 1915 at Monroe Street, Hoboken, that Francis Albert Sinatra was born in an upstairs tenement room. His
mother, Natalie—known as Dolly—was barely five feet tall and
had a bad time delivering him. The baby had scars from the forceps
used by the doctor, and he nearly did not survive at all. The scars remained throughout his life, and the reason for the difficult delivery
may well have been his remarkable weight at birth of thirteen
pounds.

Both parents had immigrated to the United States from the same
Mediterranean region. Martin Sinatra came of Italian stock from
Sicily, while Dolly hailed from farther north at Genoa. Martin was
a shipyard worker, more particularly a boilermaker. Hoboken, of
course, was already well developed for docks and ship repair work,
while it was also becoming important as a railhead terminus. The
Delaware, Lackawanna, and Western Railroad ends there and the
city was also served by the freight lines of the Erie, Lehigh Valley,
Pennsylvania, and New York Central railroads.

Martin was having some trouble securing regular work in the
docks, but he began appearing also in a number of bantamweight
boxing bouts, where he became quite a local favorite. Throughout
these and their later years, however, Dolly was really the driving
power in the immediate Sinatra circle—and beyond it. A pleasant,
dark, dynamic woman, she loved the family but was perhaps even
keener on social and political work than on domesticity. With her
various external commitments, she sometimes left Frank to be
looked after by his grandmother.

By the spring of 1917, when Frank was beginning to walk, America entered the war. Martin was too old to enlist, so he continued his checkered career at the docks, working in a bar, boxing, and later working for the Hoboken Fire Department. This last job turned out to be the one that occupied him for most of his life.

Hoboken assumed an even busier appearance when it became the main embarkation port for the young idealistic doughboys of the American Expeditionary Force. On their way to join the troopships along the quays, they sang "Over There"—eager to be sailing and fighting. Or else they rendered "Alexander's Ragtime Band," one of the first hits by the bright young composer Irving Berlin. The world of popular music was changing. The whole world was changing.

All too soon, the doughboys were over there. Some came back. Others did not. The war was won, and Dolly Sinatra meant to play her personal part in winning the peace, too. The immigrants of Hoboken needed help from people like her if they were to secure their full rights and avoid being oppressed or exploited. She wanted to turn the American dream into a reality for all.

While she was busy at various meetings, Frank's grandmother Rose and an aunt used to take turns looking after him. And if he ever felt a lack of motherly attention at this period, he must have absorbed from Dolly that social conscience and sense of justice that influenced him so much throughout his later life.

From a curly-headed boy of two, he grew progressively more slowly, despite having been nearly twice normal weight at birth. And he gradually seemed to acquire that hollow look that remained with him at least into maturity. It almost became his hallmark. From Dolly he had inherited the genes resulting in penetrating ice-blue eyes and the wide-eyed look that stayed with him so appealingly.

By the 1920s, Dolly seemed to be in everything. She was an active committee member of the local branch of the Democratic Party. That was as radical as the United States got. And as well as politics, she sang at church socials, since she was a good Catholic, while also finding time to act as a midwife. Her ambitions for the family were reflected by helping her husband to get a good-paying job in the Hoboken Fire Department. Perhaps the most significant of all of Dolly's interests was singing. Maybe Frank got it partly from her. Frank started to grow up during the Roaring Twenties but was necessarily left alone by his parents for quite a bit of this time. He was quoted as describing this particular period as follows: "We kids had nobody to turn to but each other. All I knew were tough kids on street corners; gang fights; and parents who were too busy trying to make enough money for rent and clothes. We found a release for our loneliness and poverty in vicious gang wars. We started hooking candy from the corner store, then little things from the five-and-dime, then change from cash registers. Finally we were up to stealing bicycles."

This rather lurid memory may have been exaggerated a little as he recalled the vacant lots and the hostile Hoboken background. Or it may have been an early example of one of the many apparent paradoxes in his temperament. Contrast his memory with that of an old neighbor and friend of the family who knew him as a quiet boy who was good to his parents and who wore rather fussy clothes. He must have had a hard time from the other boys if his mother did dress him in rather goody-goody attire. Anyway, we know that Dolly did want him to grow up to be a gentleman.

Frank had the final word on that early era of boyish escapades: "I'm convinced I might have ended up in a life of crime if it hadn't been for my interest in music."

In 1928, Frank attended David E. Rue Junior High School, where he was recalled more for his interest in, and impersonations of, film and radio stars than for scholastic talent. The very first time that the topic of music crops up in the Sinatra story is when he went to A. J. Demarest High School, not far away. Here, he studied and also performed with the school band and glee club. This was probably his earliest taste of applause, though no mention could be recorded of any solos yet.

The idea of music was still embryonic in his mind. Occasionally, Sinatra would walk down to the waterfront just to look at the flow of life on the Hudson. Downstream a little, round to the right, and five miles out as the crow flies, he could just see the upper limbs of the Statue of Liberty, already fast becoming a symbol to the world of the kind of country America claimed to be—or aspired to become.

One evening he climbed up to Castle Point, a part of Hudson Park built on a rising rock framing and overlooking the whole busy riverside scene. From here he could survey everything—from Jersey City all the way south to the Palisades. Behind him, the sun had set, leaving in its wake a streaky pink trail touched with turquoise high over New Jersey. But it was always the view across the Hudson that took his breath and fired his wild young imagination.

New York.

What magic words, even then. The towering temples loomed away toward the East River. And as the day died, the city's great clustering columns winked alive with light: blurred blocks of amber against the blue night sky. Downtown Wall Street to the right; midtown Manhattan ahead and left. Just that brief ferryboat trip over the river and a different world unfolded. Paul Whiteman would be playing the latest jazz with his big band. But it might as well be an ocean or a world away just then. For Sinatra, New York was still a far-off dream, as yet less than half-formed in his mind. The reality was Demarest High.

Frank's grandmother Rose had died when he was about twelve. This loss had upset him a lot, as she had helped to bring him up as much as anyone. That was around 1928. The family had never made much money, but ironically when the Wall Street crash came in the following year, they were in fact becoming better off. So 1929 meant a move to a more pleasant neighborhood than the tenement-type street. By his fourteenth birthday, Sinatra's personality started slowly to develop and bloom. No hint yet of what might be in store for him—that one day he would be singing a song actually called "New York, New York."

He was still slim, even skinny, but he already had a degree of individualism. Dolly went on with her work in local affairs, but now that they had a little more money, she saw that Frank wore as many clothes as they could afford. After all, clothes were always an outward sign to the world at large—or at least the smaller environment of Hoboken. Frank himself was quite keen on dress even then and had a particular passion for sports coats, the transatlantic rage of the very early 1930s. He also seemed to have acquired that enduring love of hats, for he was to be seen frequently in an ample trilby.

Yet, despite his fancy for clothes, Frank was never soft. In the tough area of his preteen youth, he had to be able to defend himself against some of those other boys who really were inclined to be hooligans. And now that he was in his teens, he was ready for all comers. There is the story of the two police officers who stopped to ask him where his smart outfit had been bought. When Frank made some suitably antiauthoritarian retort, they went for him. He tried to resist but they lashed into him, beat him up, and ruined his clothes. From then on, he was said to have disliked the police force, but he may have mellowed later. Not that mellow was a word readily associated with Sinatra! Fighting and singing. The two scarcely seemed to go together, but to Sinatra there was nothing incongruous between them. Hoboken fostered the fighting, the Latin blood the singing. And after all, his father had done a sizable amount of prizefighting. The times that Sinatra had sung at Demarest High hatched a vague idea in him that this might be what he really wanted to do in life. The 1930s were to be the golden era of radio and he would gradually come to realize all the possibilities presented by this mass medium. And there were always the movies as a subconscious dream. Since the development of sound with movies, there had dawned the early years of the musical, with great composers commissioned to write for them.

Frank left Demarest High without completing his final year there by mutual consent between the school and himself. His parents were not exactly pleased and directed him to a term or two at the local Drake Business School. Even before he left Demarest High, however, he had been earning a little cash by helping on a local newspaper delivery van. And when he came to leave both schools, there was a clash of ideas about his future. The notion of becoming a singer had barely taken seed yet, but it was there enough for him to voice the concept to his parents. Dolly did not mind, but Martin insisted that he find a proper paid job. Singing seemed a wild idea to him.

Naturally, Frank thought of newspapers, since he had been delivering them. He had a mental image of possibly graduating to star sports reporter. The reality proved rather different. He got a job on the local *Jersey Observer,* becoming copy boy for both the city editor and the sports editor—rather grand titles for their respective posts. His bent was much more toward sport than finance. At that stage, he still had ideas of staying with the paper and trying for promotion to the reporting staff. The thought of covering sports events and getting paid for it sounded attractive to him. But during the 1932–1933 period, the appeal of journalism faded. He felt he was not going to stay with the paper just to run around for other people. Why should he, when he had a voice? So the idea was crystallizing at last.

When the family tried to talk to him about a real career, it was then that he broke the news seriously that he wanted to take up singing in a professional way. Frank had listened to those early 1930s hits of Bing Crosby on records and on the radio. He used to sing them more and more, both in the quiet privacy of his own room and elsewhere about the house. Dolly had said at first, "Why don't you want to be something nice—like a doctor or an engineer?" But from the moment that she realized he was serious and could not be swayed, she started to do everything she could to try to help him. After all, he was her only child and if that was really what he had set his heart on, she couldn't change his mind. She knew him well enough for that.

So at this stage (around 1932–1933) Frank was still trying to earn money at odd jobs found by himself or through relations. But as well as these, he was veering increasingly toward music. He was also growing into a darkly good-looking lad, with his main characteristic being those three-dimensional blue eyes and an engaging smile. His voice remained an utterly unknown quantity—and quality—but he quietly became more determined to break into the world of music. All he had as yet was a passionate feeling that he could do it, for he certainly didn't have any musical training.

But at least he knew now what he wanted—that was the key thing. Journalism had been stillborn. It was going to take years of guts to get across the Hudson to the bright lights. That gap of the river could seem to symbolize the struggle ahead. As yet, the future remained unknown. He had no illusions about it. But he was young, with the perennial optimism of youth.

Frank picked up tips from the Crosby numbers being released on record: songs like "Please" and "Thanks." Dolly set about trying to get him dates for work. And both Dolly and his two uncles encouraged him with such practical help as providing him with the sort of clothes he would need to make any public appearances. All that remained to be found were the actual dates.

Dolly threw all the energy she usually reserved for more public affairs into trying to get Frank started somewhere. She toured and scoured the district, calling on all the local Italians who had restaurants or clubs. And counting on her fellow countrymen's love of music at most times, she suggested to one after another that they give Frank a break. Long experience had instilled in her some strong powers of persuasion, but there was nothing so special about a seventeen-year-old boy wanting to sing—especially as he came from Italian and Sicilian parents. It would be more surprising if he had not been inclined toward it. And Italians were understandably reluctant to consider paying someone to do what was to them such a perfectly natural activity. Frank, of course, was trying his hardest, too. One of his other vocal idols was Billie Holliday. He learned much from listening to records by both Crosby and Holliday.

Franklin D. Roosevelt took office as president of the United States in 1933, with the full approval of the whole Sinatra family. Something had to be done if the slump sparked off by the Wall Street crash was to be reversed. Yet, despite the mixed conditions prevailing throughout the country as a whole, Frank started to get the odd engagement, with the emphasis on odd. But he had begun. At this stage, he was using a megaphone to amplify his voice with the little groups accompanying him. Then he invested in a fairly primitive portable sound system and some sheet music.

The dates started to come, always after any daytime work at the time. No matter, he could claim to have started his singing career. Around 1933–1934, Frank first appeared at the local Hoboken club called the Azov with Matty Golizio accompanying him on the guitar. Both boys were of the same age and both felt that they were on the verge of a fortune. But they weren't—although this did prove to be the beginning of several years' association professionally on and off. Meanwhile, if Frank wanted to sing for a living, he had to take anything offered him—meager as it might be. He could not pick and choose. This might mean handling the vocals at beer parties or rundown roadhouses. The price of admission to the beer parties was in the region of less than fifty cents, so Frank's pay remained proportionately small and sometimes nonexistent. But it was all experience. At that phase, this must have ranked as much more valuable than money.

The great thing was that Frank sang. And right from the outset he refused to compromise over his choice of numbers. He stuck to the standards of the 1920s or to the newer classics being written every year by the phenomenal crop of composers in the 1930s: Cole Porter, Irving Berlin, George Gershwin, Jerome Kern, Richard Rodgers, and Lorenz Hart. What a collection. He was lucky to be growing up amid such a choice of writers, and he was wise and mature enough to take advantage of what they offered. Always he had an uncanny knack of choosing the best songs and imprinting them indelibly with his personally definitive version.

Dolly persevered on his behalf. Sometimes it meant just a one-nighter for the Hoboken Sicilian Cultural League. But then she might persuade a friend of hers, Joseph Sampers, to let Frank sing at the Union Club also in Hoboken. This turned out to be quite a long spell, by his recent experience, lasting between one and two months. But it came to an end when mother and son Sinatra tried to get Sampers to invest in a "radio wire." This would have meant that broadcasting companies could have relayed from the Union Club on the air, but Sampers felt such a scheme to be beyond him. After all, he explained to them, he only had a small club. The question of "the wire" proved to be a stumbling block more than once around this time. Restaurateurs could or would rarely bring themselves to risk so much money in return for the gamble of possible fees from radio plus the less tangible value of publicity accruing as a result of broadcasts.

But both Dolly and Frank were stagestruck by the radio. If she could not help him to get on it yet, she had assisted in providing the precious equipment he needed: the microphone and amplifier sound system, which he carried around in a rhinestone case especially made for the purpose.

It was nearing the mid-1930s that things eventually started to happen for Frank. In the summers of 1934 and 1935, Frank first got to know Nancy Rose Barbato, a dark and hauntingly lovely Italian girl. By 1935 he was in his twentieth year, while she was barely seventeen. Frank was on a vacation at an aunt's beach house down the New Jersey coast when Nancy really began to notice him. She heard him, too, humming a tune to a ukulele he took around with him. From then on, they were with each other all the time, or whenever he was not away on singing dates. Nancy counted as his first serious girlfriend.

Years later, one of his great numbers was "At Long Last Love." They were quite near the popular New Jersey Atlantic resort of Asbury Park during those summers at the beach house. Doubtless it seemed more like Granada, as the song suggested. On one memorable summer evening, the two of them went to see and hear Bing Crosby singing in Jersey City. If Sinatra had not already set his heart on singing, he certainly did thereafter.

It was about 1935 when Sinatra first met Hank Sanicola, who worked as a song plugger and played the piano in his spare time. The friendship would last for many years, for Sinatra was always loyal to trusted companions. Whenever he could, Sanicola arranged for Sinatra to sing at some one-night stand or a longer date around the state of New Jersey. Sinatra was still on the wrong side of the river, the wrong side of the tracks, but he was beginning to inspire faith in friends. They could glimpse his potential. Moody though he was sometimes, he burned with intensity, too.

Then occasionally one of the local clubs would give him a spell singing solos with their particular little group of three, four, or five musicians. Often, Sinatra found himself doubling as a waiter as well as singer. At least he never had to sing while actually serving, but changed his jacket before stepping up to his own portable microphone outfit. His pay for these two-in-one jobs amounted to precisely $15 a week.

That first break into radio came at last. It had to, really. It was all a matter of time and timing. Three local lads performed under the name of the Three Flashes. Frank made a specialty of collecting musical arrangements and renting the four of them to schools and club bands, with himself as the featured singer for a small additional fee. The quartet was wondering how they would get on, when one of them suddenly said, "I know—let's try the Major Bowes Amateur Night. We can't lose anything."

September 1935 was the date of destiny, when they auditioned to go on *Major Bowes and His Original Amateur Hour*, as it was known in full. They were accepted just as they had auditioned, as a trio and a solo singer. Major Bowes had the idea of linking them as a single act, and the Hoboken Four was born. On the air at New York's Capitol Theater, they sang "Shine" and Sinatra sang "Night and Day." This Cole Porter classic was rendered by him hundreds of times after that, yet on each occasion it was as if he had just discovered its magic. The following month, Sinatra and the other three took part in two short films for Major Bowes and these were actually shown, albeit only for a few days, at Radio City Music Hall.

Part of the prize for winning in the radio show—which they did—was a Bowes Vaudeville tour right across America to the coast of California—on real live stages. It was Sinatra's first taste of being on the road. Two recent Jerome Kern numbers were added to the act, both from films made by Fred Astaire and Ginger Rogers. The songs were "The Way You Look Tonight" and "A Fine Romance," both classics to this day—two-thirds of a century later. All this proved incredibly valuable experience for Sinatra, but exhausting physically and financially. Although they did appear in Los Angeles and San Francisco, their performances were in smaller towns on the whole. Sinatra arrived home three months later as broke as at the start.

At least he had broken the ice into the magic realm of radio, even if it was only an amateur hour. Nor was his next radio break exactly earth shattering. By offering his services for free, he got a spot on the local Jersey City radio station, once more with Golizio on guitar. Sinatra put over popular songs with a certain tentative style somewhere between reticence and assurance. Yet, all the while he was striving to improve and he did gain confidence. This went on weekly for some time, developing into programs in Jersey City, Newark, and even New York itself. The programs remained only minor ones, though, and he was still a way from the Columbia Broadcasting System or the National Broadcasting Corporation— the famous CBS and NBC networks. All he got in return for these radio appearances was about a dollar a week toward his fares! Regardless, it was a change from singing at weddings, political meetings, and Union Club dances.

So the local radio station grind went on, as many as eighteen times a week. The ferry fare from Hoboken to Manhattan cost four or five cents, but that was still all Sinatra received for his efforts. The publicity was priceless, however, and Sinatra actually trod the legendary sidewalks of Tin Pan Alley. His twenty-first birthday on 12 December 1936 came and went. He was a man and was finding that the streets of New York were not exactly paved with gold or even dollars. Later, he recalled that spell of his life, "I sang my heart out nearly twenty times a week. Nancy always encouraged me, listening to all my dreams."

In 1938, Frank was very close to Nancy and one day while they were listening to Crosby on a record, he told her, "I'm going to sing like that." During the spring, Frank had his mother, Sanicola, Golizio, and Nancy all encouraging him—as well as other friends who had recognized his promise. Sanicola took over his business affairs, such as they were, and then the next minor break arrived. Not the big break yet, but that had to come, thought Sinatra.

He was planning to ask Nancy to marry him, so he wanted some steady work and pay. Harry Schuchman, a friend of his, had heard that a roadhouse called the Rustic Cabin was looking for a singing master of ceremonies who could double as a head waiter. Sinatra had had dates at a number of other roadhouse-type clubs, but the Rustic Cabin was known to be a classier club than any he had yet encountered. It lay on Route 9W, near both Alpine and Englewood, New Jersey. The pay hardly seemed lavish at $15 a week, but it was more than he had been used to on a regular basis. Whether the money came from management or tips seems open to question, probably partly from each. Sinatra's duties went on nonstop, comprising ushering customers to their tables; acting as vocalist with the resident band, which included Schuchman on the saxophone; and actually singing between band numbers with accompaniment from a mobile piano! Sinatra sustained this grueling routine throughout the summer and into the autumn of the Munich crisis in Europe. He loved every evening he was there. Adolf Hitler seemed a long way off as Frank and Nancy became engaged.

He was still earning the same modest amount on his twenty-third birthday and also when they were married on 4 February 1939 at Our Lady of Sorrows Church in Jersey City. The private record that Frank made and gave to Nancy as a wedding present was called *Our Love*. This symbolic title and lyrics were set to the haunting theme from the Tchaikovsky Fantasy Overture to *Romeo and Juliet*. It was music that I heard for the first time about then—in both its forms. After their honeymoon, Frank and Nancy lived in a three-room apartment at Number 12, Audubon Avenue in Jersey City. Frank got a raise from $15 to $25 after the marriage, while Nancy helped with the cash by continuing to work as a shorthand typist. Frank owed a lot to her support in these crucial formative years. She was always there to exhort him as a loyal wife.

The Rustic Cabin looked an inviting and welcoming little roadhouse on the outskirts of the built-up area. With the gradual return of comparative prosperity to the country, quite a lot of people regularly drove the short way out there for an evening meal on those spring nights of 1939. Part of the attraction was undoubtedly the music, Sinatra's vocals, and the chance to dance to some of the current radio hits.

This was virtually a high-water mark for dance bands, both in Britain and America. Certainly a peacetime zenith before the war storm broke. Just to recall the names of these bands evokes an era never to return—unfortunately. Among the British bands of the 1930s: Ambrose, Geraldo, Henry Hall, Harry Roy, Jack Jackson, Joe Loss, Roy Fox, Oscar Rabin, Carroll Gibbons, Maurice Winnick, Jack Payne, Lew Stone, Victor Silvester, and Nat Gonella. And over in the States, of course, the list is legendary and astounding. There were the two Dorsey bands, under Tommy and Jimmy.

Added to these Artie Shaw and his dazzling clarinet; Benny Goodman's, too; Glenn Miller was coming into prominence; plus Ray
Noble, Harry James, and those two jazz giants, Duke Ellington and
Count Basie. Artie Shaw's "Begin the Beguine" is still played regularly today.

Generally speaking, vocalists were still just singers and not stars.
Crosby was an exception. The pattern was usually for the big band
to have a couple of good singers, perhaps a man and a woman. They
sat on the stage looking rather superfluous until the chorus came
along—when they would sidle up to the unwieldy microphone, deliver their lines, and return to their seats again.

As an example of a star in embryo in this era, Sinatra had already
sung with the unknown Dinah Shore, later to become the American
forces' sweetheart during World War II. The standard being set by
these vocalists was high and some like Sinatra and Shore became
stars in due course. But even as band vocalists they were a remarkable crop. For instance, Tony Martin sang with the Ray Noble Band,
Bob Eberle with Jimmy Dorsey, and Jack Leonard with Tommy
Dorsey. I always used to like Ray Eberle as well as Bob. Ray, of
course, sang with Glenn Miller in their absolute heyday.

So it was in this setting of strong competition that Sinatra aimed
to make headway. It was a challenge he met unconsciously every
day he sang. A singer or an actor—or anyone else for that matter—
has to gauge how long to stay in any one place or job. He or she cannot control fate, but it is no use hiding lights forever in some small
corner, expecting one day inevitably to be discovered. On the other
hand, if someone has talent like Sinatra possessed, you could safely
bet that sooner or later it was bound to be recognized. But the stages
toward this happening remain interesting—possibly the most absorbing of all in the development of a career.

Frank had been at the Rustic Cabin for the best part of a year. He
and Nancy were both idyllically happy through these first few
months of their marriage. Yet, soon he would feel impelled to try
something bigger and better. A singing head waiter was hardly the
extent of his ambition. Already the girls used to come to the Rustic
Cabin specifically to see and hear him. And already his sights were
shifting toward wider horizons.

While Sinatra was thinking of linking up with a band under Bob Chester, who played at the roadhouse some of the time, something happened that changed his life forever. He and Nancy heard that the trumpeter Harry James had recently left Benny Goodman and was planning to branch out with his own group. With Nancy's financial help, Frank had some publicity photos taken to deliver to James, offering himself as a vocalist. The timing was perfect. James had actually borrowed $4,500 from Goodman in return for the latter having one-third interest in the new band. James was not finding things all roses, though, even to base a band on his brilliant trumpet. At this particular time, he happened to be in New York with his wife, Louise, a vocalist herself with a baby face.

James knew that he needed more than just good arrangements and a golden trumpet. He wanted to find the variety of a good male singer. While working in New York, Harry and Louise were listening to a local broadcast while relaxing in their hotel room. Louise knew Harry needed a male singer.

"Harry, come and listen to this boy sing," she called.

What they heard was Sinatra on the radio from the Rustic Cabin. They looked at each other. James had already seen the photos from Sinatra. So as it transpired, Sinatra did not have to make the next move in his singing career. It was done for him. On the very next evening, as May was yielding to the longer eastern seaboard evenings, someone special dropped into the Rustic Cabin. This was always how it happened in fiction, but now it was fact. Real life in late May 1939.

Of course, the someone special was Harry James. And, of course, he was not there by mere chance. James was present in person to see if Sinatra would be the kind of singer to create the right kind of contrast to the swing played by his band in many of its orchestral numbers. Contrast and balance, these were the keys to a successful group. James sat quietly, unannounced, at a table listening to Sinatra singing in the flesh—always a more informing dimension than on record, radio, or television. Sinatra had not been getting anything extra for the daily radio relays on three New York stations, but the publicity had finally paid off.

Sinatra happened to sing the Cole Porter classic "Begin the Beguine." This is perhaps the most popular song ever written and proved a fortuitous chance. The voice was pure if thinner than later. But its quality of youth and musical style were undeniable even then.

James liked what he heard and saw. On the spot he offered Sinatra the job of vocalist with the new band, which was already on the road. So there and then at the Rustic Cabin the modest Sinatra salary of $25 a week became trebled to $75 a week. He could hardly wait to get home that night after the show to break the news to Nancy. The extra $50 a week seemed a small fortune after the years of scrimping to keep fed, clothed, and fit for the role of popular-singer-to-be. Now it looked like the scrimping had been worth it. This was his first big break. The Harry James Band was still comparatively obscure and Sinatra was still largely an unknown quantity, but they were both young, in America, and on their way.

CHAPTER TWO

POISED FOR STARDOM

1939-1942

In June 1939, at twenty-three-and-a-half years old, Frank Sinatra joined the Harry James Band in Baltimore. That was the great thing about the eastern states: so many cities within reasonable reach. Then he made the symbolic step of crossing the Hudson into New York itself, more specifically for an engagement that the band had at the Roseland Ballroom.

After a matter of mere weeks with Harry James, Frank made his very first record on the historic date of 13 July 1939. The setting was Columbia's New York gramophone studios. During this halcyon summer season, Sinatra was still frail-looking, though he had been known to sport a pipe in the manner of Bing Crosby. And with the pipe in the left-hand corner of his mouth, the inevitable trilby was tilted slightly backward. Slight as he might have been in build, the burning blue eyes and sudden shy-seeming smile concealed a man determined to succeed, by his own talents plus extreme effort. His hollow, slightly haunted face was balanced by high cheekbones. This was Sinatra in 1939, poised for stardom, with a floppy paisley bow tie or a large loose conventional one, a watch on his left wrist, a ring on the little finger of his left hand, and usually dressed in a single-breasted suit, though sometimes a double when actually singing.

The two titles recorded at the now historic session were "From the Bottom of My Heart" and "Melancholy Mood." No catalogue number is available for the latter song nor can any be traced for two other pairs of songs recorded later that same year: "My Buddy" and "It's Funny to Everyone but Me," and "On a Little Street in Singapore" and "Who Told You I Cared?" Jimmy Dorsey recorded the Singapore number very successfully with Bob Eberle on the vocal, possibly accounting for the absence of the James-Sinatra version from the files.

"From the Bottom of My Heart" was actually issued with the ballad "Here Comes the Night," while the other pair released at this time was "All or Nothing at All" and a special trumpet-cum-vocal version of the classic "Ciribiribin." Most people familiar with the Sinatra life also know the ironic fate of this recording of "All or Nothing at All." The facts will emerge a little later in the story. Incidentally, the *Frank Sinatra Discography* and Nancy Sinatra junior both give the date of that session as 31 August 1939, whereas Fontana Records dates it as 17 September. It doesn't matter that much, except that between these two dates Germany invaded Poland and World War II began.

What was Frank really like in those first, far-off months with Harry James? Although he had not yet developed a voice immediately recognizable as his own, he already possessed a certain style. Perhaps not as polished as it would become, but with the hint of real quality in store. The famous version of "All or Nothing at All" was surely his record and not James's. It contained a trumpet solo but was obviously made as a vocal vehicle for Sinatra with the orchestra very much in accompaniment. He was singing practically throughout its running time and his enunciation shone through at once. Even then it was virtually flawless. Every word came across audibly in an unhurried, distinct style.

Already, too, his voice revealed the real sincerity and conviction that characterized it ever afterward. As well as meaning every syllable, he had developed the instinctive knack of near-perfect phrasing—and stressing the significant word or words in any given lyric line, however good or bad the song. Throughout the record, Sinatra created the right mood, which was matched by a nostalgic saxophone backing. Right to that final word he brought off just what he intended. It was quite a phenomenal effort for a young singer. The song became the first one of his actually issued for sale, but it made no more than a ripple in the mainstream of music.

That fall, the band moved to the West Coast, but its members were having a tough time making ends meet. For the record books, however, 8 November marked a significant date as the session in the Los Angeles studios of Columbia Records. The two titles were "Ciribiribin" and "Every Day of My Life." Nancy went with Frank to California, and like the rest of the band they were getting extremely short of money. The band was on the move most of the time, desperately booking dates. By the end of the year, they were all back east again. Then came the next momentous stage in the story.

After four or five years with the Tommy Dorsey Band, their male vocalist, Jack Leonard, told Dorsey of his intention to leave. Dorsey started the search for a worthy replacement. It was around the turn of the year when he came to hear Sinatra for the first time. Just as Harry James had done, Dorsey offered him a job at once. The Sinatra magic was working.

"How much are you getting with James?" Dorsey asked him.

When Sinatra told him, the bespectacled bandleader immediately blurted out, "I'll double it."

So in one night Sinatra jumped from a promising $75-a-week vocalist into the $150 range. That was ten times what he had been earning at the Rustic Cabin a comparatively short while before. The Harry James contract had been for a year, but the trumpeter was not the sort of man to stand in someone's way: he let Sinatra go, waiving the outstanding five months or so. "No strings," he told Sinatra. Sinatra left the Harry James Band one night in the depths of that freezing winter and actually felt pretty bad about it. But James bore him no grudge, no hard feelings, and twenty-eight years later they appeared together at a Las Vegas reunion show. Sinatra had been slowly working his way up for seven years from those earliest Hoboken and district dates—now he was on the verge of undreamt-of glories.

It should be remembered that to be with Tommy Dorsey in January 1940 meant to live alongside such instrumentalists as Ziggy Elman, trumpet; Joe Bushkin, piano; Buddy Rich, drums; and, of course, the velvet-toned trombone of Dorsey himself. And although it seemed strange for Sinatra to be singing with the Dorsey orchestra, from his very opening appearance the applause began to hit him over the footlights. Not yet quite overwhelming, but enthusiastic enough to be encouraging for a newcomer with the band. He actually joined the Dorsey outfit while it was on tour during that notoriously wintry weather. Sinatra took the train from New York to Chicago and on to Rockford in late January.

The Tommy Dorsey Band was a big name already—that meant quite a difference from the Harry James set-up. The Dorsey vocal group singing with the band was known as The Pied Pipers, three men and one woman. Jo Stafford was the woman who led them, yet another starry name from this era. Sinatra joined them on specific numbers, too, but right from the start Dorsey had realized Sinatra's potential appeal and gave him solo vocals whenever he could.

As early as 1 February 1940, only a week after Sinatra had joined the band, he recorded his first songs with Dorsey: "The Sky Fell Down" and "Too Romantic." The latter tune came from a current Bing Crosby film and marked the start of the long, friendly battle between the acknowledged "king of the crooners" and this new upstart. By singing Crosby songs, Sinatra was actually inviting comparisons. Later that year followed other Crosby hits recorded by the Dorsey-Sinatra combination: "April Played the Fiddle," "I Haven't Time to Be a Millionaire," "East of the Sun," and "Trade Winds."

Fortunately, Sinatra was already used to the hard grind of being on the road. Sometimes the engagements were one-nighters, a week in Indianapolis, or a four-week debut at the Paramount Theater in New York. Sinatra was still being billed halfway down the program, alongside Buddy Rich and The Pied Pipers, but this could be called the start of the big time. It would get bigger.

After only two or three months, Sinatra was profiting immeasurably from the experience of studying and singing with the fastidious Dorsey. Sinatra had already acquired the art of breath control: how to hold a note for a long time and how to move from one to another with no apparent break for breath. Now he was beginning to realize some of the undreamt-of possibilities open to his voice. If Dorsey could slide up and down the scale on his trombone, why shouldn't Sinatra be able to do the same with his vocal cords? After all, Dorsey's notes emanated first from his larynx. They didn't just materialize in that smooth-sounding trombone that caught and reflected the spotlights on stages from Milwaukee to San Francisco.

It was a slow and tiring business, yet exhilarating at the same time. Sinatra was soon established as an integral part of the Dorsey outfit. He had proved himself a worthy successor to Jack Leonard, even though some of the band had been suspicious of his abilities at first. They were all on stage for six or seven hours a day and Sinatra sang dozens and dozens of songs during that phase: songs he had to learn and know by heart. Multiply the days into weeks and months, and it is clear that he got through several thousand numbers a year. Before he had finished this famous and formative era with Tommy Dorsey, he had recorded over a hundred numbers with the band.

During their first year together, Dorsey told Sinatra, "There's only one singer you might listen to—Bing Crosby." At that stage, no one yet realized that another popular singer might emerge as good as Crosby—or better. Sinatra kept at it all day, every day. He made it his life to get better and then better still. He sang more slowly, more softly, and with more heart than anyone had tried to do before him. Only by his breath control could he maintain the notes and the flow—and phrasing and rhythm. And all the time, too, he went on concentrating on Dorsey the instrumentalist. Sinatra said, "I figured if he could do that sliding phrasing with his horn, I could do it with my voice. I bend my notes, gliding from one to another without abrupt breaks—just like a trombone."

It was not often that Sinatra spoke about his technique, but this was certainly one of his many trademarks. And all the time, he knew that Dorsey felt truly sympathetic toward his singing: always a reassuring thought for him. The following vivid cameo by George T. Simon gives as good an impression as possible of Dorsey, bandleader, and Sinatra, singer, working together: "Anyone who remembers Tommy Dorsey—and of course that includes Frank Sinatra—remembers one of the most talented, one of the most dynamic, one of the most colourful, and one of the most unpredictable men the music world, or any other world, has ever known."

As so many of us did, Sinatra obviously recognized and appreciated Dorsey's great talent. Consequently, it had quite an effect on
him. Sinatra was already a good singer when he joined the Dorsey
band in January 1940. He'd been making great strides with the
Harry James Band. But though he wasn't a bashful boy—Sinatra
was never bashful, so far as any of us ever knew—he was in a sense
a retiring sort of singer. His phrasing was always impeccable, always full of music, but if you listen to some of the early sides he cut
with James, you'll notice an uneasy tentativeness like a young boy
out on a date who isn't quite sure of what he's supposed to do.

Dorsey helped change all that, not so much by instruction as by example. If you had any sort of ear—and Sinatra had always had an
amazingly good one—you'd have to notice and admire the way
Dorsey blew a melody line. His breath control was fantastic. What's
more, he also had an uncanny musical sense, a way of both drawing
out and drawing from a melody, of tying phrases together in the
smoothest sort of way. Largely because of Dorsey, Sinatra learned to
phrase and to breathe more surely and more smoothly, as did Jo
Stafford and the other singers whom Dorsey had strongly influenced.

Dorsey affected Sinatra in other ways. Call it osmosis or whatever you like, but much of the sentimental-gentleman-of-swing's
sometimes gentlemanly and at times maybe a little less gentlemanly
personality infiltrated Sinatra's. For one thing, Dorsey was a fire-
brand who would take no guff from anybody. In those days, so was
Sinatra, and when you're as young as he was at that point, all you
need to strengthen your own convictions and actions is to be around
an even more dynamic and successful boss who's doing just what
you've always wanted to do.

Sinatra was admired and well liked, not only by the thousands of
fans who were constantly swarming around the bandstand, but also
by the many talented musicians within the band. He would never
stand for any musical malarkey and, like Dorsey, he backed up his
strong musical convictions with equally strong musical action.

When Sinatra decided to leave Dorsey, he showed no lack of confidence at all. Those of us who had known him all along never expected anything else.

For just as Sinatra spread himself into all phases of his business, so did Dorsey twenty years before. No doubt about it, Dorsey was a dynamic, colorful, and controversial man. As Sy Oliver, whom Dorsey hired six months before Sinatra joined the band and who scored many of its biggest hits, points out, "Tommy was like ripe olives. You either liked him a great deal or not at all. In many ways, Sinatra has just as definite a personality. I love them both. I'll tell you this: they're two of the few people who hired me who didn't tell me what to do." Few top managers bestow such praise. "Something else about the two of them," Oliver concludes, "both of them have always known exactly what they were doing and what they wanted."

Certainly as 1940 wore into the summer the two were seen more and more at the front of the traveling bandstand, wherever it might be, Sinatra with one hand clinging to the slender stand of the microphone; Dorsey with his trombone in one hand and his free one timing a downbeat for the band to round off one of Sinatra's songs.

Perhaps the paradox of Sinatra was already emerging. So he was never the bashful boy. We have established that. Yet, in these still early days of his blooming career, he certainly conveyed a sincere modesty, even self-effacement. This could be accounted for partly by his being still just slightly unsure at twenty-four—a romantic age—and the fact that he was singing straight love songs on the whole. Ballads, they were often called. Naturally, he had to possess a large measure of self-confidence to perform at all, plus the stamina and grit to have sweated and sung around all those admittedly dreary New Jersey dives. This did not diminish the overall effect of transparent honesty and integrity in every number he approached—indeed it increased it.

With the band touring all over the States, Frank and Nancy did not see much of each other during the first hectic months of 1940. Their first child, Nancy Sandra, was born on 8 June at Margaret Hague Hospital, Jersey City. Sinatra and the band were actually in Hollywood at the time. Over in Europe, Britain had just survived the epic evacuation from Dunkirk, so as yet it knew nothing at all of the blossoming young singer. America seemed like another planet to British people. I was mad about Deanna Durbin about then and somehow received a letter from her. California could have been in the Andromeda system instead of just 6,000 miles distant.

Meanwhile, the Tommy Dorsey Band members spent most of their short-term lives on one-nighters, hustling into one of the monster Greyhound coaches to be driven through the night to their next stop. If they were very lucky, they got to a hotel for a day or even two, but often they had to sleep on the road.

Many of the appearances were broadcast, and the name of Frank Sinatra began to be known to the younger generation who danced to the Tommy Dorsey music or merely listened to it over the radio. This was the new post-Depression generation who either studied on campuses or worked in drugstores or offices. But many of them now had cars of their own and enjoyed the new-found freedom of boy-and-girl relationships in America in the summer of 1940.

By the beginning of June, when Nancy was busy having her first daughter, the outfit had somehow managed to squeeze in ten recording sessions as well as all the traveling dates. The eventual tally of Sinatra recordings with the Tommy Dorsey Band topped a hundred in the two and a half years or more they were together, so these sessions were just the early ones. It was all exhausting, to be sure, but the endless excitement generated their energy for it. Sinatra loved the life. Who wouldn't? It was what he had dreamed of through the 1930s. The great thing about being with a big national-name band was that it automatically had a huge following that snowballed from the past years—the golden 1930s, a ready-made mature audience, plus a younger one growing up.

Records meant jukeboxes, that all-American phenomenon that had spread like prairie fire from the Atlantic to the Pacific, along with soda fountains and freedom. The youngsters collected the records and played the very latest releases as they toyed with their ice-cream sodas and made dates. Everything seemed set fair for Sinatra. Even the songs continued to be special. Apart from the vintage Cole Porter/Jerome Kern/George Gershwin/Irving Berlin, the new tunes had an extra quality of romantic innocence. He could hardly miss with such songs as "Shake Down the Stars," "I'll Be

Seeing You," "Imagination," "Fools Rush In," and "It's a Lovely Day Tomorrow."

On 23 April 1940, he cut "I'll Never Smile Again" with Dorsey and The Pied Pipers. For some reason the record was not issued, but exactly a month to the day later, they did it again, released it, and it sold a million copies before the summer was out. That meant more money from extra fees from record-sale royalties and radio appearances. Throughout that fateful summer, the band was mainly on the East Coast, broadcasting regularly from NBC in New York. As the Battle of Britain was being decided in the skies over southern England, the American airwaves carried more and more music by Sinatra. "Our Love Affair," "I'd Know You Anywhere," "Stardust," and "Oh Look at Me Now."

He recorded this last tune nearly sixteen years later for the longplay (LP) record *A Swingin' Affair,* but the original version sounded just as good. The song was actually written by Joe Bushkin, Dorsey's pianist, and this is how jazz critic Benny Green described the record: "Sinatra's voice production and sense of phrasing on that record are models of their kind. For one so young, it is a performance of astonishing poise and maturity, tuneful, melodious, respectful of the writer's intent, and laced with the hints of an impish humour which we know today is part of his temperament."

Despite the lighter touch, the direct romantic approach to the love songs of the day was the familiar formula for 1940–1941. Sinatra was still mastering techniques and it probably had not occurred to him consciously that there were many ways a song could be presented. Twenty years or so later he knew it well, when he lived these wonderful Tommy Dorsey Band days all over again on the LP *I Remember Tommy.*

During the fall of 1940, the Battle of Britain was won. October was busy for both the band and Sinatra. It marked the start of a six-month NBC radio show from New York. The difference about this particular format was that the theme was really a talent program for amateur composers. Sinatra had to assimilate new songs every week. And in the same month they all somehow found time to make a film, which was released the following year. Add to that the Sinatra/Pied Pipers/Dorsey recording of "I'll Never Smile Again" hit the top of the American charts. I suppose that the record was also the first time I remember hearing Sinatra sing, in late 1940.

The Christmas season proved far from restful for any of them. It meant a four-week return run at New York's Paramount Theater, and with impeccable commercial timing they released the record *Without a Song* the week after the show closed. Roosevelt was inaugurated for a third term and Sinatra went wild with joy. Soon, he was destined to come in yet closer touch with the U.S. president than just as a supporter of the Democrats and the people they stood for. Sinatra had not forgotten those multiracial immigrants. How could he? He was the product of two of them.

In early 1941, Sinatra was still absorbing from Dorsey, not only instinctively improving and honing his singing by being with such a professional organization, but also acquiring the invaluable knack of pacing a series of songs. The kids at the Paramount or the kids who hung around the bandstands of the midwestern cities did not want to be lulled into insensitivity by a succession of slow numbers— though they liked a dreamy one as well as anything. Contrast added bite and spice to each tune, each program. A fast band number stood in its own right and also created anticipation for his next song.

A photograph from 1941 summed up the atmosphere evoked by a Sinatra song. The band played, The Pied Pipers sang, and Sinatra was crooning into the main microphone. He was wearing a light suit, dark tie, and the obligatory handkerchief in his breast pocket. How many hankies did he give away in his long life? But the crucial clues in that picture were two teenage girls. One was dancing with a boyfriend and looking very dreamy. The other girl was simply standing alone beneath Sinatra, hypnotized, transfixed! Of course, this was nothing new. They used to look like that at the Rustic Cabin, but now it was happening on a bigger scale—at all points west across America.

Las Vegas Nights was the prophetic title of that first film; quite a coincidence in view of Sinatra's later and legendary association with the gambling mecca. He sang "I'll Never Smile Again" in the picture. On the sheet music cover he was wearing a big bow tie and was featured with The Pied Pipers. Sinatra had long ago gotten into the habit of immaculate cleanliness and dashing dress. Even on tour, while some of the band were wearing rather off-white attire, Sinatra went out of his way to ensure clean clothes daily and to take a shower or bath more often still. Just as he had collected sports coats in his teens, now he spent more money on smart suits for shows. And he tended to choose good hotels and meals, too, often treating members of the band. This was the start of his legendary generosity.

As the Dorsey entourage went on its endless engagements, they played at bandstands, dance halls, on the stages of America's greatest cinemas, and were heard regularly over the 3,000-mile coast-to-coast radio hookups. From the $150 a week basic salary Sinatra had earned in 1940, he was getting twice that and more. Four hundred bucks a week! That was some pay back in those distant days.

So Sinatra was being seen on the stage and on film and heard on records and on the radio. Somehow, the band squeezed in all these four media. And Sinatra gained his first States-splash recognition when he topped the poll by *Billboard* magazine to become the number-one male vocalist of 1941. Continuing the success story of that year, Sinatra actually collaborated with writing the lyrics for the song "This Love of Mine," which was recorded by himself and Dorsey. Then it was back to the Paramount for a further three weeks in the early fall. Only now, instead of Dorsey and Sinatra, it looked like Sinatra was as big as, or bigger than, the band. We are not really sure what Dorsey thought about the way it was going, but for the time being, Sinatra was bringing in the business—in the shape of thousands of teenagers. More girls than boys, but a good mixture. It had already crossed Sinatra's mind that sometime soon he would try to sing solo—without the benefit of the Dorsey name and band backing him. But not quite yet.

Pearl Harbor, 7 December 1941. The pick of his twenty-nine recordings with the Tommy Dorsey Band during that year were "Without a Song," "I Guess I'll Have to Dream the Rest," "Blue Skies," "Violets for Your Furs," and "How about You?" But Pearl Harbor came before the last one had been pressed for release.

America had been giving the Allied cause all the help possible short of actual armed forces. Now, the country had become committed. And popular songs took on an immediate and new significance—especially any lyrics linked to parting and absence. Men

were beginning to be drafted and leaving girlfriends and wives behind. And like the doughboys who had sailed from Hoboken and
elsewhere in World War I, some were destined not to live long.
Sinatra underwent a medical examination almost at once, but due to
an eardrum punctured during the time of birth, he was graded 4F
and could never enlist. Later on, as well as his regular output of
work, he made a total of some sixty V-discs, which were noncommercial records especially for American service personnel. This formidable number was spread over the war years as a whole, first with
Dorsey and later with his first real musical director, Axel Stordahl.

The start of 1942 could be dated as beginning the change-over
period for Sinatra as Dorsey band singer to Sinatra as solo performer. The Tommy Dorsey outfit admittedly had a sizable string
section and totaled some thirty players and singers in all. Nevertheless, Sinatra was bound to be just one of this many, although an important one. But on 19 January 1942, he made his first records as a
solo performer, backed by Stordahl for these first four titles. Stordahl was particularly keen on orchestrating for string accompaniment, so right for Sinatra ballads.

The four titles were "The Night We Called It a Day," "Night and
Day," "The Lamplighter's Serenade," and "The Song Is You."
"Night and Day" was of course the classic that had brought him luck
on the *Major Bowes Amateur Hour*. Those early Stordahl records, or
some of them, managed to cross the Atlantic somehow—despite the
U-boat war and other hazards.

Spring 1942 brought yet another big month at the Paramount
Theater. It was beginning to be the second home of the whole
Dorsey organization. Most of them felt as if they hardly had a
home. Now Sinatra was twenty-six. Two years of nonstop singing
seemed to have flown by with Dorsey. Frank only got home to
Nancy and their daughter at the times when he was in the environs
of New York. He began to feel nearer the phase when he should
take stock of the present and consider his future. Many people
would have been satisfied to stay with Dorsey indefinitely. Dorsey
expected him to do so. But the scale of Sinatra's success made him
feel that he ought to branch out soon. Another million-seller hit
record convinced him of it. In sweltering weather just three days

before the significant celebration of American Independence Day 1942, he recorded "There Are Such Things," which did as well as "I'll Never Smile Again." The phrase "vocal refrain by Frank Sinatra" was adding huge sales to the Dorsey records and making money for all connected with them.

Sinatra had warned Dorsey months in advance that he wanted to leave, but the bandleader tried to ignore it. The records had been rolling off the presses, to be snapped up avidly throughout the States: *Stardust, Daybreak,* and *Street of Dreams.* Sinatra's last number with the orchestra that was actually issued was recorded on 2 July 1942: "It Started All Over Again." Meanwhile, they were still having one-night bookings in the big cities—and across the Canadian border in Montreal. Then more regular radio programs were interspersed with summer dates at many of the East and Midwest cities, including Washington, D.C.

Despite disagreements and legal wrangling, Sinatra finally left the Tommy Dorsey ensemble on 8 September 1942. His singing successor had been introduced a week or two earlier: Dick Haymes. This was a yardstick of the vocal talent available at that time, and a measure of just how good Sinatra had to be to stand out above the rest. He had always been a bit of a gambler. but this looked like being the biggest risk of his life so far. It was one thing leaving Harry James for Tommy Dorsey. He couldn't really lose. But this was something quite different. To leave Tommy Dorsey for a dream: that he had it in his capacity to become and remain the leading male singer of America.

It was autumn in New York—not yet a cue for a song. Frank came home to Nancy and New Jersey. Amid acrimony about Sinatra allegedly breaking his contract, Dorsey and his outfit went their own way. The final settlement cost Sinatra $25,000, but even this was better than the threatened sum—one-third of all his earnings for life!

Just about the time of Sinatra's twenty-seventh birthday in December, he got his first job since leaving the band. He was given a star billing at the Mosque Theater in nearby Newark, New Jersey. He had come close to home once more, but in a very enhanced status. The radio and record sessions over the previous three years had paid off more than even Sinatra had realized. The girls of Newark besieged him. The local press had given him a good advance build-up as a Hoboken-born boy made good, but the reaction was surely something less local, more universal.

The word "bobby-soxer" really dated from around this time. Synchronizing with it seemed to be the fever generated by Sinatra among the teenage female populace. Newark was not far from New York City, so Robert Weitman, the manager of the great Para-mount Theater in the Big Apple, took time off one bleak afternoon during December to go over the river to see "why throngs of bobby-soxers were yelling and fainting." Despite the rather unpromising setting of Newark in midwinter, he soon found out why. If they went wild over Sinatra in New Jersey, why not in New York and on a larger scale? Weitman offered him a fair two-week contract. The astute manager did not really expect to invoke an option to keep Sinatra longer if desirable, but the clause was in the contract all the same.

Weitman had three ingredients in his formula for filling the ex-panses of the Paramount. There was a new Bing Crosby film show-ing; a good basis. There was Benny Goodman, his clarinet, and his orchestra. And in the solo spot there was Sinatra. Even though Sinatra had already made a name, no one was really prepared for what happened next—least of all the Voice himself. And as they say nowadays, the rest is history.

CHAPTER THREE

THE SWOONATRA ERA

1942-1945

The date: 30 December 1942. The place: the Paramount Theater, New York. As well as screening the first run of films by the Paramount company, the theater featured the familiar stage show—with a continuous performance from before noon till late at night, seven days a week. Benny Goodman with his clarinet was known as the King of Swing. He was booked to appear with Sinatra for a fortnight. Sinatra's starting salary was $750 a week. The cold facts did not prepare anyone for what followed.

The sensational wave of mass hysteria started even as Sinatra's taxi reached the theater. Once inside, he and Goodman prepared for their first entrance. The audience consisted of 5,000 teenagers, mostly girls. Goodman and Sinatra were to share the show with the new film, but the girls had not come to see Bing Crosby. The bandleader was waiting in the wings with Sinatra as the announcer prepared to speak. Goodman had heard of Sinatra, but nothing much more than that—despite his growing fame. The theater was packed, crammed from the front stalls to the back balcony. The time could not have been better: right after the Christmas holidays.

The announcer made the introduction, "Ladies and gentlemen, Frank Sinatra."

"Frankie-e-e!" The bobby-soxers screamed and screeched. Hundreds of girls clutched their heads, opened their mouths, and the Frank Sinatra era was born. It went on for over half a century.

"What the hell is that?" Goodman queried. It was really a rhetorical question, though, as he soon realized that the girls had not come to hear him, his band, or the other singer, Peggy Lee.

So opened 1943. Nancy was behind him at this stage, as ever; and Hank Sanicola; impresario Manie Sacks; and a bright press agent, George Evans. It was Evans who decided to try to exploit the apparently endless source of female emotion by planting a few selected girls in the audience to start the swooning. It may have begun like that, but Evans need hardly have bothered really. Before the first fortnight was over, no one could have distinguished between the cheerleaders and the masses. They had merged into one.

The bobby-soxers were so called because of the cult of wearing short, ankle-high socks, twinned with saddle shoes of the period. They screamed, swooned, moaned, and even danced into the capacious Paramount aisles. They went weak at the knees as they writhed about in musical ecstasy. Goodman soon got used to it all, having experienced something approaching it when he launched the big band swing era back in 1934. Clutching his classic clarinet, he smiled benignly at them, like some distant uncle indulging thousands of proxy nieces.

Sinatra shrugged his expressive shoulders and responded to them from his very soul. They swooned afresh at his swooping, soulful phrases and they refused to let him go. Day after day it went on. Crowds milled around the marquee outside the Paramount. Girls sat through performance after performance, despite the efforts of the manager to get them to move. The theater was sold out solid for four weeks and then Goodman and his band left the show, because of prior commitments elsewhere. But every seat was still sold.

The attraction was Frankie. He was the main event—as at Madison Square Garden three decades later. He had already been dubbed "Frankie" by the fans, who grew both numerically and in intensity throughout that memorable month of January 1943.

Robert Weitman kept Sinatra on for a further four-week spell. The fee for this fresh booking ran into thousands of dollars a week and he was worth it. By the end of the spell, Sinatra's reported weekly sum reached $25,000. The same spectacular scenes were reenacted through February. The band backing Sinatra now read as Johnny Long, but the rest of the scenario remained the same. Girls queued for hours and then came back for more. Often, they waited all night for the first show. Then they sat through show after show if they could—for four, five, up to six shows a day— physically refusing to be removed. Sinatra stood the pace well. The Tommy Dorsey years had given him a good grounding, and anyway this was what he wanted, what he had craved, all these years: success. Now he had it in a dramatic damburst. Somehow he kept level-headed.

While Sinatra's mother made his floppy bow ties for him to wear under the spotlight, whether on stage or off, the girls pursued him, fighting for fragments of his clothes—buttons, shirts, ties, cuff links, anything. They were all ripped out regularly in the frenzy of female passion. The fans even tugged at his hair, plucking out strands of it. It was Sinatra more than the swooners who was likely to need the nurses who were always kept ready at the Paramount during those winter afternoons and evenings. Behind the scenes, the girls scrawled loving messages in their current lipstick colors. They wrote across mirrors, walls, corridors, anywhere, as if compelled to express themselves in some tangible form. It cost the theater management a small fortune to keep the place clean, but they did their best and no one ever objected. Audiences were all witnessing and participating in a unique phenomenon. One of the commonest phrases found in every conceivable color of lipstick was simply this one, "I love you, Frankie." And in the audience at Madison Square Garden thirty-odd years later, quite a number of those same bobby-soxers were there as middle-aged fans. And still saying, "I love you, Frankie." That's loyalty.

But back to February 1943. While the bobby-soxers were busy listening to Sinatra pouring his heart out to each one of them, other people were trying to describe, define, and analyze the vocal quality he created. "A thin singer with a thin reedy voice" was one candid comment, probably by a male critic. Another saw him as "a younger Lincoln"—not a bad visual image. Yet, a third heard his voice this way: "When he sings, it's like being stroked by a hand covered with cold cream." Of course, there were always detractors and these started as soon as Sinatra's success did.

Psychologists tried to explain the Sinatra cult. One saw it as "escapism and substitution" for love among the masses of moaning girls. Another called it "one of the elemental instincts of female kind—the urge to feed the hungry." This analyst equated the yearning, beseeching quality of the young Sinatra's voice to the plaintive cry of a hungry child, noting that the frail, even famished, look of the singer fitted in with this conception. Not that Sinatra ever needed to look hungry again. Or ever to be short of mere money. Around then, he already had some fifty suits and twice that number of trousers! Not to mention the equivalent quantities of shoes and jackets. He still loved those light-colored shoes to contrast with the rest of his outfit.

Right in the midst of this maelstrom of female adoration, Sinatra had a film released that had been made the previous year. This rejoiced in the rhyming title of *Reveille with Beverly.* The seventy-eight-minute picture featured Ann Miller, three dance bands—Bob Crosby, Duke Ellington, and Count Basie—plus a song by Sinatra, "Night and Day." Naturally, this all helped the Sinatra bandwagon gain speed through February.

Still on the subject of psychology, just at the key moment, Manie Sacks pushed Sinatra a bit further along his fabled route. Sacks was then vice president of the Columbia Broadcasting System (CBS), and he had been following Sinatra's progress ever since the switch to Tommy Dorsey. One of the top radio programs was CBS's *Your Hit Parade,* a weekly nationwide review of the most popular current numbers. Sacks invited Sinatra to join this top Saturday night radio show from 6 February on, and he became an instant hit all over again.

Next came a twist in the recording saga of Sinatra. He was signed by Columbia Records. The company recalled his single of "All or Nothing at All" and how it had sold only 8,000 copies. It reissued the same Harry James–Sinatra track. By midsummer, it had topped the half-million mark and eventually had the distinction of being his very first million-seller. *Downbeat* magazine ran its annual popularity poll and Sinatra headed the major section of favorite male vocalist. This was to be no passing phase or fancy. The appeal of Sinatra changed age groups over the decades—but this marked the start. A bobby-soxer said later of those days, "When I used to go almost every evening to hear him, it seemed as if he was looking right into my eyes and I was the one among all the thousands in Radio City he was singing to."

Despite the undammed flood of female adoration and all the radio fame, the night that next clinched the arrival of Sinatra as more than just a passing fad came when he was booked to appear at the exclusive uptown Rio Bamba Club on East 57th Street. The address was No. 151 to be precise. The date: well, not so precise but between 11 and 17 March. The club was near the most fashionable section of the city and abutted Central Park. As the Americans of the day would have said, it was classy.

This represented a real challenge in a different setting. The audience members were all adults, and they had paid more than the price of a Paramount seat for their evening's entertainment. The press was there, too. The tough columnists and critics could virtually make or break a performer. The question on all their lips was this: Is he really as good as he is made out to be?

Sinatra sensed that the night would go one way or the other. All or nothing at all. The story of his whole life. But by now he had acquired the confidence bred by success. No longer was he the young fledgling vocalist from the wrong side of the river struggling to make good.

The club's atmosphere approached fusing point. Sinatra felt the same electric tension for the first few seconds before he started to sing. He came on to polite applause. No one swooning. No hysteria. What would happen next? It was now real time. The spotlight hovered around rather uncertainly before settling squarely on his slender 120-odd-pound frame. He clung to the mike as if for support—twiddling with it and looking around with a slight sense of desperation. He had a suit with padded shoulders a bit too heavy for him, while his huge bow tie flopped down like some spaniel's ears.

But as soon as he started to sing, surrounded by the tight-packed horseshoe of tables, everything and everyone in the darkened nightclub fell pin-drop quiet. Then they all went wild, mad, potty. He sang "That Old Black Magic" and they were in his spell. The club had been hard up before that opening night. Sinatra took less then $1,000 a week and in a very short time it was solvent again. People fought to get bookings and even stood to hear him sing.

After that, Sinatra swept to universal success, stardom, and acclaim—by the ability to sing a love song with total conviction. You could say that to reach this point so young, he had already come through four necessary stages in his approach to his art—and it was an art—participation, involvement, commitment, and dedication. It would be a demanding life. And yet, and yet, this still marked merely the beginning. From then on, his life could never be completely his own in one sense, yet infinitely more satisfying than if he had remained unknown.

Sacks and songwriter Sammy Cahn were just two of the notable people in New York show business who cherished the memory of that night at the Rio Bamba. Cahn later wrote such hits as "Come Fly with Me" and "Come Dance with Me" (with Jimmy Van Heusen), as well as many other Sinatra classics like "All the Way" and "Time after Time." And to Cahn, Sinatra said quite simply, modestly, "I'm going to be the top singer in America." From then on, he was really already just that, but comparatively immature by later standards that he would set himself.

After the eight-week Paramount run, the Rio Bamba, and the regular radio programs, these are a few of his spring and summer 1943 dates: singing "God Bless America" in Central Park; a second benefit, this time at Madison Square Garden; four more weeks at the Paramount; and a big-scale success at the Manhattan Playhouse.

Two shows with symphony orchestras led up to the next milestone. The first of these classical ensembles was the Cleveland Philharmonic Orchestra, followed by a concert with the Philadelphia Philharmonic. These dates culminated in a concert at the famous Hollywood Bowl. After a group of short classics by the accompanying orchestra, Sinatra strolled on to the vast arena stage. He had decided to dress in a manner suited to the setting and wore a white tuxedo jacket with a dark bow tie, dark trousers, and dark shoes. Backed by the ample string orchestra and a guitar to his right, he sang "Dancing in the Dark," "Night and Day," "You'll Never Know," "The Song Is You," "Ol' Man River," and

"All or Nothing at All." There was no doubt about the reception. The audience, which approached 10,000, stood in acknowledgment, and Sinatra had conquered California just as he had New York. And incidentally, with that single performance at the Hollywood Bowl he had obliterated a large deficit hanging over the arena. While in California, Sinatra contracted to make films for RKO Radio and he did so almost at once. Somehow, he also found the time to sing in aid of American war rallies, without any fee, of course.

Amazingly, he juggled his schedule to sing throughout October and November at the famous Waldorf-Astoria in New York while also launching a long solo radio show with CBS.

Sinatra's first feature film, *Higher and Higher*, was released in time for Christmas 1943. In it he played himself, but even that called for acting ability. The five numbers he sang were "You Belong in a Love Song," "The Music Stopped," "I Saw You First," "A Lovely Way to Spend an Evening," and "I Couldn't Sleep a Wink Last Night." I remember both the film and the records as being my first real encounter with the Sinatra touch. And yet it has to be said again, how immature he still was!

Sinatra took it all surprisingly calmly for a man still in his twenties. For, of course, the adulation had not come overnight, despite the Paramount razzmatazz. He had worked for a decade on it already. Yet, success was bound to make a difference. He and Nancy had moved into a new white house in Hasbrouck Heights, New Jersey, and he got back there as often as he could after the shows. Young Nancy turned three that last summer, and Frank and Nancy tried to keep their lives on an even keel. He is quoted authoritatively as saying of this era, "In Nancy, I found a beauty, warmth, and understanding. Being with her was my only escape. But later on I was edgy and irritable, and Nancy and I found ourselves arguing over trivial matters. I thought another child would cement our marriage and the following year Frank Jr. came along."

When the new baby did appear, they named him Franklin after President Franklin D. Roosevelt, who received Sinatra at the White House later in 1944. Roosevelt had always been one of Sinatra's foremost heroes, for he embodied everything Sinatra had ever stood for. A man devoted to the rights of men and a champion of people who—like the Sinatras—came from the wrong side of the tracks.

Now, Sinatra was on top, though, and was finding that life had its problems wherever he was. Somehow, he had to try to balance his home life against this rather frightening fame. Home meant Nancy. Nancy cooking him spaghetti, looking after the family, advising him on money matters, and altogether doing all she could to help him. But they did not find things easier when their new home was almost continuously assaulted by batteries of girl fans. Making the easy trip from anywhere in the greater New York area, the bobby-soxers stole into the garden, kissed the white walls of his house, or scrawled love lines across them. Sinatra was never safe night or day, and the more enterprising fans actually tried to penetrate into the house or peer in through the windows to steal a momentary sight of their idol. Some of them lugged ladders up against the house to climb up and see him sleeping.

This was all very flattering but hardly made for a stable family life. Nor was it any easier when Sinatra had to stay overnight in New York. The telephone operators at his hotel had to cope with hundreds of calls a day from girls trying to speak to him on any pretext under the sun. The "Swoonatra spell" spread to wherever he might be appearing, whether one-night stands or longer dates. Queues of girls crocodiled around all the buildings adjacent to the particular theater. And then when he finally appeared on stage, the same wild screams and swoons erupted. Sinatra always had a penchant for hats—and these proved easy game for the girls ambushing him for souvenirs. First they removed the loose items like hats and handkerchiefs, before going to work on the buttons and bows—until not a lot remained of his clothing.

Even in the midst of the war, the story of Sinatra percolated across the Atlantic and by the summer of 1943 Britain had definitely heard of "this young man who looks as if he needs a square meal," as the *London Daily Mail* described him. The same newspaper went on to report, "Women have gone mad about the man. When he sings in a curious, soft, effortless—almost girlish—voice, something happens to feminine listeners. They shriek: 'Here I am, Frankie, come and get me!' Or: 'Frankie, you're killing me!' Others swoon and some have stormed the stage to try and kiss the little crooner. In fact, things have become so delirious that a group of psychiatrists have been called in to study the problem."

Through this crucial 1943–1944 period, a total ban was operating that precluded members of the U.S. Musicians Union from accompanying any records. To overcome this, Columbia Records managed to organize a vocal background for Sinatra and these voices were known as the Ken Lane Singers. Between July and November 1943, Sinatra recorded eight numbers with this group, six of which were issued. The best-known pair was "I Couldn't Sleep a Wink Last Night" and "A Lovely Way to Spend an Evening"—both from *Higher and Higher.* After the three Ken Lane records, a whole year passed before Sinatra had his next recording venture. By then the ban was over and he could record to the sensitive backing of Axel Stordahl, an association destined to last for eight years.

Meanwhile, still in 1943, one interlude interrupted the chain of conquests. Someone had the idea of Sinatra singing with the New York Philharmonic Orchestra. Although the music critics were forced to admit he had a pleasant voice, they noted a calm reception from many of the audience, even if the girls were as enthusiastic as ever. Perhaps this setting was not a very wise choice at that stage in his career.

But Sinatra never stood still. That is why he was bound to make a few mistakes. It is always easier to stick in the same rut and not risk anything fresh. But in the end, the capacity to branch out proves to be not only rewarding but also actually life-enhancing or at least life-sustaining. Sinatra's venture into films was touched with success from the start: commercially if not always artistically! As usual, Hollywood was hurrying to take advantage of a new marketable commodity, or to cash in on a "hot property," as the film boys expressed it. Sinatra was always that—and still is, even after his death.

When *Higher and Higher* was generally released, audible sighs echoed around all the cinemas where it was shown. By now the press was calling him anything from the "Thin Thrush" to the "Gargoyle Groaner." Looking through his singing schedules for this year, it seems incredible how he fitted it all in and yet remained sane. In January 1944, Sinatra not only toured the United States to entertain servicemen and servicewomen, but he also made the first of many visits to the Hollywood Canteen to sing to them. The men there seemed to be as wild about him as the girls! Somehow, he retained his existing slot in the radio show *Your Hit Parade* while actually launching a new one bearing his own name: *The Frank Sinatra Show.* As he was in the middle of a broadcast from California, Frank Jr. appeared in Jersey City. Although Sinatra was making another film for RKO Radio, *Step Lively,* Metro-Goldwyn-Mayer (MGM) smartly moved in to sign him up for a long contract that would later result in some memorable musicals.

But all was not smooth sailing—or singing. Some of the Republican newspapers under William Randolph Hearst indulged in a real vendetta against Sinatra, accusing him of trying to avoid military service. In fact, he had always attempted to enlist, ever since America entered the war. The real reason for the smears lay in the fact that Sinatra supported Roosevelt, while Hearst was doing everything he could to discredit both Sinatra and Roosevelt. While all this went on, too, Sinatra brought the family out west to Los Angeles to live. It seemed as if he would be spending much of his time there and the aim was to try to keep the family structure intact. Already, there had been rumblings of a rift—not so surprising with 3,000 miles between components of the group.

Step Lively was released during the summer of 1944. Sinatra was teamed with George Murphy and he bestowed his very first screen kiss on costar Gloria De Haven. Murphy was already well known as a dancer in film musicals, while Sinatra's songs were penned especially by that classic team of Julie Styne and Sammy Cahn, still in their youth like Sinatra. He sang his four songs "effortlessly," as the *London Daily Mail* said. And what songs they wrote in those days. These were just four typical tunes in just one typical Hollywood musical: "Some Other Time," "As Long as There's Music," "Come Out Come Out Wherever You Are," and "Where Does Love Begin?"

While America was watching and loving *Step Lively,* Sinatra started filming his first vehicle for MGM. And while the Americans and their Allies were busy invading the Normandy coastline on the immortal beaches of Omaha, Utah, and others, the Sinatra boom was building up even higher. By 1944, Sinatra had to be backed by quite an organization to cope with all that was involved in being a star.

Already he had been quoted in the press as the highest-paid person in the world. As long ago as the Tommy Dorsey days—not so far back—the girls had been writing in the hundreds asking for photographs. He had a supply of picture-postcards printed to cope with them. The numbers then totaled less than a hundred a week. Now, the fan mail was 3,000, 4,000, and up to 5,000 letters a week. An office staff posted signed pictures of him to high school girls in every one of the forty-eight states, every single township across America. The press and publicity side fully occupied press agent George Evans and some other staff. They sent out those glossy prints—like the one I got from Deanna Durbin at exactly that time, even in the midst of the war.

When Sinatra made his frequent personal appearances, bodyguards had to search his hotel in advance for girls hiding just to meet him—or rather more. They tried concealment everywhere: in laundry shafts, fire escapes, elevators, under beds, and in cupboards and closets. Sinatra never neglected to do what he considered his duty to the fans, but he did draw the line at some of the more extreme methods they employed to get at him. But he would also think philosophically that the time to start worrying was when they didn't want to see him. And he had that happen to him later in life.

A memorable interlude in all this rather frightening hero worship came when Sinatra visited Washington, D.C., in September 1944. Sinatra did his own bit of hero worshiping over Roosevelt, contributing financially to the president's campaign funds in his quest for an unprecedented fourth term in office. While Sinatra was rather in awe of Roosevelt, the president was reported as telling him, "Mr. Sinatra, you have restored to women something they lost fifty years ago—the charm of knowing how to faint!"

Among all his other work—for the war and on his own behalf— Sinatra found the time and energy to sing free of charge to Democratic meetings during the presidential election campaign that fall. A small return, he felt, for meeting Roosevelt at the White House. In the same season, he made a short film for the purpose of helping to sell war bonds. Then the most historic date in this wartime era came in October. To most Americans, Columbus Day is something special, marking as it does the day when Christopher Columbus first sighted Watlings, now San Salvador, in the Bahama Islands. Columbus Day 1944 was when the bobby-soxers went wilder even than they had done on Sinatra's earlier visits to the Paramount Theater.

On this return date to the place where it all really started for him less than two years previously, thousands of girls ran wild in adjacent Times Square. There had been nothing near to equaling it in American show business history. Oblivious of their surroundings in the familiar elongated Times Square, 30,000 of them converged in one solid Sinatra-mad mass. The cause of it all was that the audience for the first morning show refused to leave the Paramount to let others inside. The queueing crowd surged, sweated, swore, and swooned. It was a case of passionate rage at being thwarted from seeing their idol.

All the traffic stopped in the celebrated neon-sign square and also the streets intersecting it. Broadway ground to a halt. The heart of New York stopped beating. Police and other emergency services rushed to the female mob, but they could do little in the face of the serried rows of bobby-soxers struggling either to get into the theater or to glimpse Sinatra when he came out. And when most of them predictably could not gain admission, they tore the box office to ribbons. The teenage Amazons wrought their vengeance in the only way open to them. It seemed that nothing could stem the hysterical appeal that Sinatra stimulated. It was as if he generated such a positive and potent charge that it was not earthed until it reached the receiving audience. It was electrifying. The girls did not pause to analyze their emotions or actions—they simply howled for him! The scenes that day went down in history as the Columbus Day Riot—and all while the Allied forces were still fighting for their lives in Europe and the Pacific. But it must be borne in mind how much the voice of Sinatra and the music of Glenn Miller meant to the soldiers.

Meanwhile, the shows at the Paramount went on from 9:00 A.M. till after midnight. The later it got each day, the greater the scenes. The girls just would not get up and go during this continuous performance. Among a capacity audience of several thousands, only 250 or so would leave at the end of the first show. Girls sat through shows for six, eight, or more hours, and if they did not swoon at Sinatra, they often fainted for lack of food or drink. After a day of emotional stress, they were drained—yet even then they refused to leave until the attendants came along and got rid of them by force. One girl sat through fifty-six consecutive shows in eight days! Seven shows a day for over a week. If Sinatra is significant to you, this does not seem absurd—I might have done something similar! If Sinatra means little to you, you would think she must have been mad!

The fee quoted for his Paramount appearances was $7,500 a week, but Sinatra's earnings were, of course, much more. The fan clubs spread to all states, and his radio shows brought fresh frenzy—not only at the actual broadcasts but even at the rehearsals. In fact, you could say that there was pandemonium wherever and whenever he appeared. And the kids used to gather at their local soda fountains for a Frankie cocktail—a chocolate soda, with tinted whipped cream squeezed in the shape of a bow tie on top of it. The tie and his sharp hats seemed to symbolize the Sinatra cult. The innocent cocktail had some associations with one of his nostalgic numbers recorded during the last winter of the war, "Homesick That's All."

This song had a direct appeal to every teenager, with its references to the activities they all shared: chocolate sodas, the junior prom, the ball game, and graduation. Among the fan club members, a new slang arose when exchanging letters. They signed off "Sinatrally Yours" or "Frankly Yours." And if they thought of a postscript, it was not a "PS" but an "FS." Innocent days. One special fan club bore the title The Slaves of Sinatra—being known to themselves as "'The girls who would lay down their lives and die for Sinatra' Club!"

With the approaching end of 1944 came the end of that union ban on accompaniments to records. Sinatra launched into his long friendship—professional and personal—with the arranger Axel Stordahl. Stordahl had worked as an arranger for Tommy Dorsey, a high recommendation in Sinatra's eyes—and ears. Sinatra made a sufficiently generous offer for him to change. Sinatra could probably afford it, for his average yearly income over the two years since leaving

Dorsey was some $750,000. Needless to say, his expenses ran at the same sort of astronomical level.

Bing Crosby recorded a highly successful version of "White Christmas" by Irving Berlin. So did Sinatra with Stordahl and they each sold something like a million copies. The timing was commercially impeccable. This title was just one of about a score of songs Sinatra recorded in four New York sessions with Stordahl over the period. Others included the slow blues number "Stormy Weather" and the swingier, if melancholy, "Saturday Night Is the Loneliest Night of the Week." Though the latter was faster, it had some of that "lonely figure" appeal of Sinatra about it. Sung at an unimpeachable tempo, these recordings still lacked the sublime sense of rhythm and "delayed phrasing" he acquired later on. "Ol' Man River" tested his lowest notes, reminding us that not only did he enunciate so well, his actual accent was remarkably pure for someone with a limited formal education. On the same day that he made the Jerome Kern classic "Ol' Man River," he recorded "Nancy," too, but this version was not issued then. The hit recording reached the public in 1945. Other numbers in this famous group were "Embraceable You" and "She's Funny That Way." So he was still very much rendering ballads rather than really swingy compositions.

The burst of recording sessions virtually overlapped with one another. From a vintage collection in January 1945 came the celebrated "Soliloquy from Carousel," "The House I Live In," "Put Your Dreams Away," and "Nancy." Some people thought that the last title referred to his wife. Others believed that it was intended for Nancy Sandra, who was five years old and growing up in California. Sinatra was by then finding it quite a strain keeping his family life running in parallel with the public adulation and adoration.

During the victory year of 1945, Sinatra undertook two projects very dear to him. He received no fee for either of them—but money never meant much to him. It came and went and came again. Both of these themes had a social connection. The first was the noncommercial film *The House I Live In*. This short feature was made to help spread the acceptance of racial and religious tolerance in both

America and the world. Sinatra jumped at the chance to do something constructive toward a favorite theme, for which he always actively crusaded. For his performance in the film, the Academy of Motion Picture Arts and Sciences awarded him a special Oscar. He had already made the record of the title song—one he sang so tellingly nearly three decades later at the historic Madison Square Garden concert in 1974.

The death of President Roosevelt on 12 April 1945 came within a month of total victory in Europe. "The President is dead" were the words uttered solemnly over the radios of America. It meant more of a loss to Sinatra than to some of his compatriots. Something seemed to have gone out of his life, even a little of the reason for living.

That spring, Sinatra had to attend a U.S. Army medical in his home area of Newark, New Jersey. The punctured eardrums had prevented his being drafted on a previous occasion in 1943. Now just the possibility of his going carried significance to millions of girls. Inevitably, the news leaked out about his medical and some of his most extreme fans hurried over to Newark to protest.

Spring can come late around New York and the whole region was still clad in a dusting of snow. When they thought that Sinatra might really be drafted, they went berserk. Some of the girls displayed all the characteristics of lemmings. They dived headfirst into snowbanks at the U.S. Army unit, yelling, "I don't want to live anymore, Frankie." Others prayed in the chill of a nearby church, asking for him to be spared, while still others, shivering and sad, waited hour after hour for him to emerge from the unit. When he eventually did so, only the military police prevented him from being injured in the stampede of screaming girls. In the event, they did not lose him after all—and nor did we. The authorities decided that he was doing a job of national service already and that it would be better not to call him after all.

Sinatra had already sung at service shows across the country and also raised big sums for war bonds and similar national projects. He had always had the dream of entertaining U.S. servicemen overseas, too, but the smears against him in the Hearst press had prevented or dissuaded the State Department from granting him a visa to do so.

At last the victory in Europe (V-E) was achieved. V-E Day came and went. So in June Sinatra was finally invited and allowed to go over to the European theater of operations to help entertain the troops who had won the victory. He and Phil Silvers went to North Africa and Italy and appeared at a number of centers during one of his lesser-known tours. A memorable moment at midsummer was when he visited his parental homeland of Italy for the first time. He had a feeling of familiarity with both the place and the people, even though they had been on the enemy side during the war. But he had no truck with fascism and so found special satisfaction in singing to an eager, excited audience of Yanks and others in the Forum of Rome, at the exact spot where the dictator Benito Mussolini had spouted such diatribes of hate. Sinatra sang about love. The troops thought about girls back home, cheered, and yelled for more. Frankie gave it to them. He was always a great giver. Just at that moment, the world still lay at his feet. But near the same spot, many men's hopes had gone astray, faded, or ended—from Julius Caesar onward.

What would the future hold for Sinatra?

CHAPTER FOUR

HOLLYWOOD

1945-1949

Victory over Japan Day. By a happy chance, *Anchors Aweigh* opened around America on or near 15 August 1945. The national mood was naturally euphoric and a film about two U.S. sailors on leave could hardly have been timed more perfectly. Of course, it was made in the previous year, but it became Frank Sinatra's first stupendous cinema success. Costarring dancer Gene Kelly, singer Kathryn Grayson, and pianist Jose Iturbi, it had all the ingredients of a smash-hit MGM musical. The ambitious film ran two and a quarter hours and Kelly taught Sinatra quite intricate dance routines that looked nonchalantly executed. Sinatra took it all in his confident stride and the whole production exuded the breezy air of the U.S. Navy. Incidentally, the picture was produced by the celebrated Deanna Durbin director Joe Pasternak. Sinatra sang five Julie Styne–Sammy Cahn numbers: "What Makes the Sun Set?" "The Charm of You," "I Fall in Love Too Easily," "We Hate to Leave," and "I Begged Her." They were all tailored to Sinatra's voice and public and he sang them straight, in his pure, slightly high, tone of that vintage. In the last one, "I Begged Her," he brought out a hint of humor along with other innovations. Sinatra and Kelly became close friends thereafter. And another lasting friendship was launched soon after the film was released.

Sinatra got back from Europe in time to record two of his best songs from that era, "You Go to My Head" and "These Foolish Things." The better the song, the better he sang it. This is true,

49

though later on Sinatra learned how to skirt over shortcomings in lyrics and even tunes by improvised variations.

Fortunately for him, however, the 1940s were overflowing with fine numbers and he was never afraid to go back to older standards when he felt like it. How about these titles for sheer songwriting quality? "Where or When," "All the Things You Are," "Over the Rainbow," "Day by Day," "One Love," and "Begin the Beguine." Add a few other quintessential ones, too—"You Go to My Head," "Laura," and "Time after Time"—and it soon becomes clear that the list is endless.

Sinatra could even turn on the blue-eyed charm enough to persuade Columbia Records to let him conduct its own tame symphony orchestra. He did not really read music, yet somehow he created a recording so good that the members of this very professional body applauded him afterward!

With all this activity, the pressures were showing signs of telling on him. He made a million dollars in the first nine months of 1945. It was rather ironic that just as the record *Nancy* was selling so widely, the strain of his engagements was stretching the ties of his family, which one part of him valued above all else, and did so throughout the rest of his life. Both Nancy senior and junior felt his absence as a husband and father figure. It was the start of an all-too-familiar show business story. Financial and career success; marriage failure. Sinatra said, "Endless tours, night-club work, and other business activities kept me away from home. We drifted apart. When I was offered a long-term film contract by MGM we moved to California and there I determined to make our marriage work." But Hollywood has never been notable for its generally beneficial effect on the institution of marriage. The trials and temptations are often beyond mere mortals.

Meanwhile, the fall of 1945 brought back *The Frank Sinatra Show* to the air, and it continued to be heard weekly until 1947. A week or two after Sinatra started the show, he was signing the final autograph at the CBS stage door in Hollywood when a young black man spoke to him. His name was Sammy Davis Jr. and he had been dancing on the same show as Sinatra several years earlier while touring with the Tommy Dorsey Band in Detroit. Davis and his father were down on their luck. Sinatra invited him to see the radio show the following week as one of the audience in the studio. Sinatra asked Davis to see him after the broadcast, and the lifelong association began from that very night. It must be remembered that the color question was a vexed one back in the 1940s, but Sinatra never wavered in his support for racial equality, however unpopular it might have made him with some Americans. And it did. There were, in fact, repercussions from the film *The House I Live In,* with Sinatra being both praised and vilified, depending on people's particular views on civil rights.

The three aspects of his persona progressed in parallel through 1946: his professional life, his social outlook, and his family connections. It was a hard juggling act and one of the three balls looked increasingly droppable. Actually, the final weeks of 1945 had meant a return to the frenzy of New York: three weeks at the Paramount and a fortnight back at the Waldorf-Astoria. Looking back at 1946, Nancy junior later put the number of songs he recorded during the year at fifty-seven. A nationwide tour that spring embraced one week at the Golden Gate Theater, San Francisco. The glittering marquee said it all: Frank Sinatra in Person. The Pied Pipers and Big Revue. Axel Stordahl and his Radio Orchestra. Frank Sinatra singing his latest Columbia recording hits. And above it all, the Face that went with the Voice. The Face blown up to about twenty feet tall. At the bottom of the billboard: On the screen—*Riverboat Rhythm.* Patrons certainly got value for money in those heady days. Outside the Golden Gate, a sprinkling of sailors' hats could be seen, almost like extras from *Anchors Aweigh.* And so it went on. That was just one week in a typical tour.

Sinatra devoted much of his energies to his still-new film career. Toward the end of the year, MGM released the screen biography of the composer Jerome Kern. Sinatra had made a cameo appearance in this large-scale production, singing the climactic number of "Ol' Man River." This was always one of his specialties, perhaps in view of the connection with black people. The film was called *Till the Clouds Roll By.*

Meanwhile, the Sinatra family was still intact if a little shaky. Frank had already been introduced to Ava Gardner, who was then

still married to film star Mickey Rooney. Nothing had yet come of
that initial encounter. But the temptations were there. One of the
early ones was the attractive Marilyn Maxwell. Nancy senior overlooked this indiscretion. There had been one or two before this, and
there were bound to be others. Perhaps she knew it.

In 1947, Sinatra and America were entering the fifth year since
that star-making date of 30 December 1942 at the Paramount. People were settling into their routine of peaceful lives, bobby-soxers began to grow up, television was still just under the horizon, and
MGM films and Columbia records were thriving. If 1946 had been
Sinatra's "record" year, 1947 topped it with the remarkable total of
seventy-one numbers committed to disc. If I had to choose three of
the best, I would quote the haunting "The Nearness of You," which
takes me back to a time in my own life; "Autumn in New York,"
ever evocative of a city I had yet to encounter in the flesh; and "Stella
by Starlight," which reached the top ten in the American hit parade.

Sinatra was often singing for charities—Jewish and cancer at this
time—and despite all the dimensions of a full life, he made a special effort never to be too busy to keep abreast of current affairs, nor
did he neglect reading of all kinds. One of the historical writers
who had an influence on the opinions held by Sinatra all his life was
Tom Paine. The author of *The Rights of Man,* written back in 1791,
had fought for the colonists in the War of Independence. Paine had
been born in England but died in New York. Sinatra could quote
Paine quite extensively and he also followed the activities of Congress keenly. He was still a strong Democrat sympathizer.

This did not seem to be enough for him, though, so as well as listening to political lectures, he spoke out for peace and racial tolerance. One day during a union crisis in the 1946–1947 era, Sinatra
stood up before a microphone to talk to the people about civil rights.
One woman called out, "Sing us, 'Saturday Night,' Frankie." Another voice yelled, "Yes, Frankie, please. And 'I'll Never Walk
Alone.'" Sinatra did not smile. "I'm here as a citizen," he said, "If
you want a song, you'd better get someone else." Then he began his
speech.

The reference to walking alone is a reminder that in many ways
he was a loner, in his own words. That is what he would always be,

however many friends or admirers he had. Perhaps that was a penalty of greatness. Perhaps it was just how he was made. Even though he may have walked alone, he never needed to feel alone. Even in those days he must surely have got that message. People loved him.

He made another million dollars in 1946 and a legend for lavishness and generosity started in earnest. When he went out to Hollywood alone during the war, Sinatra had stayed at his Sunset Towers apartment. Now with Nancy, he had a lakeside house in the San Fernando Valley. Soon they would be moving into a bigger and better home.

In his wardrobe, Sinatra had amassed some fifty suits, plus quantities of shoes, sports coats, and trousers. The cuff link collection was in full swing, too, being put at a value of thousands of dollars. The Sinatra group at the time included Hank Sanicola and writer Don McGuire. Two of their hallmarks were dark shirts and extravagant cuff links. Sinatra never hoarded his money, nor did he spend it solely on himself. He started a habit of giving away real gold cigarette lighters engraved with messages of affection to his friends. Reports varied on their overall number and value, one estimating that 400 lighters distributed by him had been worth over $40,000. All that by 1947!

No signs showed yet of any dip either in his income or his popularity, the two of course being closely interconnected. He had long decided to accept the inevitable and enter into the spirit of being a star. He knew that everything he did, everywhere he went, would always be news. He never went out of his way, however, to court publicity, and he always held passionately that even public figures were entitled to have their private lives respected as such. He was still fantastically successful on radio and records and in films. These were the figures quoted at the time. Columbia was issuing at least one new record a month. These records' total yearly sales soared up to the $10 million mark and brought him royalties of $250,000. His weekly radio show was worth an annual $500,000. He could get as much as $200,000 for one film. And when he appeared live for a stage show, his fee was at least $25,000. Of course, these figures are approximate, but they are near enough to convey the general idea that Sinatra was a success, commercially as well as artistically, to his own exacting standards.

The champagne fizzed. There were the times when Frank and Nancy went out together. But . . . there were times when he also saw other women. As already mentioned, the blonde Marilyn Maxwell. And Lana Turner, the glamorous and talented star of such films as *Ziegfeld Girl*. For periods, Frank and Nancy became estranged, but then they thought of the children and tried to smooth over their difficulties. They moved into a wonderful new house in Holmsby Hills, Hollywood, and Nancy settled down there with the two children. They all lived behind a ten-foot-high wall for privacy, while in the garage reposed three or four cars. Quite modest by Hollywood standards. For their own sakes, and for Sinatra's career, they still hoped to solve the marital problems. Could they? Lee Mortimer was one of William Randolph Hearst's newspapermen who had been making life hard for Sinatra. Sinatra had been photographed in company with Lucky Luciano, a known mobster. Mortimer used the so-called evidence to accuse Sinatra of associating with such men. The Federal Bureau of Investigation was also always digging into his background for connections with crime or communism. Things came to a nasty head on 8 April 1947, when Sinatra happened to be at the same restaurant as Mortimer. Someone told Sinatra that Mortimer had called him "a dago son of a bitch," whereupon our hero physically attacked the journalist. Mortimer saw to it that the police arrested Sinatra, who was later granted bail. But the incident cost him a lot. The case did not come to court and a settlement was made in favor of Mortimer for $9,000 plus an apology from Sinatra. The cost proved much more than financial to Sinatra, however, and the alleged connections were hard to disprove for a long while. Yet, ironically, only days after this incident Sinatra was given the Thomas Jefferson Award for his prolonged work against racial intolerance.

The sequel to this entire episode came quite swiftly. In an open letter on MGM studio letterhead, Sinatra wrote about his troubles and thanked his fans and friends for believing in him. The Sinatras somehow continued to prosper, with the unstinted support quoted in his open letter. Doubtless, MGM was behind this, but nevertheless it did confirm the sympathy felt for him by the public. The eventful month of April included a concert at New York's revered Carnegie Hall and a charity benefit down in Texas. Then, in a typically thoughtful and generous action, Sinatra arranged for his support at a New York engagement by Sammy Davis Jr., his father, and his uncle. The trio never forgot Sinatra's kindness in offering them this break.

That summer Sinatra was filming *It Happened in Brooklyn,* with the location sequences actually being shot in New York for added authenticity. This was not yet done frequently by Hollywood companies, but it reached its apotheosis later in the classic New York musical *On the Town,* which was filmed to a great extent in the Big Apple. *It Happened in Brooklyn* was a postwar story and a starring vehicle for Sinatra. He sang half a dozen or more numbers, including even an aria from Wolfgang Mozart's *Don Giovanni,* "La ci darem la mano." Kathryn Grayson accompanied him, and Jimmy Durante was thrown in for laughs. The young Peter Lawford was also in the cast and Sinatra was a friend of his for many years after the film.

Frankie sang six other songs in the picture. The most enduring of them all was "Time after Time," but the group represented a strong handful. "Brooklyn Bridge" was really an example of a tune and lyric written to order; "It's the Same Old Dream" was a typical Sinatra ballad of the period; he also sang "I Believe" and "Black Eyes." One of the snappiest of all was the duet rendered with Durante, "The Song's Gotta Come from the Heart."

One of the intriguing things about retrospective looks at a star's career is noticing how other performers of the same vintage were developing in parallel. That September, Sinatra reappeared on the radio series *Your Hit Parade* and singing in the same shows was the young female vocalist Doris Day. Her film career lay wholly in the future, but already she displayed that unique singing style and obviously felt thrilled to be on the same program as Sinatra, who was a few years ahead of her in stardom.

In October, Sinatra's hometown of Hoboken announced that 30 October would henceforth be known as Frank Sinatra Day there.

Frank and Nancy both attended the ceremony, together with parents Martin and Dolly. Turning to records made at the time, Fontana Records later issued a double LP called *Sinatra Plus*. This compilation contained twenty-seven of the best recordings he made between 1944 and 1952. Many of these came from the 1946–1947 era and reflected his straighter style of the late 1940s.

Here are a few parenthetical memories of some of these numbers: "Bess," not too exciting, nor suited to his voice; "The Things We Did Last Summer," evocative of the real swoon style; "Time after Time," solid but not with the authority of a later version; "All of Me," faint stirrings of the swingier Sinatra to come; "Sweet Louise," one of the best of this vintage and one of his first real shots at jazz— "gay abandon," as Benny Green put it; and "I Concentrate on You," painstaking but painful compared to later interpretations. So Sinatra was still somewhat immature beside the future to unfold before our eyes and ears.

A fortnight after receiving the freedom of Hoboken, Sinatra opened yet another grueling booking at his second New York theater home, the Capital. There was no sign yet of any abatement in popularity, with up to eight performances daily. Nowadays, people grumble at appearing eight times weekly!

It seemed that something happened near the start of each year that would or could affect the Sinatra marriage. The previous New Year there had been the Marilyn Maxwell affair. Now in the opening month of 1948 Sinatra sometimes stayed overnight at a friend's place rather than going home to his lakeside residence and Nancy. Ava Gardner lived very near and she described how they met first for a dinner date that led to "heavy necking." Was it a one-off evening? Only time would tell.

Sinatra's last RKO Radio film involved straight acting and only a single song, "Ever Homeward." The title was *The Miracle of the Bells* and he costarred with Fred McMurray. Sinatra was cast as a priest, a far cry from film parts to date and slightly out of character, too! His fans were not really ready for such an unlikely transformation, although it did foreshadow many dramatic roles ahead. Later that year, *The Kissing Bandit* made for MGM seemed an equally strange casting. In this one, Sinatra was rematched with

Kathryn Grayson and there were four songs to lighten the ludicrous story: "If I Steal a Kiss," "Señorita," "Siesta," and "What's Wrong with Me?"

The Sinatras were still together despite the extramarital interludes. On 20 June 1948, Frank himself drove Nancy to the Hollywood hospital for the birth of their third child. Christina arrived early, to be known as Tina later on. The family still seemed an anchoring post in Sinatra's existence, but there would always be those other women. It was a fact of his life. The children got used to Hollywood as their home area. Sinatra's screen and radio career went on. There were more charity events, ever a part of his activities. The previous Christmas he had sung at a Los Angeles hospital and now in the summer it was an appearance in Music for the Wounded.

By the standards of previous popularity, 1948 proved to be a bad year for him. For the years immediately after the war, he had topped a poll as "popular singer of the year" but in 1948 the recordings were below par and his radio show had begun to show signs of slippage. As another ban came into force in 1948 by the American Federation of Musicians, the year was almost an utter blank as far as records were concerned for most singers—including Sinatra. As he was a life member of the union, he did not wish to contravene the ban in any way. Sinatra was depressed during this year because of both his career and domestic events. He had three children and a lovely wife, but Nancy knew they were not really in a stable, permanent relationship. Frank loved her, of course, but it would never be enough—and Ava Gardner was still in the offing. Both Sinatra and Gardner were big MGM stars, in spite of Sinatra's slight slip in popularity ratings.

He was back in the recording studio right at the start of the New Year 1949. Two of the tunes selected were sure classics, but they were not well received critically: "Some Enchanted Evening" and "Bali Ha'i." Perhaps Sinatra's mind had been distracted by the thought and vision of Gardner. Neither could forget their first encounter and then in February 1949 they met again at a show business party. A fresh date followed and it looked like it was getting serious.

During the 1948 lull in recordings, Sinatra had made a big feature film for MGM that was now shown in spring 1949. It was a

strange period mixture of baseball and vaudeville, both beloved
by American audiences. Sinatra and Gene Kelly were reunited,
this time as a couple of ball players—with the shapely Esther
Williams thrown in for luck. The film was released in America
under the title *Take Me Out to the Ball Game* and in Britain as
Everybody's Cheering. As well as the title song, five other vaudeville numbers graced the project: "Yes Indeedy," "O'Brien to
Ryan to Goldberg," "The Right Girl for You," "It's Fate Baby It's
Fate," and "Strictly U.S.A."

This was promising to be a rocky year for Sinatra. The powerful
female columnists in the States, syndicated coast-to-coast, drew repeated attention to his extramarital actions, while even his inner ad-
visers were warning him of the consequences of continuing to flout
conventions with ill-advised behaviors. Sinatra was really getting
criticized for a variety of reasons and from a variety of fronts. There
was bound to be an adverse reaction from his public in time, for
much of the American backbone was at that time severely moral
and unforgiving of sexual lapses. Apart from the family problems
getting bad publicity, McCarthyism was also gaining ground in the
United States, and along with many other liberally minded stars in
Hollywood, Sinatra came under scrutiny for quite mild civil rights
views and utterances. He could never be linked to communism, but
Senator Joseph McCarthy did his best to undermine many careers
in California and elsewhere. While all this turmoil was going on,
the Sinatras made their move from the lakeside house to an even
more luxurious mansion situated nearer the film studios. The os-
tensible reason was to patch up the family scene for the public image by being at home more during his limited spare time.

This move happened in the middle of 1949. But before the year
was out, Sinatra and Gardner appeared indiscreetly together. The
same week as this event, Sinatra's new blockbuster film for MGM
was seen. Once more he was with Gene Kelly, in the marvelous
musical *On the Town.* The plot: three sailors on shore leave and,
of course, three girls. Two of them were brilliant dancers, Vera-
Ellen and Ann Miller, and the whole picture scintillated with its
imaginative modern choreography and sheer verve. To recapture
its essence, you have only to recall the number "New York, New

York." Some of the scenes were shot on location in New York City and although the style may have become dated in the intervening decades, contemporarily speaking, it was rightly recognized as avant-garde. The other two players in the sextet were Betty Garrett and Jules Munshin. Among the enduring images from the film is one of Sinatra and Kelly hurrying through the turnstiles in the Times Square subway station, while their dance routines certainly became more advanced and adventurous than formerly. The other songs were "Come Up to My Place," "You're Awful," "Count on Me," and the title tune, "On the Town." Sinatra always loved New York, where some of his immortal triumphs happened.

Records were really still a barometer of Sinatra's popularity. In this tail-end of the 1940s, he made an amazing number with Axel Stordahl. Practically all of the 281 numbers from 1943 to 1952 were conducted by Stordahl and it is to the arranger's credit that the standard of the accompaniment never fell below being superior for that particular period. No one could expect more than that.

As a sidelight, it is interesting to recall how many well-known singers collaborated with Sinatra at odd times over these years. As far back as 7 November 1946, he did a special recording with Dinah Shore and the Kay Kyser orchestra called "It's All up to You." This was for the Good Health League and was in fact given away by the health department in North Carolina. He teamed up with the velvet-voiced Shore again in the following year for a commercial recording of "Tea for Two" and "New Romance."

Pearl Bailey helped him with "A Little Learnin' Is a Dangerous Thing." And, of course, in that era there would have been Americans who might have considered singing with a black woman, even a star like Bailey, as something calling for careful thought. This did not seem to occur to Sinatra. Rounding off the list of glamorous girl singers, Doris Day joined him on record to make "Let's Take an Old-Fashioned Walk"; Rosemary Clooney sang alongside him in "Peachtree Street" and "Love Means Love"; and finally the sultry pin-up girl Jane Russell made "Kisses and Tears" with Sinatra. But on the whole, I have always felt that he was at his best when in sole control. If you spent vast sums of hard-earned money to hear Sinatra, you did not want to have to share precious time with anyone else, however apparently special.

By the end of 1949, Sinatra had been right at the top for seven years. He had naturally met and made friends of a huge proportion of entertainers, artists, and composers. He always preferred creative characters to the "coffee drinkers," as he used to call them. He never made any secret of it.

In these years, too, Sinatra managed to make some enemies without much effort. Some people abhorred his liberal politics, even though all he ever advocated was social respect for all humanity. But he advocated it actively. He never stood for anyone being called a "nigger" or "dago" within his earshot. It made him mad, and when he got mad, anything might occur and occasionally did! He had the guts and energy to live by his principles, which were both simultaneously complex and simple. Some people were beginning to say that Sinatra was getting a bit too big for all those shoes of his. Perhaps there was a grain of truth in this, for he was only human after all. December 1949 marked his thirty-fourth birthday. His foes got something to bite on. The Ava Gardner affair really erupted. Their lives were about to go into free fall.

CHAPTER FIVE

ENTER AVA, EXIT NANCY
1950-1953

Frank Sinatra had fallen for Ava Gardner from the start. There seemed to be a certain inexorability about it. His marriage was already strained before Gardner, but this looked like it would bring about the final break. There was no purpose in blaming people for things like that. Three adults were involved: Nancy, Frank, and Ava. But there were three children, too: Nancy, Frank, and Tina. Sinatra was far from perfect, but he never forgot his family for a moment. Yet, it still made no difference to the outcome. Rather like a Greek tragedy, events unfolded at this stage. Despite the arrival of Tina in 1948, Nancy and Frank remained divided. They put on an appropriate face for family publicity pictures, but the gap widened irredeemably from December 1949 on. Years later, Gardner said that this was when she and Sinatra had made love for the first time.

In late January 1950, Sinatra's press agent and longtime friend George Evans died from a heart attack. Sinatra attended the funeral in New York and on the next day flew on to Texas, where he was due at the opening of a new hotel in Houston. Gardner turned up there, too. Inevitably, they were seen dining with the local mayor at an Italian restaurant. Sinatra had his not-unusual altercation with a press photographer during their dinner, with the result that the story became big news right across America.

Gardner had already been married twice, each time to a man connected with music. There was that dynamic young bundle

Mickey Rooney and also the clarinet-playing bandleader Artie
Shaw. Both men were eventually much married. To my young and
innocent ears, though, all that Shaw meant then was his classic rendering of "Begin the Beguine," still remembered half a century
later. Gardner had not really been very interested in Sinatra at first,
but the more elusive she made herself, the more strongly Sinatra
sought her. She had chosen to come to Houston after that first love-
making. Needless to say, the press made the maximum possible of
this fresh turn in Sinatra's always storm-swept private life. He was
becoming far from the former diffident young crooner. Gardner
said, "One thing I am sure of is that Frankie's plan to leave Nancy
came into his life long before I did." The domestic drama went on.
And about a fortnight after the Houston story broke, Nancy told
the world that she was filing for a legal separation. The irony was
the date of this announcement: Valentine's Day 1950.

This spell certainly piled the pressure on Sinatra. Manie Sacks
had left Columbia Records and his successor, Mitch Miller, had not
really identified with Sinatra's work. Nevertheless, it should not be
imagined for a moment that Sinatra's career collapsed as soon as the
Gardner story hit the streets. It did not. The process was slower and
less spectacular, spread over one, two, or even three years. In that
spring, for instance, Sinatra was in quite jaunty form on record,
making nine numbers with a bright, brassy new band behind
him—George Siravo's. Several of these titles have been issued over
and over again: "You Do Something to Me," "Lover," "The Continental," and "Should I." These and the rest all hinted at a new Sinatra in embryo, one breaking with the old sweeter stage of his life
and career and beginning to aim toward a new sharper, harder
phase that was more rhythmic, biting, painful, and mature. As yet,
it was only a straw in the wind of change. A lot still had to happen
to him first. Amid all the outburst from family-based opinion
throughout the States, Sinatra somehow managed to go on singing.
Well, he brought it all on himself, people said with little sympathy.
Anyway, after a Jewish charity concert, he started a stint at the Copacabana in New York, safely a continent away from California.
Gardner was there out front for over a week before going to Europe
for filming.

The strain finally manifested itself on Sinatra, however, and just before the end of the spell at the nightclub, his voice started to go and he was hemorrhaging in his throat. This was not so surprising, since in addition to the three nightly club shows, Sinatra was coping with five radio shows a week plus Sunday appearances. It all became too much and the body rebelled. A final blow followed when MGM canceled his film contract.

After a rest and recovery from the vocal trouble, Sinatra flew to Spain to be with Gardner during May. But as proof that the affair did not constitute a death blow to his career, he was back on radio shows, while a recording of "Goodnight Irene" got into the upper half of the top ten in the American hit parade. In fact, when Sinatra and Gardner came to Britain at the beginning of July, things were still fairly flourishing between them and in his career. The films may have stopped temporarily, but he had just signed one of those astronomical contracts—this time for a television series. It would be his very first television appearance and it came later that year on 7 October. But meanwhile they were in England.

Gardner took a flat in Mayfair, while Sinatra went into hiding nearby—somewhere in Berkeley Square. I think of it whenever I walk diagonally across the square on my way to the Curzon Cinema or elsewhere. Hardly to be wondered at, Sinatra refused to discuss his friendship with Gardner, confining his press communications to the television contract with Columbia and his forthcoming booking at the London Palladium. This was to be Sinatra's first live appearance in Britain. In the immediate postwar years, there had been talk of a tour, but it had fallen through—probably because he had been too busy back home. At that time, British housewives actually had the temerity to protest that they would rather have dried egg than the dollars that would have been paid to him in exchange currency. What an unromantic lot! But amends were about to be made.

Sinatra had one of his brushes with the press on the Friday evening before the Palladium week opened. He took Gardner to the first night of a new Noel Coward musical, *Ace of Clubs*, at the modern Cambridge Theatre just off Shaftesbury Avenue. Less than seven years earlier, I heard my earliest real symphony concerts in the same theater during the war. Sinatra and Gardner had scarcely settled in their seats before a photographer flashed a shot of the two together. Sinatra leaped up from his stalls seat, his blue eyes blazing, and was quoted in the press as saying, "Unless you give me that negative here and now I'll sue you so hard it will make your hair stand on end."

The photographer did not oblige him, making a quick getaway from the theater and into the maze of back streets north of the Covent Garden market area. It was not far from there to Fleet Street and his newspaper offices. Sinatra had started a long battle for privacy without much hope of success. But being the man he was, he could not help making his protest, however futile it might prove to be.

Three nights later, the great plush curtain swung apart at the Palladium, revealing Sinatra in evening dress with bow tie. The fans cheered his fifteen songs, still mainly slower ballads. For light relief he did a takeoff on Bing Crosby. The reception rivaled the early days at the Paramount, with teenage girls going crazy over such numbers as "Bewitched" and "I've Got a Crush on You." He included "Ol' Man River" and there was also the song that could have been the story of his life: "I Fall in Love Too Easily."

He sang with his heart, as ever. The palms of his hands were frequently turned outward expressively, as if in sheer supplication. All the audience could see, against the matte-black background and his black suit, were these hands, the white shirt, and the familiar face so involved and engrossed in each song that it became utterly unselfconscious. True, the fans squealed, but perhaps with slightly more British inhibition and restraint than the bobby-soxers back home. Gardner sat right among them in the vast audience.

All that week, from Monday, 10 July, to Saturday, 15 July, Sinatra filled the Palladium, and then he flew to Blackpool to appear there with the British orchestra, the Skyrockets. He arrived to cheering crowds at the holiday resort, then approaching the zenith of its season. Sinatra made two appearances at the 3,000-seat Opera House. For the first performance, it was three-quarters full, and for the second one, the theater nearly met its capacity. Five thousand people in one day was good enough. The applause certainly made up for the few gaps.

Before leaving Britain, Sinatra met the Duke of Edinburgh at Clarence House in London and agreed to come over again the following year to do a charity show for the National Playing Fields Association. This was one of the duke's particular interests. Sinatra also announced that he intended to devote all the royalties of a forthcoming record to youth recreation in Britain and to send sports gear over as well. These were early examples of a lifetime of philanthropy for youth and other causes close to his heart.

As a memento of the summer weeks he and Gardner had spent in Britain, Sinatra recorded "London by Night" with Axel Stordahl in September, just before the start of his television series. Sinatra met Carroll Coates, the young composer of the song, soon afterward in New York. Coates's verdict on Sinatra was "charming and intelligent."

Back in the States after the British interlude, Frank went straight into an Atlantic City series of shows, while Nancy still grieved over the breakup of the family. She and the children were all deeply affected by it. The television run was launched in the fall. *The Frank Sinatra Show* was seen at peak viewing time on Saturday evenings and continued to be broadcast a regular number of times over the ensuing couple of years. The CBS television series was complemented by a radio show also starring Sinatra, which went out the following day, Sunday, each week. So the American public was still seeing and hearing a lot of Sinatra, considering that he was allegedly entering the doldrums of his career.

The press pursued Sinatra and Gardner like wild beasts after their prey. In desperation, the couple fled to Acapulco for a few days, but were besieged before, during, and after the trip. Hardly a restful break. And all was not necessarily smooth between the pair themselves. Gardner was still sometimes on the run, with Sinatra hotfoot after her. So it became almost a Keystone Cops vision. Before they eventually got together legally, Sinatra made two transatlantic flights following her—and spent some thousands of dollars in phone calls. This was so different from Sinatra's normal trouble of having to ward off women. There were frequent cases like that of women who arrived asking for his autograph—on their brassieres. And the society woman who got as far as his hotel bedroom somewhere, loosened her fur coat, and revealed nothing—or everything. Things like that never seemed to happen to mere writers like me!

Sinatra and Gardner had been together in Spain, the United States, Britain, and Mexico. He was still obsessed by the emerald green eyes of the actress, who was considered to be one of the most beautiful women in the world. Even Nancy junior had to admit as much when she was taken to meet Gardner for the first time at a tender young age.

Frank asked Nancy to divorce him, but she hung on throughout 1950, possibly hoping that he would change his mind. She had the three growing children to consider. Furthermore, as a Roman Catholic, she could never treat divorce lightly, or even countenance it at all.

In 1951, Sinatra recorded over a dozen titles for Columbia Records under the auspices of their recording boss, Mitch Miller. "I'm a Fool to Want You" could be thought of as symbolic of the Sinatra-Gardner liaison, and in fact Sinatra had a strong influence in shaping the lyrics of the song. It certainly came over with the to-tal conviction of real-life experience and not just a fictional number.

In May 1951, Nancy eventually made the following simple, digni-fied statement to the press: "I have regretfully put aside religious and personal considerations to give Frank the freedom he has so earnestly requested." No one could fail to read the anguish between those few lines and to feel some emotion—whether sympathy for Nancy and the children, or dislike at the way Sinatra had acted toward them.

Amid all this private drama, Sinatra had been making yet an-other fortnight's booking at—yes, where else?—the Paramount. Not quite the same swoon era now, but still a star performance. This phase in his life as one of decline has been exaggerated by var-ious sources for various reasons or dramatic effect when telling the Sinatra story. On the musical front, things did get a bit worse—but only by the phenomenal standards he always set himself and by the ultrahigh levels of his popularity over the previous decade. It was not so much that he had flopped, for even throughout 1950 and 1951 Sinatra never fell below second in the major popularity polls for male singers. Most performers would welcome that sort of def-inition of "decline"!

But he was feeling the effect of strain through the dual combination of private and public life—and how they interacted with each other. There was the friction of the 1949–1952 years with Columbia Records set against the background tension of his personal life—self-inflicted but spread all over the newspapers of the world. There was nowhere to hide from the publicity. The press loved the story. Then there was Mitch Miller, who had become the manager of artists and recording at Columbia in 1950. Miller and Sinatra did not see eye-to-eye. As most people knew, Sinatra was agreeable to being advised but never ordered.

The *Frank Sinatra Discography* quotes Sinatra's comments in *Hit Parade* magazine. Referring to Miller, Sinatra said, "He is a fine musician, one who played woodwind on some of my earlier sides, but I can't go along with Miller as a recording manager." Then he added, "I rejected so many tunes that my business managers began to hound me to accept one." One infamous title actually was called "Mama Will Bark." I think most people would have been on Sinatra's side in ridiculing this one. The astounding fact was that he agreed to sing it at all.

One session Sinatra did enjoy was a highly nostalgic reunion with Harry James, whom he had left on that wintry day so long ago. While the Festival of Britain had got into its summer stride on London's artistic South Bank, one afternoon in July 1951 Sinatra joined James and his trumpet on the following: "Castle Rock," "Farewell to Love," and "Deep Night." James bore Sinatra no grudge for leaving him.

Over the final three years with the Columbia outfit, Sinatra tried several groups other than Stordahl without ever finding the perfect formula: Hugo Winterhalter, Morris Stoloff, Jeff Alexander, and the well-known Percy Faith. But it would eventually turn out to be George Siravo who ushered in the next phase of Sinatra's singing career. Or you could say the next phase but one, because by summer 1951 the well-publicized slump still lay ahead of him.

The television series ended for the season in June. By his standards it had not been a total success. The month after the Harry James session, Sinatra was flying down to Mexico City with Gardner. Their courtship was still proving turbulent—and very public.

Then in August they flew to Acapulco for another few days. There, they had a quarrel outside the Beachcomber Club, set on Acapulco Bay, and so the stresses were spilling over into public gaze. Not very edifying. On their return to California, Sinatra was alleged to have driven his car at William Eccles, a press photographer, at the Los Angeles airport. As in the instance of Lee Mortimer, Sinatra was advised to send the journalist a letter of apology, which he did. The story made headlines throughout America. So the dramas went on unabated, but shortly afterward Sinatra and Gardner told the press that they were engaged and would marry as soon as it became possible.

Sinatra's long and legendary affection for Nevada started in August when he fulfilled a two-week spell at a Reno casino. But straight after that the drama resumed. He was feeling an underlying depression with his life then, despite the degree of success most men would have welcomed. He and Gardner were staying in a rented house beside Lake Tahoe when a quarrel occurred. Gardner returned to her Hollywood home leaving Sinatra more depressed than usual. He took some sleeping tablets on top of a few drinks—probably Jack Daniels. The next thing was that his friend Hank Sanicola was ringing Gardner that same night. Gardner recalled the message, "Frank's taken an overdose." But when she got back to Lake Tahoe the next morning, he was sitting up after a good rest. "I thought you'd gone," he said to her. She was very annoyed but forgave him "in about twenty-five seconds." Needless to say, the press managed to turn the account into a "suicide attempt."

Then immediately after the Reno booking came Sinatra's debut at the Desert Inn in Las Vegas. This could hardly be called a slump, especially as another series of his television shows followed in the fall.

The public and private personae went along in parallel. The same month as the Las Vegas date, on 30 October, Nancy obtained a divorce decree and was awarded custody of the children, one-third of Sinatra's future income, and two homes. Despite the apparent bleak finality associated with such proceedings, Sinatra still managed to remain on close terms with the children, whom he worshiped in his own way. Nor was it, indeed, the end of seeing Nancy. Which says something for all five of them.

This was the traumatic timetable involved in getting married a week later. On 1 November, Sinatra qualified for residency in the state of Nevada by having lived there for the past five weeks. The next day they got a licence to marry, after Gardner had finally agreed to do so. On 7 November, they were married in Philadelphia at the home of Manie Sacks's brother.

The idea had been to avoid publicity, but it did not work out as planned—as throughout the Sinatra-Gardner saga. A seven-tier cake adorned the occasion, which was attended by Dolly Sinatra. So after Mickey Rooney and Artie Shaw, Ava took Frank as her third and last husband. He was quoted as saying to her after the ceremony, "Well, we finally made it." But that proved to be far from the happy ending to the romance. Life rarely turned out to be as tidy as the Hollywood films depicted. Meanwhile, they were photographed cheek to cheek with Frank wearing a white carnation.

Sinatra had made the film *Double Dynamite* for RKO Radio earlier, with siren Jane Russell and the inimitable wisecracker Groucho Marx. Remember that surname for the future of the story. Only two numbers graced the film and Sinatra really only had one of them, "Kisses and Tears." It is hard to come to grips with the mentality of a company that had Sinatra contracted to it yet produced a vehicle that gave him a single song; rather like composing a ballet and including only one solo spot for the ballerina. There was nothing intrinsically wrong with the picture, but it wasted Sinatra's talents at a time when they really needed to be nurtured and developed.

True to his word, a month after their marriage Frank returned to London with Ava. He had promised to sing in the London Coliseum Midnight Show in aid of the National Playing Fields Association. There were no scenes, no angry words. The honeymoon was not yet over. They dined with the Duke of Edinburgh at the Empress Club. Ava looked darkly devastating in white satin under coffee lace. At her throat shone a necklace with matching gems in her ears.

Sinatra said, "The Duke asked me to help the Association, because I had done similar work for children in America. With the Variety Club of Great Britain, we organised a big Anglo-American charity show. We could not have done it without the Duke's great encouragement and support. He is one of the most congenial and nicest people I have ever met. I am hoping to make this an annual event. I have given my pledge to the Duke to come back next year."

Prince Philip and Princess Margaret both attended the Coliseum show, and Margaret could frequently be seen in later years as a prominent member of audiences at Sinatra concerts in Britain. A devoted fan!

But over in America, the public had not taken the Gardner romance too well. The country had that strong puritanical strain running through it—for better or worse—and it would clearly take time for the people to adjust and accept what had happened in the Sinatra family. Added to this, the press was retaliating for Sinatra's brusque behavior toward it. It stressed the fall in his record sales and called his voice a croak. The truth was more complex. Sinatra was ill and his throat was liable to hemorrhage again as on that previous occasion in New York.

Failure, like success, can come with a snowballing effect. True, the record sales did fall. His television series came to an end. And there had been alleged disagreements with costar Shelley Winters during the shooting of his latest film, *Meet Danny Wilson*. He attended its premiere in San Francisco and the reviews were quite reasonable. Yet, in spite of no fewer than nine good songs, the film did not make much money for anyone involved. The *London Daily Mail* said fairly that "the Sinatra voice is still pleasant." This picture did give him some straight acting experience, which might be useful for him if the immediate signs of his singing career were anything to go by.

The story of *Meet Danny Wilson* rather resembled Sinatra's own show business career to date, but in retrospect it really seems incredible that a film with these nine numbers could not succeed totally: "You're a Sweetheart," "Lonesome Man Blues," "She's Funny That Way," "A Good Man Is Hard to Find," "That Old Black Magic," "When You're Smiling," "All of Me," "I've Got a Crush on You," and "How Deep Is the Ocean?" What a collection of classics. But the truth was perhaps that time had moved on since the heady days of the 1940s and the public had yet to realize that many of these songs would last for the rest of the century—unlike the rock and pop music that followed.

This leaner time had not come overnight, nor was it catastrophic for Sinatra. While chronicling the apparent downward curve in the career, it is hard to reconcile it with yet another fortnight at the legendary Paramount Theater. The drummer Buddy Rich and his band were the backup for Sinatra, but the engagement did not have to be extended due to demand. Those immortal bands of Tommy Dorsey, Glenn Miller, Artie Shaw, and the rest were out of favor— or on the way out. And the teenage girls were married and had settled down with different lives. Many of them, anyway,

So 1952 looked like being a "hinge" year for Sinatra. The door could swing open again for him, or it could shut in his face. He was not the sort of character to accept a slap in the face from anything or anyone. Which way would things go for him? Publicly and privately? The two undeniable temperaments of Sinatra and Gardner clashed. Perhaps that was what created the chemistry. When they were not kissing, they were liable to be quarreling. The dilemma was described in these terms: when Sinatra was down, they got on well, but by his very nature he could not stay down.

Ava was in Africa during April 1952 filming Ernest Hemingway's *Snows of Kilimanjaro* with Gregory Peck, the great star of the time. She was reported to have said at the time, "I can't wait to get back to my old man. I miss him terribly, and I'm flying to New York where he's doing personal appearances with his picture. We hope to go to Honolulu at the end of April for a holiday and a concert for Sinatra. He'll sing at the Royal Hawaiian Hotel. And in June he opens at the Coconut Grove in Los Angeles."

Sinatra's records for Columbia dwindled in number during 1952. Nevertheless, two of the titles were long associated with him. These were "I Could Write a Book" and "I Hear a Rhapsody." In fact, in June 1952 Columbia canceled his contract. How wrong could it get?

But let us take the story in sequence. Ava thought that Frank was singing better than ever, but a Hollywood gossip writer, eager to anticipate or precipitate any trouble to befall Frank, wrote, "Big rise, big fall." Despite the differences caused by their tempestuous natures, Ava was as good as her word and did in fact fly to Honolulu with Frank in April, thereby incurring suspension by MGM.

Sinatra sang in Honolulu. And according to reports of one particular concert, this marked a crucial personal point in his career. He could have gone under, given up, but he didn't. He turned the test into a triumph. The date was at a Hawaii county fair and it was raining. The concert was held in a tent before a small but eager audience. Sinatra responded to this challenge. He realized that they represented his real public. He sang up to a score of his hit songs, to the very best of his ability. To the *Honolulu Advertiser*'s Buck Buchwach, Sinatra was reported to have said, "Tonight marks the first night on the way back."

I suppose the important thing was that Sinatra had not despaired. It did not matter that the Hawaii and Los Angeles dates proved inconclusive and that the dip in his career continued. Then the *New York Sunday Mirror* columnist Sheila Graham said, "Mr. Sinatra's next picture had to be canceled because the last one laid a bomb. His agents have left him, he has sold his office building. The 200 Sinatra fan clubs have dwindled to four and his fan mail has shrunk to a trickle—all in a year."

Notwithstanding the confirmed quality of his singing at this stage, the decline went on. The rows between Ava and himself went on, too, and while he was appearing at the Copacabana in New York each night, Ava made him mad by going out on her own. In a fit of jealousy, Frank told her that he was going to shoot himself. It was reported, or fabricated, that he did actually fire two shots—one into the bed of their hotel room. Another time the intention seemed really there, for Sinatra was brought around after breathing from an unlit gas stove at Manie Sacks's abode—also in New York. The summer of 1952 was a dark phase.

The strange story of his downward slope appeared all the more unaccountable as only three weeks after the *New York Sunday Mirror* article almost writing him off, Sinatra went into the Columbia studios to record some of his last titles with Stordahl for that company—and his style hinted at a great new quality in embryo.

For the first time in his career, he gave an irrefutable sign that he had a fresh range and style of singing within his grasp. The key number was "The Birth of the Blues," which he hardly ever felt obliged to record again after that summer day of 3 June 1952. He revealed an exciting new jazz awareness, full of sweeping phrases. This was no longer Sinatra, but simply a singer of love songs. Now he blended the sweet with the swing in a heartfelt blues. Tommy Dorsey could hardly have done it better on his trombone.

The whole session seemed symbolic. It disclosed the same appealing loneliness of his past voice, with the blues of his present undeniable confusion—and yet there was buoyancy bursting through as a hope for his future. Add to this number the "Hipster Exuberance" (Benny Green) of "Bim Bam Baby," and we imagined we could see how Sinatra would survive any trials still ahead of him. It was as if he was determined to show them he could not be finished off that easily, summarily. In the parallel of a later age, it was like John McEnroe saving a succession of match points and going on to win at Wimbledon or Flushing Meadows.

17 September 1952: this is a well-documented date of Sinatra's final recording for Columbia in New York. It had been a momentous decade with the company. The record was symbolically entitled *Why Try to Change Me Now?* Later, he would be signing up with Capitol Records, but just then the career still looked tottering. And so did his second marriage.

The same scenes were being reenacted with Gardner. In October, Sinatra was making a guest appearance on his friend Jimmy Durante's television show. It was a Saturday-night transmission and Sinatra did not get back to their Palm Springs home until Sunday morning. He found Gardner there with his former girlfriend Lana Turner and one or two others discussing him in critical terms. He got so furious that he was reported to have phoned the police to ask them to come and eject them from the house. No one ever quite knew the end of that particular story.

Sinatra always had a temper. Sometimes it was directed into positive channels, when he helped to correct some injustice or other. But his mood was liable to be loosed on someone dear to him. This outburst may have followed others earlier that month about Gardner's decision to accept an offer to go to Africa on location to make the film *Mogambo* with Clark Gable. Sinatra was fed up and at a low ebb. He was always at his best when busy and just then there seemed to be virtually no work for him.

But no one could say that Frank and Ava led dull lives. Ava found out that she was pregnant but for a variety of reasons decided to have an abortion—without Frank's knowledge. Meanwhile, Sinatra happened to be reading the James Jones best-selling novel *From Here to Eternity.* He became fascinated and even obsessed by the character of Private Angelo Maggio. He felt that this might have been written for him. And he was also aware that scripting and casting happened to be imminent for a film adaptation of the book. Ava was also aware of his strong feelings about the story and the part in it that Sinatra craved. Buddy Adler and Harry Cohn were working on the script and in charge of casting the picture. Ava arranged through a mutual friend to meet Harry for dinner one evening. Talking about the forthcoming film to Harry and his wife, Joan, Ava suggested that Frank would be exactly right for the role of Maggio. Harry was actually head of Columbia Pictures, which would be making the film, and he agreed to consider Frank.

Despite their previous rows about Ava accepting her film role in *Mogambo,* she decided to go ahead and left for Kenya to start her scenes with Gable and Grace Kelly. Sinatra went with her. She had called his bluff. But this was still destined to be an eventful November 1952. They had only been out there about a week when Sinatra got a telegram from his agent inviting him to fly back to Hollywood to discuss the role of Maggio. He took the next available flight, leaving Ava to carry on filming.

"Can't you see?" he urged the producers. "Maggio's me. Please let me play the part." But they were still tending to think of him in terms of his singing, and anyway they had several other actors ready to do screen tests for the role. They told Sinatra that they would test him if none of the others turned out to be right. There was more than one star name in the short list already, men who had made film reputations as straight actors, so it seemed pretty hopeless for Sinatra to expect anything to come of it. He seemed to sense that he needed this chance, this change, at that particular moment in his life, and so he felt especially frustrated at not being allowed to test for the part. Sinatra could never sit idle for long and now he seemed more restive than usual. He contacted Ava and told her he was flying out to Africa to join her there for Christmas.

It was good for him to see her again. But with all of them busy filming, Sinatra felt slightly out of things. All his hopes seemed to be concentrated on the outside chance to test for a supporting role in a film. For most of that week, he brooded about the location of *Mogambo.* Then one day he went missing. He had gone into nearby Nairobi. Years later, Grace Kelly recounted what happened next. She was introducing Sinatra at the celebrated 1970 Royal Festival Hall concert in London. This was how she described the scene in Africa all those years earlier:

> I remember a Christmas time in East Africa many years ago. We were all getting a bit glum and gloomy at being away from home at this time. Frank decided to take Christmas in hand. He disappeared into Nairobi and returned with just about every Christmas ornament the city contained—and one Santa Claus suit. He came back to the bush where we were all on safari. At Christmas Eve we gathered in a clearing under a starry African sky. There in the centre was a huge mantelpiece with all the ornaments. Frank even talked John Ford into reciting *The Night before Christmas* to us. And this wonderful evening ended with sixty Congolese Africans, barefooted and with their blankets wrapped around them, singing French Christmas carols to us. It was a wonderful Christmas—thanks to Frank.

Sinatra's cajoling paid off. He got his reward. The cable came. None of the actors who had made the screen tests satisfied the producers, and so Sinatra sped back to Hollywood on the next available flight. He had the script of his test scene with him and he studied it to the exclusion of all else as he flew nearly halfway around the world. He arrived on the set for the test early one morning. He knew the scene word-perfect, gesture-perfect. During the long hours of those flights from Kenya, he had somehow almost become Angelo Maggio.

The producer was quoted as saying, "Almost from the first take, we knew we had it."

But they had to see all the tests commissioned before they could come to a definite decision. Frank could not stand the suspense of hanging around Hollywood to hear the verdict—so he flew back to

Kenya and Ava. By the time she had finished the film, Ava was pregnant for the second time. She told Frank about it, and between them they decided on the same course of action that she had taken originally. So an unlikely scenario ensued of Ava Gardner and Frank Sinatra at a nursing home near Wimbledon on the southwest outskirts of London.

Then it was back to the United States once more—to the continuing publicity surrounding the couple. The influential gossip columnists were of course syndicated throughout the whole of America and so any item from Hollywood—real or concocted—was disseminated everywhere. And Sinatra and Gardner were still good for the gossip. The two matriarchs of the 1950s were Hedda Hopper and Louella Parsons. Rather like the New York theater critics, they could virtually make or break the careers of actors and actresses.

In January 1953, Sinatra had been so keen, so crazy, to get the Maggio part that he offered to do it virtually for free if necessary. Meanwhile, after a couple more singing engagements in Boston and Montreal came a real upsurge in his fortunes. In April he signed a contract with Capitol Records, one that would bring him in proximity to such star arrangers as Billy May and Nelson Riddle. And that very same month, Capitol released Sinatra's version of "Three Coins in the Fountain"—later to become an Oscar winner.

By then, of course, Sinatra had heard the good news. He had been given the coveted part of Maggio. He was paid a few thousand dollars, which was very little by film standards. But Sinatra was not worried about the money. This meant much more. The chance to act, to prove himself. Perhaps his last chance? He had not forgotten the two comparative flops only a year or so earlier. Nor had Hollywood, where "you are only as good as your last picture."

In April, too, the filming for *From Here to Eternity* began in Hawaii. They all went out there: Burt Lancaster, Montgomery Clift, Deborah Kerr, and Sinatra. The famous setting was Pearl Harbor, Honolulu, in 1941. Sinatra would either make the grade or be exposed by the others' professional abilities. Gardner was away, working in Spain. Sinatra found that the only release from himself was in work, and he threw all his infinite capacity for caring, feeling, and suffering into the role of Maggio, the anonymous, tough soldier who died victorious, beaten but unbeaten. The man who was everybody and nobody. The character crystallized all those fellow Italian immigrants of Sinatra's hometown, and all the humble of humanity. Much of the anguish of his recent life must have been transmuted into the portrayal. The producers finished the film, but no one yet knew how it would emerge, how he would fare.

While Sinatra had been busy creating Maggio, the Internal Revenue Service (IRS) now entered the scene, which was something he could have done without just then. IRS officials filed a claim for $110,000 in income tax against him. The fee from the film would not go far toward meeting this claim. The Sinatra marriage was still running its predestined furrow. He and Gardner were still kissing or throwing things at each other—a Latin-style love affair. Sinatra had spent a day or two in Britain before working on Maggio, planning a tour for a little later. And while he was there, he attended the Variety Club of Great Britain Annual Star of the Year presentation, which was made to Jeannie Carson. Her very name makes it seem a long time ago now.

While the technicians set about editing *From Here to Eternity* prior to its premiere planned for later in 1953, Sinatra undertook his projected European tour. Although he was feeling happier having completed the film to the best of his acting ability, this tour did little to help him in his career—except as part of the overall pattern of his experience of life.

The international press was still against him and it reported that he refused encores at Turin, stressing that Italian audiences had asked for their admission money to be refunded. But they cheered Ava, who went with him. He was also said to have halved an appearance in a Swedish amusement park to catch a boat across to Denmark. These reports did not read well but, as we know only too well, the press can be very selective and subjective. For instance, to counterbalance the adverse side of the coin came news from Knokke in Belgium. The manager responsible for Sinatra's three concert appearances there said, "Never have there been such scenes, never such extraordinary attendances!"

The reliably melodic Billy Ternent and his orchestra accompanied Sinatra for his only real tour in Britain. The places he played included Dundee, Glasgow, Liverpool, Birmingham, Bristol, and London. The tour started on 14 June. In Dundee, his first audience numbered 586 and the second house twice as many—in a cavernous 3,000-seat theater. Unabashed, Sinatra asked them all to move down toward the front where he could see them better! He got a very good reception. He had learned by now to take rough and smooth, and he knew he was still in a rougher patch than in the past.

From the moment of his first concert at the Granada Tooting, it was clear to all who really cared that Sinatra was singing better than ever. Even Mike Butcher for the *New Musical Express* wrote that "his visual manner of selling a song is an object lesson in unexaggerated mastery . . . his range and power seem greater than before." Other critics sounded favorable, too, detecting "an extra spring in the singer's stride." On 11 and 16 July, he made special guest appearances on Cyril Stapleton's radio band show. The orchestra was wild in its praise of Sinatra's musicianship and general mastery. The success of the British tour as a whole can best be judged by the advertisement Sinatra took in the musical press before leaving the country:

> Farewells are never pleasant and with my flight tonight to America I feel the "sweet sorrow" of partings. I have been accorded a wonderful welcome during my tour of these little Isles and I will carry home a legion of memories.
>
> Tomorrow I shall be in New York, but each day I shall cherish the thought of the very friendly manner in which I was treated by everyone on the map, up and down your country. But let this not be Goodbye, just "So long" for maybe only a few months. And "Thank You."
>
> Very sincerely yours, Frank.

As Sinatra returned to the States, he had two things up his sleeve, as it were. The first was the Maggio portrayal. The second, and equally vital to him, was the promise of a turn toward recovery in his singing fortunes. For on 30 April and 2 May 1953, he had made his first recordings on Capitol Records with two exciting new orchestras—Nelson Riddle and Billy May. Sinatra had signed the crucial Capitol contract during April and initially he also cut a trio of Stordahl orchestrations, plus one by Riddle. This was virtually the end of the fruitful Stordahl years. Around the same time, he also made another significant side, the theme of *From Here to Eternity*. Perhaps this would be a sign of good luck for both his acting and his singing career. Certainly, the arrangements reached a new standard of modern accompaniment and accomplishment.

In retrospect, it is apparent that the key time for Sinatra's upturn of fortune was this spring and summer: around the period of the British coronation of Elizabeth II. Regardless, he never really fell from esteem as deeply as the press would have liked the public to believe. It was just that judged by the dizzy success of the rest of his career the early 1950s era looked comparatively lean.

Sinatra was still obsessed with Gardner—and still married to her. They were together in London that August 1953 but the customary quarrels flared. In the Milroy Club, Park Lane, the two of them began to disagree in raised vocal tones. The proprietor of the fashionable club asked them to quiet down a bit.

"Don't crowd me," said Sinatra, still in a heated state.

Frank and Ava did not seem to be able to spend time together without violence erupting. People observed it as a love-hate relationship. Both of them appeared possessive and temperamental. Perhaps they were too much alike in vital ways. Gardner said, "This guy Frankie just has Italian blood which bursts out and we quarrel. It's one of those things. At one time I'm crazy about him and then all of a sudden I'm not. And then I am again." Once she sat up all night playing his records after he had gone away somewhere. The emotional seesaw went on at the apartment they shared in the leafy Regent's Park region of London during that August. When they got back to New York, they went to separate hotels and did not speak to each other. Sinatra's mother tried to intercede, but it was no use.

While this roller coaster of a romance juddered along its rails, *From Here to Eternity* opened in August. The reviews were ecstatic and the box-office business presaged record-breaking proportions. Sinatra's Maggio was one of the talking points with the reviewers and the public alike: underdog Maggio bullied by Ernest Borgnine.

But the differences between Frank and Ava widened and rough-
ened. On 2 October, they made a show of being seen at the
Mogambo opening in New York, but afterward Ava went on to
Palm Springs while Frank pointedly did not. Instead, on 19 October he began a week's singing stint at the Sands Hotel in Las Vegas.
Nancy Sinatra quotes him as singing "They Can't Take That Away
from Me," "Day In–Day Out," "All of Me," and "Just One of Those
Things." The last classic looked like being the epitaph for the marriage. Less than a year after the marriage had taken place, on 27 October MGM announced that the fated love of Frank and Ava
seemed to be at an end. Ava told the press that she would settle in
Madrid and would also be considering divorce. By that time, a bullfighter had appeared on her scene, if only as an ardent admirer.

By November, Sinatra was coping with radio shows three times
a week, which ran for several months. But he was still in a bad way,
more from his personal relationship than professionally. The public
announcement of the separation affected him deeply. His weight
then was never very much for his height of 5 feet 10 inches. But he
lost weight. George Wood, his agent and friend, stayed with him all
the time, to see that Sinatra did not go to pieces. There was the dan-
ger that he might drink and not bother to eat or sleep properly. But
he still could not get Gardner out of his system. She was due to
travel to Europe to film *The Barefoot Contessa* with Sinatra's close
confidant Humphrey Bogart. So Sinatra prerecorded his radio
shows to free himself to try to go with her. But on 19 November, he
was admitted to a New York hospital suffering from mental strain
and exhaustion. As soon as he could, and against the advice of his
doctors, he staggered out of the hospital and flew to Europe, armed
with presents, with the aim of seeing Gardner.

They met in Madrid, but Ava was already seeing her friend the
bullfighter. Then she had to go to Rome. Frank flew back to the
States, but just before Christmas he phoned her asking if they could
meet in Rome over the holiday. Ava agreed but said she would still
divorce him. He flew over and they met for the last time in the volcanic marriage. Then they parted. Now just thirty-eight years old
and immeasurably more mature than when he had met Ava, Frank
finally went home alone to a New Year and a new life. There

seemed to be a certain inexorability about it all. Twenty years earlier, he had started singing. Eleven years before, the Paramount had happened. Already, he had crammed the experiences of several lifetimes into this life span and given millions of people memorable moments.

And yet, and yet, it had hardly all started . . .

CHAPTER SIX

FROM HERE TO ETERNITY
1954-1957

The New Year—1954—started well for Sinatra. He must have made a mental resolution to try to put his troubles behind him and to concentrate on his career. For just in the way that things had been piling up against him—Sinatra even seemed to be against himself sometimes—they now seemed to be turning in his favor. A losing streak has to change sometime. But it was not mere luck. He had fought back and was once more in control of his life, as far as anyone can be.

First proof of this came early on. In the 1950s, it took several months for a film to be generally released. The *Los Angeles Examiner* was just one of many newspapers reviewing *From Here to Eternity*. It wrote, "It is visible even from here that Sinatra will be among the first next Academy time." And the proof of Sinatra's comeback was not long delayed.

On 25 March 1954, at the Pantages Theater in Hollywood, the film world held its great annual occasion: the announcement and bestowal of the Academy Awards for the previous year's motion pictures. There had been the usual forecasts from both the press and the public, and as the time neared for the actual awards to be made, an electric atmosphere tingled through the starry theater. This was the night of the year for the filmmakers and all associated people. Frank attended with his children Nancy and Frank Jr. but had also gone with the good wishes of Nancy senior and Tina. Quite a family.

From Here to Eternity collected eight individual awards. But the most moving moment of an evening charged with the usual emotion came when one particular Oscar was announced. Mercedes Mc-Cambridge opened an envelope and read the words, "The award for the Best Performance of the Year by a Supporting Actor goes to . . . Frank Sinatra for his role as Maggio in *From Here to Eternity.*"

The applause broke in waves over the air.

Sinatra was sitting there with his children. They looked across at him and exchanged nods for a second. Then he stood up, kissed each of them, and "sprinted" (in his own words) to the stage to collect the familiar statuette. Immaculate as ever, Sinatra appeared quite composed—outwardly. The sign of the ultimate professional. Barely a year earlier, he had gripped hold of the chance of this part instinctively, almost as a lifeline to a sinking man. And he played the part instinctively, too, "the gutsy little Italian American who dies a tragic death." Now, he gripped the Oscar tightly, too. As a reporter was actually heard to remark with a total lack of originality but a lot of truth, "That's show business for you!" Afterward, Sinatra recalled missing the party and going for a long walk around Beverly Hills, still clutching his precious Oscar.

Dismissed as a dismal washout by some only a year or two earlier, Sinatra now plunged into work almost with a frenzy for it. The part in his next picture suited his mood of resilience. No doubt that he emerged from these times enhanced in stature in every way. He played a cold-blooded killer in *Suddenly* and made the character suitably ruthless for the role. The film was not released until later in 1954.

More important to the Sinatra story, however, was the resurgence in records. Back on 9 December 1953 Sinatra had recorded "Young at Heart" with "Take a Chance" on the B side. On this pair, he was accompanied by the smooth swing of Nelson Riddle. These arrangements seemed to be bringing out something new in the Voice. It was as if at last an arranger had realized that he should never try to fight the vocal but frame it lovingly. Never compete, only complement.

Sinatra and Riddle found that they got on ideally and they went straight into a project for two LPs. The 78 rpm and 45 rpm records were passing. The 33 rpm was here. It was ten inches in diameter and could take up to eight songs. The two new projects were *Songs for Young Lovers* and *Swing Easy*. They were recorded on 5 and 6 November 1953 and 7 and 19 April 1954, respectively.

Capitol Records issued the albums in 1955 and 1954, respectively. Both proved to be best sellers. The public leapt on *Swing Easy* after having its appetite whetted by the single *Young at Heart,* which was also released in 1954. The switch back to success was almost funny. There would be a million potential customers all ready and waiting for the LPs. The extraordinary recovery of Sinatra during the golden year was not yet complete. He had catapulted back into the top ranks of radio, television, and films. But best of all perhaps to him came the news of recognition for his two 1954 records. *Swing Easy* had only been released in August, but zooming forward a few months, *Billboard* announced the result of its yearly disc-jockey poll as follows:

Favorite male singer—Frank Sinatra

Favorite single record—*Young at Heart*

Favorite album—*Swing Easy*

After this triple crown came the regular popularity poll run by *Downbeat* magazine. It almost went without saying that the outstanding male singer verdict was voted to Sinatra. And rounding off the musical press triumph, the third magazine, *Metronome*, also ranked him as the year's top male vocalist.

By a stroke of commercial genius, Capitol later combined the two hit LPs into one sixteen-song record. The sleeve of this album graphically conveyed the revolution that took place between the swoon and swing phases:

It's the new Sinatra. Not the kid in his twenties who was sending the kids in their teens. Now he's a young man in his thirties, and he's singing to the world. He's more mature, his musical insight is deeper, his voice richer. He's

no longer just another good pop singer called Frankie Boy. He's a great
singer of popular songs. He's Sinatra. As Nelson Riddle, who so beautifully
arranged and ably conducted the album, comments, "Frank is a wonderful,
intuitive singer. He's got it all in him."

Let's look at these records. *Songs for Young Lovers* was recorded
before Sinatra was free of his emotional conflicts. The remarkable
fact was that he made it just ten days or so after the announcement
of the Ava Gardner separation—and a fortnight before going into
the hospital owing to mental strain and exhaustion. There were
bound to be romantic numbers in the group, but he brought the beginning of a less-sugary, more-spicy style to them. Or perhaps they
were chosen not to be too saccharine. Few other singers could make
"Violets for Your Furs" sound so sincere. "A Foggy Day" inspired
a slightly jaunty approach. And there was one of his all-time favorites, "I Get a Kick out of You."

To flip forward five months of his life, imagine Sinatra at the
recording studio on those spring days of April 1954 making *Swing
Easy*. On one day he wore a large polka-dot tie with a dark jacket
over the top. On the other, he still sported a large tie, but it was
plain this time. The pattern on that session came from a checked
vest under his jacket. On both days, the first thing he did as he settled himself in the studio was to undo the top button of his shirt and
to loosen the big knot in his tie. Then he felt freer. He tipped his
bright-banded hat farther back on his head, glanced through the
sheet music for the first song, and nodded to Riddle. They had
worked out the arrangement in advance, naturally, but this would
be the first time Sinatra heard the finished product live. He listened
to the band playing it through; then they went into it again, this
time with Sinatra filling in the vocal gaps.

"Okay. Take one," called a recording man across the floor.

From the second that Sinatra sang the famous Cole Porter
opening to "Just One of Those Things," the pace and style of the
record had been set. This was going to usher in a new standard in
the history of American popular music. They all sensed it. The
reign of Riddle and Sinatra. Sinatra would have wanted it described like that—not the other way around. He always showed

generosity in crediting arrangers and composers alike. As he said, they were "my peers."

There was more brass, there were fewer strings. But brass used with taste and restraint. "I'm Gonna Sit Right Down and Write Myself a Letter"—here he really started to "trombone" it up and down the scale. "Wrap Your Troubles in Dreams"—he developed the idea of the pause effect, to underline a key word or note. Thus he sang "wrap" and then paused before "your troubles." He was really starting to sing like a musical instrument. "All of Me"—letting rip as solo brass might do. "Get Happy"—sounding just that, joyous. He was in a different frame of mind from five months before. The band could tell it. The listeners would tell it, too. The record showed it. "Taking a Chance on Love"—as the song said, things were mending now, and he stressed it by some slick changes of lyrics. He certainly sounded as if he had got a grip on life again just like he sang.

The film *Suddenly* earned him impeccable press reviews. It had been a daring idea to cast Sinatra as the ultimate villain—a murderer—but it did him no harm professionally.

Sinatra and Sammy Davis Jr. were firm friends by this time, so Sinatra felt really bad when Davis lost his eye in a car crash that November. But as usual with his friends, Sinatra offered practical help. Davis went to him before anyone else and Sinatra handled everything—not in any sort of sentimental way, but practically and often humorously. They were friends for life from that point forward.

Now in another New Year—1955—Sinatra was in such demand that he really had to juggle his schedule to fit in filming with concert dates. Sinatra decided to take fourteen-year-old Nancy along with him on his tour of Australia in January. The audiences were all enthusiastic, though the press seemed to be gunning for him. To Nancy it was one of her first adventures into the big adult world of entertainment.

While they were away, Sinatra's film *Young at Heart* came out to a favorable response all round. As well as the hit title tune, there were other classics including "Just One of Those Things," "Someone

to Watch over Me," "One for My Baby," and "You My Love." Sinatra renewed acquaintance with his costar Doris Day, with whom he
had last sung on the radio six years earlier. Of course, the connection
is apparent between his role as a saloon-bar pianist and one of the
numbers, "One for My Baby." The film boosted the single record of
Young at Heart, naturally, and also the LP *Songs for Young Lovers*—
who can forget "My Funny Valentine" and "They Can't Take That
Away from Me."

The album *Wee Small Hours* was recorded on 8, 16, and 17 February and 4 March 1955. He made it with a small rhythm section
under Riddle. An unusual factor was that the album really had been
recorded "in the wee small hours of the morning." The small size
of the group gave the sessions an intimate air, while a nightclub atmosphere was created by the presence of a specially invited audience. Sinatra was always sparked particularly by personal contact
with any audience and this experiment turned out very successfully.
And the audience responded and reciprocated by being charged
through his presence.

"I Get Along without You Very Well" and "I'll Be Around" were
two of the top numbers in the album. And as if linking his twin careers together by design, the last song recorded at these nighttime
sessions was "Not as a Stranger," the theme song from his newest
film of the same name.

This film looked like it possessed all the ingredients of a distinguished work. Which it was. The producer was Stanley Kramer.
Naturally, he had seen Sinatra's performance as Maggio, as well as
several others on film, and he felt that Sinatra could be right for one
of the main roles. Kramer said, "Sinatra's range is fantastic. He can
do anything. He is no longer just a singer, but an actor who does
songs. As a world star, he could beat Brando."

Sinatra felt very much in sympathy with the leading male star in
the picture, Robert Mitchum. Both tended to be rebels in their respective ways, refusing to be tied down to the conventions either of
Hollywood or indeed of the world at large.

Despite its rather mixed critical reception, *Not as a Stranger* proved
to be a powerful one, set partly in a hospital. Its main theme was
medicine itself, with both men playing young doctors. They gave

portrayals in the more realistic style of acting only just emerging around the mid-1950s. Even Gloria Grahame had her own style of realism. Sinatra was gaining more and more facility for identifying himself with his characters. It was quite uncanny, really, when his background before entering films had been entirely as a singer. But then he always went for dedication and perfection in the art forms. He was a strange mixture, striving for this perfection, expecting it as a matter of course in others, yet still with human failings and frailty.

Marlon Brando was a star admired by Sinatra. Judy Garland, too, always meant a great deal to him. She had the same thing in common with Sinatra. She gave all she had. About that time she had been making her late British film *I Could Go on Singing,* with that other great star Dirk Bogarde. The fact that she sang and acted as long as she did was due, at least in some degree, to Sinatra's friendship. For she was just one of the many whom Sinatra helped over the years and decades. Even back in 1955 he was once more doling out presents, even a Cadillac! Dozens of friends—and even an enemy!—wore jewelry or other trinkets he regularly handed out, whether he could afford to provide these gifts or not. And only a year or two earlier than this, he was worrying about how he could afford to keep the family home going for Nancy senior and the children.

But much more than this, he really assisted people in important, positive ways, with his thoughts and his time. Judy Garland had sustained a bad illness that threatened to affect her whole career. It did, in fact, mar her performance in the film remake of *A Star Is Born.* Judy was in Boston, when she became really ill and had to go straight into the hospital. The next few months were fateful ones for her and might have meant the premature end of her career. Sinatra knew her already, of course, but from the very moment he heard of her illness he went out of the way to make sure that she received flowers from him every day that she spent in the hospital. Not only this, apart from visiting her himself, he arranged a special surprise flight of her friends from the film world to appear and help cheer her up. Sinatra's innate sense of rightness and fitness of occasion did not falter. At a period when Garland had too much time to lie around and think, this gesture made her realize and appreciate that her friends had not forgotten her. They were waiting for her and willing her to get well again. And she did, for a time at least.

Sinatra said of Garland around that year, "Judy Garland can't relax any more than I can. It's just something inside of us—that's why we understand each other so well." Whenever and wherever she was appearing, Sinatra would try to see her. On 19 July 1955, for instance, he took Sammy Davis Jr., Dean Martin, and Humphrey Bogart to hear her sing at a show in Long Beach. This was a gesture of support from her true friends.

From this era, as at other times, came endless examples of kindness to friends—and also comparative strangers. It could take many forms. Sinatra was, of course, one of the earliest people to recognize the talent and potential of Sammy Davis Jr.—back in the hoofing days when Davis was with his father and uncle in their vaudeville act. For no other reason than wanting to help Davis get on, Sinatra encouraged him to branch out from merely dancing. Davis heeded the advice and started singing, impersonating, and even doing a stand-up comedy act, until he eventually developed into an all-round entertainer who appeared alongside Sinatra with almost equal billing.

So Sinatra helped Davis to discover himself, utilize himself, and even to laugh at himself. After the car accident, Davis later referred to the lack of attributes of "a one-eyed colored Jew"! Sinatra was against waste of potential in people. As Davis put it when asked, "He helped me overcome my greatest handicap, my inferiority complex about being a negro." Perhaps Sinatra saw Davis as a test case in his eternal struggle for equal rights for all. Certainly, Davis did a lot to justify a more enlightened outlook on racial relations in the United States and elsewhere.

Sinatra never went an inch out of his way to publicize any of these things. It would not have fitted in with his makeup at all. Sometimes they did become known, naturally. But at other times they remained the private gestures they were intended to be: kind actions from a man with an unfair reputation for having been brusque and unkind.

A friend of Sinatra's owned the Mocambo, a well-known nightclub. But when the owner died, his widow, Mary Morrison, could not cope with the financial position and felt she would have to close the club. Sinatra heard of this, and amid all his other activities he got in touch with her. He insisted that he would love to do a cabaret for her—for free. Now once more able to ask tens of thousands of dollars for a personal appearance like this, Sinatra entertained at the Mocambo twice a night for three weeks. He did not consider any possible strain on his voice from such an extended engagement. The result was that the place was packed every single night and Sinatra felt he had done something worthwhile. Perhaps the biggest compliment Sinatra could ever expect came from a hard-boiled press agent whom he had punched on one occasion. The man called Sinatra's gesture to sing free at the Mocambo "pretty wonderful."

One of the qualities that Sinatra valued most highly was loyalty. Comedian Jack E. Leonard said that Sinatra was very loyal to his friends. Leonard fell badly sick at one period in his life. Sinatra stepped on the scene, and Leonard recalled that "if it hadn't been for Frank's phone calls from the coast to cheer me up, I wouldn't be here today."

Of course, Sinatra gave masses of money to charity throughout his career, such as organizations for cancer research, Catholic societies, and Jewish appeals. More of this came to light later and on a pretty incredible scale. And as well as actually donating funds, Sinatra was always a crusader for a better world and for better understanding between peoples. He worked with as ferocious a force as in his career for such causes as the national polio drive and the National Brotherhood Week observation, sponsored by the Conference of Christians and Jews—apart from the Heart Fund and any number of other causes.

The best single instance of his help to other people as individuals was in 1955, when the distinguished middle-aged actor Lee J. Cobb was seriously ill in a hospital in Los Angeles. Cobb had suffered and survived a bad heart attack and was lying in his bed when the phone rang. It was Sinatra, whom Cobb hardly knew. They had run across each other once or twice in films that they both had acted in, but they were not friends in any definable way.

"I'm coming to see you," Sinatra announced in his customary forthright manner. Cobb could not believe it. Why would a man he

had only spoken to quite casually go out of his way to visit him?
Perhaps there was no real reason and no answer to that question. At
least, there was nothing capable of being articulated. Perhaps it was
simply because Sinatra had learned a little of life and remembered
something of what it was like to be down. This is how Cobb described what happened after he had put down the receiver that day:

> I had been very ill. In his typical unsentimental fashion, Frank moved into
> my life. I was in a low mental state then. I was divorced and pretty much
> alone in the world. I was sure my career had come to an end.
>
> Frank came to see me every day after work. He flooded me with books,
> flowers and delicacies. He kept telling me what fine acting I still had ahead
> of me, discussing plans for me to direct one of his future films. He built an
> insulating wall around me that shielded me from worry, tension and strain.

Cobb had no money at all when he eventually came out of the
hospital. Sinatra did not leave his self-appointed job half-done. He
installed Cobb in an apartment in Hollywood, covered all his expenses, and made a particular point of seeing him regularly till the
actor had recovered from the depression that had been enveloping
him before the phone had rung that day. Cobb is quoted as saying
later, "I still don't believe it. A man, practically a stranger, comes
along and maybe saves my life. I don't know if I'd have any career
at all today if it weren't for Frank Sinatra."

At about the same time as this episode, Sinatra signed to play the
part of Billy Bigelow in the film version of *Carousel* for Twentieth
Century Fox. Sinatra had nurtured a desire for this role over a long
time. He had recorded the long "Soliloquy" years earlier, too. He
actually prerecorded some of the songs before attending the first
day's shooting. But he was destined never to play the part.

The picture was due to be shot partly on location at Booth Bay
Harbor, on the peaceful Maine coastline. When Sinatra turned up
at the start of the week in question, a succession of loud disagreements ensued with the producer Henry Ephron. Sinatra gave as
their cause the fact that each scene was to be shot twice, in ordinary
35 mm and also in 55 mm for the "bigger and better" Cinemascope
screen. Sinatra was not aware of this when he agreed to make the
film, and as always, he strongly maintained that he had only one

spontaneous take for each scene—he refused. It looked like being a serious impasse and it was. Soon afterward, Sinatra said to Hank Sanicola—at his side as ever—"Let's get out of here." And they did. And that was how Gordon MacRae came to take over the male lead in *Carousel* opposite Shirley Jones.

Sinatra may not have played Billy Bigelow, but he did get Nathan Detroit. Sinatra must have been working overtime in the film studios, because he signed for one of the two male starring roles in the screen version of the stage success *Guys and Dolls*. As the elusively ephemeral Nathan Detroit, he was the proprietor of the world's "oldest established permanent floating crap game in New York." And what a cast: Marlon Brando, Jean Simmons, Vivian Blaine, and our Frankie. Simmons was the Salvation Army girl Sarah Brown; Brando was Sky Masterson, the pursuer of religion and her; and Blaine was Miss Adelaide, Nathan's girlfriend with the perpetual head cold. The film had some striking choreography. And what a score! It exuded such numbers as "Guys and Dolls," "If I Was a Bell," "Sue Me," "The Oldest Established . . . ," "Adelaide," and "Luck Be a Lady Tonight." But Sinatra did not sing the best titles— particularly the last one. That was left to "baritone" Brando. Regardless, Sinatra used it for several decades afterward in many of his concerts. Sinatra was in his element as Nathan and enjoyed making the film with Brando. It must have been a good score and show, because the Frank Loesser musical is still going strong on stage and screen in the new millennium. The British National Theatre did a wonderful stage version in the 1990s and I saw an equally memorable one. Where? At the Guildford School of Acting, where people come from as far away as California to attend! But I digress.

Days after this was shown came the next film, *The Tender Trap*. Sinatra was back in the tailored role of his, the worldly hustler with the heart of gold. Most of the film was occupied with costar Debbie Reynolds pursuing him, or pushing him, toward the altar. Hence the title. Celeste Holm added to the humor, and she and Sinatra would be seen again very shortly in *High Society*.

Meanwhile, the same thing happened here as with *Young at Heart*. Sinatra had another hit with the title song "Love Is the Tender Trap." This he sang with a certain wry humor, invented, perhaps, from recent recollections of his personal life. His "comeback" year was clearly 1955. For this was not even the first hit he had made on record. "Learnin' the Blues" was selling on a large scale all over the States. And on 15 August he made "Love and Marriage," another solid single hit. Then on 13 September he recorded "The Tender Trap." "Love and Marriage" came from a new and successful television show, so his various careers all seemed to be interacting once more. Someone should have said to that nasty gossip writer, "Big fall, big rise." Sinatra was on a winning streak, which went on for another forty years!

One of his greatest film roles was being hammered out for 1956: the part of Frankie Machine, the golden-armed poker dealer in *The Man with the Golden Arm*. A man in a peak cap and open-necked shirt staring at the cards on the table. This was the tragic imprint of a bitter but losing fight against the effects of drug addiction. In fact, heroin. So convincing was it that it must surely have saved some people from becoming addicts. Scenes that linger include the one where he tried to do without drugs and went berserk in his bedroom— heaving things at the walls in sheer frenzy. The Sinatra performance was tormented and tremendous and was received with some rapture. He was nominated for an Oscar in the Best Actor category, and he personally considered it his "finest work."

After an unbilled cameo part in MGM's *Meet Me in Las Vegas*, it was a case of "enter Bing Crosby." Sinatra's former hero and crooner par excellence. I remember Crosby back in such films as *The Big Broadcast* of 1936. Crosby called Sinatra a paradoxical cuss, adding the inevitable counterbalancing quote, "Without taking any bows, he goes about doing things for people who need help. But he can then turn around and do something inexplicably thoughtless, so unnecessary that you wonder if it's the same fellow."

There may have been some grounds for Crosby's summary of Sinatra, but often it was just that Sinatra was determined not to be pushed around and insisted on sticking up for his own rights—or other people's. On a lighter note, there is Crosby's apocryphal quote on Sinatra, which might well have been perfectly true, "A singer like Sinatra only comes along once in a lifetime—why did it have to be in mine?!"

This crowded spell of life saw the teaming of Crosby with Sinatra in the scintillating screen musical by Cole Porter in *High Society*. The film had been made straight, before the war, as *The Philadelphia Story*, with Katharine Hepburn being quite memorable. Now, MGM threw all it had into the musical version, including this daring combination of the two leading male singers Crosby and Sinatra. The two women were Grace Kelly as the ice maiden and Celeste Holm, with the added jazz attraction of Louis Armstrong. Perhaps the producers thought that the two singers would spark off the best in each other by a bit of friendly rivalry. Crosby and Kelly had the main song, "True Love," yet Sinatra somehow seemed to get the key numbers. A flash from the film recalls the scene with Sinatra and Holm—as reporter and photographer—surveying the dinner table splendor and singing "Who Wants to Be a Millionaire?" Then there was that duet between Sinatra and Crosby, "Well Did You Evah?" It was left to the songs Sinatra sang to Kelly to clinch it more as his film, "You're Sensational" and "Mind If I Make Love to You?" Although he did not get Kelly in the last reel, they became close friends after *High Society*, until her tragic death in 1982. Needless to say, both the film and the sound track were big successes.

Sinatra found time to go on campaigning for the Democrats in 1956, singing at their convention, which nominated Adlai Stevenson. Days later he played for a week with both the Dorsey brothers at the Paramount Theater. And on the screen was shown Sinatra's film *Johnny Concho*.

For this one, he had put on a cowboy suit and moved into the role of producer with his own film company. No one could then tell him what to do! The story was a Western with a difference: the presence of an antihero. The theme was cowardice. He was moving further from his original image of the bobby-soxers' delight. Acting and singing, how could he juggle these joint careers in the future? He never thought of it in those terms. Fine actor as he already was, I have always felt that while there are so many great actors, only one Sinatra-the-singer could ever have lived.

Meanwhile, the tightrope act went on. In fact, on six days earlier in the year, Sinatra and Riddle recorded the new benchmark album

Songs for Swingin' Lovers. Released in the spring of 1956, it became
the first LP record ever to get into the top twenty, and even the top
ten, popularity and sales charts for singles records. The title helped
it to sell, as well as the record sleeve. On it, a couple of lovers were
being looked on benevolently by a young-at-heart Frankie in a
turned-up-brim hat. Sinatra at forty still sounded full of bounce
and bite.

The songs had all been well chosen and arranged and they conveyed that youthful feeling right from the first track, "You Make Me
Feel So Young." He brought back several really old ones associated
with other singers, too: "Makin' Whoopee," Eddie Cantor's hit of the
early talkies, and Bing Crosby's "Pennies from Heaven." He was still
slightly restrained in his adaptation and modification of lyrics,
though he did switch a line or two in the former of these. A pair of
Cole Porter classics added class to the album, "I've Got You under
My Skin" and "Anything Goes." The incredible truth, however, was
that this favorite of Sinatra's was only added as an afterthought, with
the arrangement being finished en route to the recording session!
Those were the days. Perhaps the most inspired creations are forced
under pressure.

One of the last numbers was "Old Devil Moon" with its racy
razzle-dazzle treatment. Or someone else might prefer George
Gershwin's "Love Is Here to Stay." Not forgetting "It Happened in
Monterey," which had never sounded like that before or since. But
this was one of Sinatra's secrets. No song ever sounded quite the
same as it did before, as it received his intuitive interpretation, plus
the new Riddle touch.

In November 1956 the Capitol album *This Is Sinatra* included the
two single hits "Young at Heart" and "The Tender Trap." Another
song hinted at his affinity to the choices of Judy Garland. Sinatra
made "The Gal That Got Away," one of Garland's most effective
emotional numbers. Sinatra was awarded more annual top places in
the music magazines, and in December he was seen and heard at
both the Sands Hotel, Las Vegas, and the Copacabana Club, New
York City. But he had to cancel one night at the latter when he
heard that Humphrey Bogart had died.

That New Year's Eve, Sinatra might have been forgiven for remembering back a dozen years to the first fantastic opening at the
Paramount. Or more recently to the last time he had seen Ava
Gardner. Instead, he was looking forward—as usual. It was announced on that very day that Sinatra would star with Cary Grant
and Sophia Loren in an adaptation of C. S. Forester's best-selling
book *The Gun.* It would be directed by Stanley Kramer, the maker
of *Not as a Stranger,* and was to be called *The Pride and the Passion.*
(By way of coincidence, Kramer's obituary is in today's newspapers
as I write this.)

Looking ahead momentarily to the spring of 1957, Sinatra was on
his way to Spain for location work on the film. Gardner was still
living there, but he refused to answer any press questions about her.
One day soon afterward, he was sitting in a Spanish hotel when she
actually arrived with a friend. She saw Sinatra and sent him a note.
Sinatra did not even read it but ripped it into shreds. Feelings can
change. Later that year, they were divorced and the relationship finally ended.

CHAPTER SEVEN

REVIVAL
1957

In 1957, Capitol Records was cashing in on the stellar appeal of the newly minted Frank Sinatra. But it was also big enough to experiment and not necessarily try to repeat the formula too often. The new LP was *Close to You*. The innovative idea was to create a blend of classical and popular music in the form of an intimate chamber group to accompany Sinatra. This ensemble was the Hollywood String Quartet and the result proved worth the trial. The LP made the top ten albums of 1957—if not the singles charts! He went on to record over fifty numbers that year. The fruits of these endeavors became very apparent in some really classic albums still much remembered and played.

So Sinatra plunged on with his work, never idle and never standing still, rarely relaxing, always eager to try something fresh that might catch his interest and imagination. He never cosseted himself or his talents. When he was at home in California, he now had a marvelous modern house built into the side of a mountain in Coldwater Canyon, Beverly Hills. He lived there with a Filipino servant and when he was not away working or at parties somewhere, he spent hours roaming around this rather palatial home. Perhaps the real reason for this endless energy and his ceaseless engagements was contained in something he was quoted to have confided to a friend around this year: "I don't want to have time to think."

Sinatra had attained a degree of maturity and acquired a reputation unique in American entertainment. But at what cost to the private man?

For much of the time he spent at his home, he read or listened to music. His taste for books had always been wide—catholic with a small "c." Perhaps eclectic would be a better word. From John Keats and Percy Bysshe Shelley to Ernest Hemingway and Eric Ambler. Later on, he embraced others: William Shakespeare, Field Marshal Bernard Montgomery, Richard Condon, and more. He had to look at scripts or books connected with possible film projects as one of the sidelines of his work as a film star. Sinatra also used to tape extracts of Shakespeare and play them back to get the effect of how the verse sounded to his ear. His feeling for poetry was natural, for how else could he have phrased lyrics of his varied songs so magically? And many of the best songs certainly contained very definite elements of pure poetry—whatever snobs might say.

Words and music were the two ingredients of his songs, so once more it would have been only natural for Sinatra to love music of every kind. Apart from the world of the leading songwriters in popular music—and they were all brilliant—he developed a taste for some of the classics, too: Johannes Brahms, Jean Sibelius, Ralph Vaughan Williams, Giacomo Puccini, and other operatic composers.

His current activities received recognition again at the start of February 1957. In Chicago, *Downbeat* magazine named its music personalities of the year in the motion picture awards poll: Frank Sinatra and Doris Day. Both had traveled far from that record they made together back in 1949. Day, of course, developed from just a singer to become one of Hollywood's most accomplished actresses.

The Pride and the Passion was about the Peninsula Wars in Napoleonic times, and it called for location shooting throughout the hot Spanish summer. Stanley Kramer directed with his usual panache, but Sinatra might have been thought of as miscast in the role of Miguel. But despite mixed reviews for the film, most critics conceded that he had been up to his set standard. A typical extract from one review read, "Thank heavens Frank Sinatra decided to play the part of Miguel—Sinatra and the cannon are the real stars of this half-tremendous, half-trivial film." *Look* magazine was simultaneously publishing a piece entitled "The Life Story of Frank Sinatra: Talent, Tantrums, and Torment." No one would expect him to be ecstatic about such labels, but it had no adverse effect on his career.

Because of the inevitable time lag between making and releasing films and records, an artist is always engrossed in another project long before the previous one has been seen or heard. In this case, Sinatra was a couple of films ahead. He made *The Joker Is Wild* and then another one that was rather more memorable, *Pal Joey*. But the former was still a lively effort based on the life of Joe E. Lewis, the Roaring Twenties cabaret comedian and singer. Sinatra sang some good numbers, including the legendary "Chicago" and "All the Way," which won the Academy Award in due course as the Best Song of 1957. Jimmy Van Heusen and Sammy Cahn could thank Sinatra for his rendering, which had something to do with the award. As for the acting, one review referred to Sinatra's as "punch and polish," while *Variety* called it "a major job" in this nostalgic film, the type Americans often seemed to favor. Other numbers were "I Cried for You" and "If I Could Be with You."

Next in his long line of musicals was *Pal Joey*. He costarred with two of the most beautiful Hollywood actresses of the day: Rita Hayworth and Kim Novak. During the making of *Pal Joey,* Sinatra renewed his friendship with the platinum-haired Novak, whom he had escorted more than once in the past and who had starred with him in *The Man with the Golden Arm*. The press was always quick to link his name with any girl he happened to take out—however slight some of these encounters might really be. Some were slight, others closer: Anita Ekberg, Gloria Vanderbilt, Novak, and, coming shortly, Lauren Bacall. Anyway, in *Pal Joey* Sinatra played the beloved "gilt-edged heel," a nightclub character who imagined that all the girls must fall for him. Hayworth was the rich girl, Novak the poor one. The Richard Rodgers and Lorenz Hart musical scintillated. Sinatra sang "I Didn't Know What Time It Was," "There's a Small Hotel," "I Could Write a Book," and "Bewitched, Bothered, and Bewildered." Also, a less memorable ditty called "What Do I Care for a Dame?" But the best of all was in that classic scene with Hayworth when he delivered "The Lady Is a Tramp." Circling around her as she sat, he timed each word and gesture to a semisecond. Even the London *Times,* that usually staid newspaper, was moved sufficiently to call it "a masterpiece of timing and technique."

Pal Joey was originally a stage show and it transferred triumphantly into a hit film. The Sinatra success tended toward being cumulative now, with the sound track album to the film released that fall. Yet, Sinatra had not finished with the specter of failure. Just as *Pal Joey* was being shown, a big television series was launched, *The Frank Sinatra Show.* After a series of criticisms directed at it, the producers revised the format. The plan had been for twenty-one musical shows coupled with shorter dramas also starring Sinatra. Perhaps it was just too large-scale a project, but despite an impressive list of guests and much hard work by Sinatra, the series only lasted one season. By American standards of sponsorship, this did not really constitute a success.

What else had happened in the interim? Well, Sinatra and Ava Gardner were finally divorced just twenty-four hours after Independence Day 1957. Another album appeared, *Where Are You?* My favorite from this one was the haunting theme song from the Gene Tierney film *Laura.* Then that fall Sinatra and Lauren Bacall were seen out and about. Partly it was a case of Sinatra helping her to recover from the shattering loss of Humphrey Bogart, but it did develop into something more than that. Bacall was quoted as commenting, "I certainly want to marry again. I hate being single. I am not one of those emancipated women who like to live alone." But would Sinatra be the one?

So rave reviews for his concert appearances; three films in a year; and the strong-selling slipstream of records. What more could anyone expect? Sinatra said toward the end of that year, "I've known joy, unhappiness; success, failure; hope and despair. Good or bad, what's happened to me is my lot and I've never begrudged a thing that life has given, or taken, from me."

If that made him sound a bit too philosophical, Sinatra also needed a quick sense of humor and retort. He had it. The British magazine *Weekend* asked him, "What is your worst fault?" The answer came back succinctly: "*Spaghetti.*" I seem to remember that

I worked on that magazine for six strange months of my check-ered life!

Despite the slight setback of the television series, the pendulum took another swing—the operative word where his music was con-cerned. Sinatra made two LPs with Gordon Jenkins and his or-chestra during the year: *Where Are You?* and *A Jolly Christmas with Frank Sinatra*. This was recorded in mid-July and released in Sep-tember! Personally, I could do without themes like the latter, but we must be tolerant—as Sinatra told us!

Already in the record stores and selling well was another Frank Sinatra–Nelson Riddle classic album, *A Swingin' Affair*. As the sleeve said, "You recall the song from a happy past . . . but the beat is brighter now than you remember it . . . the orchestra is richer-sounding . . . more exciting . . . and the voice is Frank Sinatra's. It's a swingin' affair."

What emerged radiantly clear on this collection was that Sinatra lived life at a more intense pitch than the normal person. He expe-rienced and savored every minute, every morsel. He felt it, assimi-lated it, stored it, and then conveyed it to us in the mood of the mu-sic. We feel the torment torn from him in "Night and Day"; the bleakness of "No One Ever Tells You" and "Lonesome Road"; the breezy bounce of "I Won't Dance" (complete with the debut of *Ring-a-Ding-Ding*); and the driving drama of "From This Moment On." Lyrics, too, were squeezed to their last inferential syllable. To cap the success of this album, Sinatra heard that U.S. disc jockeys had voted *A Swingin' Affair* their number-one LP of the year. Each album of his was selling something like 200,000 copies and this one got into the top ten of the American charts.

What a year. And as a coda to it, Sinatra branched out as a writer! He signed this feature for the *London Daily Sketch,* published on 30 October 1957:

> Whether or not you like progressive jazz, popular songs or Dixieland, you've got to admit the enormous influence they possess outside the conti-nental limits of the United States.
>
> American music as represented by every form, good or bad, from Dix-ieland to the most complex contemporary jazz, has a more positive effect on all the peoples of the world than anything but the Marshall Plan.

I have only one reservation here—rock 'n' roll—which I consider to be the martial music of every long-haired delinquent! But more of that later.

Let's get it into our heads . . .

It's been demonstrated repeatedly that most of our music is deeply respected and admired by all manner of people.

People who, due to bumbling diplomacy on our part, have decided—in the mysterious way that whole populations arrive at decisions—that we Americans are not the most charming of all possible hosts or neighbours.

But American music—and I mean jazz—does please them. And our players are the most successful goodwill ambassadors we have.

A report by Marshall Stearn in America's *Saturday Review of Literature* on a tour of trumpeter Dizzy Gillespie and his band through the Middle East made it quite clear that one of the few acceptable points of contact we are able to make with each other is jazz.

Countries which view America as a clumsy, brutal giant reconsider when they hear our music and meet the men who play it.

Jazz is the most American commodity we have outside of our wealth and power, which are much less loved—no matter how much aid they have rendered.

As an American I say that it's our finest export. It is unique. And for that reason alone we should treat it and its makers with constant respect and admiration.

And even pop songs which I sing are a considerable force for good. Tasteful songs and musically competent orchestral background—whether the words are understood or not—help to keep the door open.

My only deep sorrow is the unrelenting insistence of recording and motion picture companies on churning out the most brutal, ugly, degenerate, vicious form of expression it has been my displeasure to hear—I refer to rock 'n' roll.

It fosters almost totally negative and destructive reactions in young people. It smells phoney and false.

It is sung, played and written, for the most part, by cretinous goons, and its almost imbecilic reiterations and sly, lewd—in fact, plain dirty—lyrics make it the martial music of every sideburned delinquent on the face of the earth.

This rancid-smelling aphrodisiac I deplore.

But in spite of it, the contribution of American music to the world has, in my opinion, one of the healthiest effects of all contributions.

Today you can hear great jazzmen in countries which before the last war knew little of our music and made no effort to examine or play it.

Whether or not it is a great art form is of no concern to us.

What does matter is that it reaches a more varied audience in the United States than any other expression, except, perhaps, baseball.

And, good or bad, it causes millions of people outside the United States to believe that we Americans are by no means as crude, mysterious or childish as our foreign policy or its representatives have often caused them to believe.

CHAPTER EIGHT

COME FLY WITH ME

1958-1961

After a lot of sifting, sorting, and rejecting, Frank Sinatra and Billy May settled on a dozen numbers old and new to fit in with the overall theme of the new album *Come Fly with Me*. The LP brought this ebullient new name of Billy May bouncing onto Sinatra's records. It was an outright winner from the start. And it is still played. Sammy Cahn and Jimmy Van Heusen wrote two top songs to start and end the record. The Billy May outfit inspired a fresh zip and zing to Sinatra, without in any way sacrificing the effect of the more romantic numbers. "Come Fly with Me" itself had some really original lines such as the one about the band in "llama land." "Around the World" and "April in Paris" were both sung tremendously lento by Sinatra with equal effect. Who can forget the final reprise word in "April in Paris"?

It would be illuminating to hear some pop stars trying to handle either "Moonlight in Vermont" or "Autumn in New York." Both are marvelous examples of mood music. The arrangements had a "freezy," frosty, crystalline brilliance. So too the sign-off number "It's Nice to Go Trav'ling" with its lines about the Hudson River. Sinatra ought to have been able to feel these lyrics, since he was born within the tang of that very river. The whole record hit a high note, even for Sinatra devotees. And I was fast becoming one!

Sinatra did a fortnight in Las Vegas. Seven words, but think for a moment what that entailed. Appearing every night. Fulfilling great expectations of all the paying customers. Hardly ever did he fail to live up to their excited hopes. Yet, that engagement at the Sands Hotel registered as just one of hundreds in his career. Thousands, actually.

Then it was straight to France for filming *Kings Go Forth*. Sinatra starred with Tony Curtis, plus Natalie Wood as a French girl. The strong story, once more from a best-selling book, featured the American army liberating the Riviera region in the late summer of 1944. And it also touched on the color question. That appealed to Sinatra. He appeared as an army lieutenant who had lost an arm. Later in the summer of 1958, Sinatra was in Monaco with Prince Rainier and Grace Kelly for the premiere there of this film made so near to their little principality.

Manie Sacks died in February, and Sinatra was with him. To be in Philadelphia, Sinatra had to meet the expenditure involved in actually suspending the American shooting of *Kings Go Forth* for two complete days. So he lost Humphrey Bogart and Sacks within a short interval. He was dragged down.

In 1958, *This Is Sinatra II,* a sequel to *This Is Sinatra,* made a year earlier, was produced. Like the first album, the new one was compiled from previous hit recordings. It featured the tune that became associated with him, "Put Your Dreams Away." Personally, I never really thought this was worthy of being such a regular signature song for Sinatra, but who am I?

The year goes on, reading like an exercise in exhaustion, but he seemed to thrive on it. Two more weeks at the Sands—and twice nightly. Or equal to a month once a night. What energy. Benefit shows in America and Europe. And then the world premiere of *Kings Go Forth*. Sinatra talked about this film in connection with race relations and trying to do his bit toward better understanding.

"If you haven't been invited, you'd better have a damn good reason for ringing this bell!" This was the two-edged welcome sign at the electronically controlled entrance gate of his Coldwater Canyon house. And bearing in mind past experiences way back to New Jersey, why shouldn't he expect personal privacy? But a lot of people were invited in this era: Sammy Davis Jr., Peter Lawford, Tony Curtis, Dean Martin, Robert Wagner, Judy Garland,

Carolyn Jones, Natalie Wood, Shirley Maclaine, Dinah Shore, and Lauren Bacall.

The house where they were all entertained was an elegant design set low against the mountain. One whole wall of the vast lounge was glazed—giving a panoramic vista on the lights of Hollywood, with the Pacific Ocean seen in the distance. Down a few steps from this great window was a floodlit swimming pool. And nearby, a private cinema. It would be superfluous to add that part of the lounge fittings included Sinatra's stereophonic record system.

As well as this fairly new place, Sinatra acquired a three-acre estate in Palm Springs at the end of 1957. This had a guest cottage at the edge of the swimming pool. Al Jolson had owned it once, so it seemed quite appropriate that Sinatra should be there. The same estate owned by two legendary singers. When he had the time, Sinatra would charter an aircraft to take a crowd of his friends down to Palm Springs for the weekend—or even just the evening! His generosity still flowed as much as ever.

But he still refused to be ordered to do anything. "Don't tell me. Suggest—but don't tell me!" Several times it seems as if girlfriends forgot this insistence of his not to be hustled or crowded or told what to think or do. After a series of speculations about the possibility of his marrying Lauren Bacall, the papers reported on 13 March 1958 that she had said they would be marrying definitely. They were together, but they didn't marry. For on 14 March he was reported to have told columnist Walter Winchell, "How can I get married again? There's nothing left of my heart!" It was to be hoped that Sinatra never used those exact words—they sounded more like a line of dialogue from a rather bad Hollywood movie than something he would say. Regardless, it was pretty obvious that the Bacall episode would soon be at an end. The press hounded them both and the real reason for the breakup is still slightly obscure. It seemed that although Sinatra felt strongly for Bacall, marriage was beyond him at that stage.

While Sinatra was in Monaco that summer with the Rainiers, the audience for the premiere there of *Kings Go Forth* included two famous Englishmen: Noel Coward and Somerset Maugham. Sinatra had known Coward for some years and always respected his opinion and advice. In a later LP, he included the Coward song "I'll Follow My Secret Heart." However, Sinatra and Coward might have been thought an unlikely combination. Sinatra spent a day or two relaxing in Monte Carlo in an open-necked orange shirt, white linen jacket, dark trousers, and a smart snap-brim straw hat.

While he had been in London the previous week, he had taken out a young actress several times to nightclubs in the capital. While he was on the Riviera, she went to work at the local theater in Ryde, Isle of Wight, off the south coast of England. She was starting a fourteen-week summer season there. Her first role was in the Agatha Christie play *Towards Zero*. Her name was Shirley Anne Field. Surely she must have dreamed of those evenings with Sinatra while working at this modest seaside theater. I remember Ryde from my childhood with its long pier and the trains trundling along it to meet the incoming ferries.

Sinatra was soon back in America filming his latest movie, *Some Came Running*. Then back again in London. He had already met Lady Beattie in Hollywood and New York. When he returned to London in October for the premiere of Danny Kaye's new film *Me and the Colonel,* the press went wild over the possibility of a romance between him and Beattie. But then three days later came another twist in the story of Sinatra and the opposite gender. He refused to comment on the question of whether he would marry, not Lady Beattie, but Eva Bartok. On 25 October, Lady Beattie was reported to have flown off to a Swiss hideaway. Two days later, she was back in London at her North Terrace home off the Brompton Road in fashionable Kensington. Sinatra was alleged to have called on her the same day.

Displaying good humor and his best manners before the queen and Prince Philip at the Odeon, Leicester Square, he said, "I did not come here to get married, though some papers would have me married more times than Farouk!" That was really the end of the Lady Beattie drama—or farce.

The next name that the press delighted in linking with him was the young American star Tuesday Weld. It was generally conceded that Sinatra always acted as a highly courteous and entertaining escort when with any girl. He observed the now unconventional con-

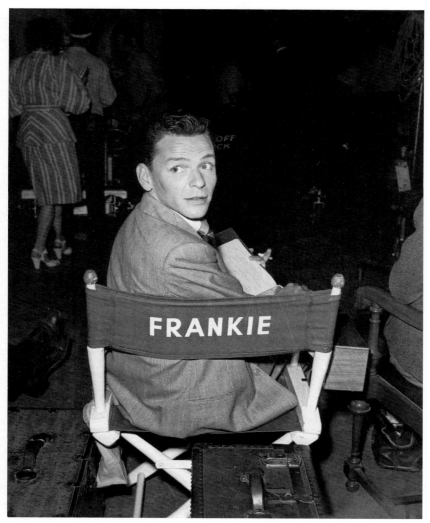

Sinatra at the beginning of his career. (Courtesy of Photofest.)

With wife Nancy and daughter Nancy in June of 1946. (Photo by George B. Evans; courtesy of Photofest.)

Arriving arm in arm with Ava Gardner for the premiere of her film Showboat *in Hollywood. (Copyright 1951; courtesy of Photofest.)*

With Donna Reed in his Oscar-winning role in From Here to Eternity. *(Copyright 1953, Columbia Pictures Corp.; courtesy of Photofest.)*

With the Rat Pack around the time of the release of Ocean's Eleven. *(Copyright 1960; courtesy of Photofest.)*

Leading Jackie Kennedy to her box at the National Guard Armory for the pre-inauguration gala staged by Sinatra to help pay off the Kennedy campaign debt. (Copyright 1961; courtesy of Photofest.)

With Janet Leigh in The Manchurian Candidate. *(Copyright 1962, United Artists; courtesy of Photofest.)*

Sinatra's performances remained charismatic and energetic, even toward the end of his career. (Courtesy of Photofest.)

ventions of sending flowers before an evening out and literally lavished attention on any consort. He talked wittily and was vitally interested in everyone's lives, as well as the topical world events around him.

Between all these dates so faithfully reported and often embroidered by the press, Sinatra managed to fit in his LP sessions, for which he always went into training a week or two in advance. He stopped smoking and he tried to get to bed before dawn. Yet nothing less than an attempt at perfection satisfied him once in the recording studio. Often, there coexisted a strange admixture of atmosphere: concentration, relaxation, and the occasional flashing joke to let off steam. All these went on more or less simultaneously. It was a galvanic kind of air. Subconsciously, he may have felt that these songs might outlive himself, so he had better summon all he had.

And when he sang, the top button of the shirt was still undone; the tie loosened; the hat tilted back rakishly, casually; and the hands perhaps pocketed, or more likely, forming some expressive reflection of the lyrics. Now a new note became apparent. Sinatra was dressing in slightly more subdued shades. Plain, medium-tone two-piece suits, with perhaps a darker plain tie. He didn't need flashiness. He seemed to have settled for two-button single-breasted suits with what the tailors would have termed a twin vent at the rear sides—hacking-jacket style. During a recording session, he might have been seen standing quite solitary near his microphone, or sitting on or leaning against a tall bar-stool type of seat. In this mood, he had made the great record *Only the Lonely.* Cahn and Van Heusen wrote the song, giving the album its overall title, and the whole record comprised classic ballad numbers. It has been quoted as being top of the American album charts for 120 weeks. Incredible as that seems, it could well be true.

Next came the companion record to *Come Fly with Me.* May and Sinatra proceeded to do it all over again with *Come Dance with Me,* made over the fortnight before Christmas 1958. And by the time they had finished the closing number, "The Last Dance," it was actually Christmas Eve. But Sinatra recorded as usual in the evening hours from 8:00 P.M. till around midnight. He got home in the early hours of 25 December and felt that he had earned his Christmas holiday. One of the mysteries of his life, of course, was how he could go on from peak to peak. The troughs were offstage, off-camera, or off-record.

The record chalked up another palpable hit. It was becoming almost monotonous—the ease with which he seemed able to maintain such standards. Playing the LPs now in their chronological order, it is possible to detect slight changes in his voice. The phase of 1956–1959 could be considered as the years when he really started to mature. The evidence was in renderings like "Day in Day Out," "Cheek to Cheek," and "The Song Is You." Little did we know what further vocal adventures he had in store later.

His career continued to be divided into acting and singing. Sometimes, the two overlapped, as in a musical film, but basically all he did could be classified as one or the other. As the returning disillusioned veteran in *Some Came Running,* he was very distinctly Sinatra the serious actor. And as had happened before and would again, he got good reviews in a picture that met a mixed reception. He liked making it, though, for it brought him close to two of his friends: Martin and Maclaine. These are names to be associated with the Rat Pack group of the era. Maclaine, shot in the last reel, actually received an Academy Award nomination for her part.

After this drama, he took a change with *A Hole in the Head.* This switching from heavier to lighter and straight acting to singing was far from unintentional. For as Sinatra said, he felt that in this way an artist stood less chance of wearing out his or her welcome over the years. Hence, *A Hole in the Head* with its lighthearted little philosophic song "High Hopes." And perhaps just because the tune was so unpretentious, it won an Oscar for the Best Song from a Film in 1959. It seemed that the golden combination of Cahn and Van Heusen wrote the style of song that precisely suited Sinatra.

In the film, Sinatra played the role of a little man tied up with one of those ramshackle small hotels down in the southern states. After the film came out, it was reported that Sinatra then had property interests in Miami Beach real estate, Las Vegas casinos and motels, and Texas oil wells. He was making over $2 million a year by 1959.

There were also a couple of albums around then. And both were regarded as classics in their own right. *No One Cares* was accompanied by Gordon Jenkins and entered the top-ten listings. The most haunting tune from the album? "Here's That Rainy Day." Then there was the LP *Only the Lonely,* which Sinatra Jr. later called "the greatest blues album ever made."

During the summer of 1959, Sinatra was busy filming *Never So Few* with his friend Peter Lawford, Gina Lollobrigida, and Steve McQueen. What a formidable quartet! Sinatra played an American captain in the Burma campaign of World War II. Part of the film was made in the Philippines to simulate Burma. Sinatra sustained an injury to his left eye during an action scene that could have cost him sight in that eye. Luckily, his eye fully recovered.

From *Never So Few* he went directly into the famed *Can-Can.* The film did not come out until the following year, but its making is still remembered by the occasion when the Russian premier Nikita Khrushchev visited the set of *Can-Can* and he and his wife were given a lunch by the film cast. Some 400 stars were there, too, and the event had Sinatra as its host.

That autumn brought a clutch of television appearances with singing friends such as Dean Martin and Bing Crosby. By now, Sinatra had met Juliet Prowse, a dancing star of *Can-Can.* Soon after completing the film, Prowse said of Sinatra, "At first, Frankie terrified me. Now I think I terrify him a little!" What would their future hold?

The winter of 1959–1960 marked the approximate start of the Rat Pack–Las Vegas period. The Sands Hotel was the locale where Sinatra appeared with the agreeably slurred singer Martin, Lawford, and risen-star Sammy Davis Jr. Joey Bishop brought the number to five, plus the occasional stars—and even John F. Kennedy. So it was also the Kennedy era; and, of course, Marilyn Monroe also frequented the Sands. The Rat Pack and the Kennedy clan were interrelated in a number of ways. And to underline the Sands group, they made the film *Ocean's Eleven* actually in Las Vegas. All five friends, including Bishop, were featured in the film. In February, Sinatra started to campaign for Kennedy's nomination as the Democratic candidate for the presidency.

Around this time, too, the Rat Pack became known as the Clan and then the Summit. One of its inner members was Lawford, who had been a friend of Sinatra's for a long time already. Five or six years earlier, Lawford had married Kennedy's younger sister, Patricia, and so with Sinatra aiding Kennedy, the Kennedy-Lawford-Sinatra relationship was closer than ever. Lawford appeared in several Sinatra films, and he and Patricia also traveled to Hawaii with Sinatra on one occasion with Judith Campbell Exner. As Judith Exner, she wrote her memoirs in which Sinatra was mentioned as part of a ménage à trois episode. But that is another story . . .

And Monroe, of course, has been the basis of countless stories, some true, others not. Sinatra introduced her to John and Bobby Kennedy, though this is not really relevant to the Sinatra saga. One poignant photograph shows Monroe sitting in the front row at the Sands with Martin, watching mesmerized as Sinatra sang. Did she and Sinatra have an affair as well?

Ocean's Eleven was released in the summer of 1960. It was a light-hearted romp about a raid on Las Vegas casinos on New Year's Eve. The five friends also welcomed Richard Conte into their group. Someone said that they hardly wanted to take their salary as the film had seemed so little like work.

In May 1960, soon after the Academy Awards had included the ditty "High Hopes," John Wayne and Sinatra had "a heated exchange" in public view at a Hollywood nightclub. The quarrel could be said to have been brewing for some time, after Wayne and some reactionary friends had accused Sinatra of being unpatriotic. The reason they gave for this rather outrageous accusation was that Sinatra had employed Albert Maltz as a scriptwriter. On the face of it, there seemed nothing wrong with that. But apparently the unfortunate Maltz had once been detained for refusing to answer questions before an anticommunist committee. Those were the days of Senator Joseph McCarthy and his infamous inquisition.

As a footnote to that quarrel, Wayne and Sinatra must have made up subsequently, for they became firm friends. Spinning forward momentarily some seventeen years, while Sinatra was in the middle of a fortnight's session at Las Vegas, he flew to Los Angeles to present the Hebrew University Scopus Award to Wayne.

No one could have accused Sinatra of sympathy with communism. But some Americans always seemed unable to distinguish between refusing to pander to such a committee and supporting Moscow. There was also the extra issue of loyalty to one's friends. With both the social and personal principles so clear, Sinatra could not possibly do otherwise than he did. He could not let an injustice pass uncorrected—large or small. It might have been a careless driver or someone trying to hound a perfectly respectable liberal scriptwriter. Sinatra did not care one iota for what people thought, provided that he lived by the standards he had set for himself. Reverting to the Maltz affair, this was an election year and Sinatra had already publicly declared himself for Kennedy. So he was fair game for the reactionary American press and political machine. Despite mass press criticism, he defended the choice of Maltz and actually took a page advertisement in *Variety* to explain why.

Films, records, concerts, and women were all part of a juggling act that he somehow kept in the air. As one ball came down, he threw another one up. Take the busy year of 1960. He met Judith Campbell—one more woman. He recorded the *Nice 'n' Easy* album. My choices from this one would be "You Go to My Head" and "How Deep Is the Ocean?" He couldn't get away from Cole Porter for long. This album went right to the top—and stayed there.

In June, Sinatra happened to be in a smart bar in Berlin with William Holden and some other friends. While there, he met the redheaded Eva-Marie Ohm, who described him like this, "He was so alive, so intense. Always looking round and asking questions, as though he were looking for something. Not nosey, but very exciting." Sinatra asked her out, but she did not go. Was this a unique event in his history? When he got back to the States, he rang her from Atlantic City and found that she had a summer holiday due. On the spur of the moment, he invited her out to Atlantic City and paid her round-trip. The resort had its weatherboard walkway beside the beach, rather like Deauville in France. Sinatra had an eighteen-show midsummer date in Atlantic City.

The two major episodes that summer, however, were the showing of *Can-Can* and Sinatra's support for the Kennedy nomination. Capitol Records had already released the sound track songs from the film. Every musical he graced seemed to be "doomed to succeed," as someone put it. This one had the basic ingredients of the

Porter tunes, Sinatra singing them, Prowse dancing, and three other sparkling stars: Maclaine, Maurice Chevalier, and Louis Jordan. Nelson Riddle handled the arrangements and Sinatra warbled four or five of the best numbers from the LP: "It's All Right with Me," "Let's Do It," "Montmartre," "C'est Magnifique," and "I Love Paris." The "Montmartre" number was a duet with Chevalier, still flourishing at seventy-something and still destined to play a memorable role in *Gigi*.

Two of the tunes remain etched in the imagination over forty years later. There was the galvanic "Let's Do It" with Maclaine in her dressing room. And, of course, "It's All Right with Me" sung by Sinatra to Prowse draped decoratively at a bar stool. The *Los Angeles Times* said of Sinatra's performance, "Frankie defies classification; he remains simply, or not so simply, a 20-year phenomenon." The Prowse affair was progressing, but read on . . .

In late May, Sinatra triumphantly sang in Japan for the first, but not the last, time. Then he was back well in time for a number of important Kennedy dates. He and Judy Garland joined talents in Chicago, and then the very next night he rendered "The Star-Spangled Banner" in Los Angeles at the Democratic National Convention. Kennedy was nominated and Sinatra felt it had all been worthwhile.

That fall heralded two special weddings. First and closest to Sinatra was the September one, when Nancy junior married the singer Tommy Sands. Sinatra gave her away and the pair were firmly entrenched in the world of show business and Hollywood. Three singers in the family, plus musician Sinatra Jr.!

Later came the marriage of Sammy Davis Jr. to the Swedish actress Mai Britt. But meanwhile it was with Davis and his bride-to-be, or Tony Curtis and his lovely wife, Janet Leigh, that Sinatra was being seen out on the town. And on these outings, Sinatra would usually be escorting Prowse. He had met Prowse in August the previous year, soon after she had arrived in America from South Africa. This first encounter happened at a party given by Lawford.

This season, too, Sinatra had a series of dates with the Curtises. He was fulfilling a voluntary commitment to sing for free in aid of funds for the Democratic Party's actual presidential campaign. The

Curtises were also aiding the same cause. And then in October, Sinatra and Eleanor Roosevelt talked together on the radio, also in aid of Kennedy.

Kennedy was elected president in early November by a small margin. Sinatra felt thrilled and so, too, were the Curtises. It seemed to augur a new age in American politics. Immediately after the election, Sinatra appeared in a real-life role as best man at the second of the year's weddings: Davis and Britt. No press members were permitted at the actual ceremony, which was held in Davis's home, as the thirty-four-year-old star did not want the occasion reduced to the level of publicity. However, later on they did relent and posed for pictures at a hotel.

Taking the Kennedy story ahead to January 1961, the sequel came after the electoral celebrations had died down. Sinatra was asked by Kennedy to take charge of the inaugural gala, to be held in Washington, D.C., in honor of the president's inauguration week. He and Lawford flew into Washington on Kennedy's private jet and began to organize the event. The only flaw for Sinatra in the whole glittering affair was that he had been advised not to invite the Davises, because of the still-vexed black-and-white marriage question. Sinatra was torn between twin loyalties: Kennedy and Davis. On this occasion, he had no alternative but to compromise and explain to Davis, who brushed it aside with characteristic style. After all, he had lived with color prejudice all his life, so it came as no shattering surprise when the Democrats felt that the couple could be an embarrassment.

Sinatra rehearsed show business talent worth literally millions of dollars. He even paid to close two Broadway shows for the night to enable Sir Laurence Olivier and Ethel Merman to take part. Olivier had been playing in *Becket* and Merman in *Gypsy,* so Sinatra simply purchased all the tickets for that date and shut both their theaters! On one of those rare nights, one that could never recur, Sinatra had the professional services of Maclaine, Lawford, Nat King Cole, Ella Fitzgerald, Olivier, Merman, and many other stars, all appearing in homage to Kennedy. Sinatra sat with Kennedy, a fitting honor for Sinatra, since he had done so much to assist in the president's victory.

My two choices from *Swingin' Session,* Sinatra's new album, were "September in the Rain" and "I Concentrate on You." The former was a prewar number that takes me back to my adolescence, while the Cole Porter classic never had a better interpretation.

It was a joyous affair, if not possessing that ultimate touch of timelessness of some of his other albums—before and after. Riddle was there, his usual quietly authoritative self, dressed not so quietly in a red-and-gray sports shirt and conducting the band with his right hand. Behind the usual scaffolding effect of the microphones and beams, the band plugged away in red cardigans, shirts, and anything wearable. In the center stood Sinatra, in a dark single-breasted suit, dark shoes, a handkerchief in breast pocket, a clean white shirt, a silver tie, and a dark hat with a wide, bright band. Music was held in his left hand, while the fingers of his right hand softly snapped in tempo. It was hot outside—and inside, too. Hence the shirtsleeves of the band.

By the time of the Kennedy inauguration, Sinatra had yet another LP in the bag ready for release in 1961. It was a case of an endless supply meeting an equally endless demand. About this time, Riddle went on record as saying that he knew Sinatra had the reputation of sometimes being a difficult man with whom to work but that he had never found him so. It was a case of mutual respect for their complementary talents.

Sinatra was coming toward the end of the fabled Capitol Record years, though he went on recording for the company until his contract ran out in 1961. But for some time now, he had been pondering the notion of forming his own record company, and on 19 and 20 December 1960 he actually made his first impressions for the new concern, to be called Reprise Records. The idea behind the name: records worthy of being played over and over again. And anyway, "reprise" was such a nice word.

Some time was to elapse before any Sinatra LPs were released under the Reprise label, but at that initial session he got a marvelous musical send-off. The band was the exhilarating Johnny Mandel and his orchestra; his daughter Nancy and son, Frank, were also there spectating and supporting, along with son-in-law Tommy

Sands, Felix Slatkin, and Prowse. A bevy of Sinatra intimates. Slatkin was at that time acting as Sinatra's musical director.

Like Riddle, Sands had never had the slightest trouble with father-in-law Sinatra. Sands was reported to have said, "I always find him very pleasant—he has certainly never hit me in the eye!" Early in 1961, the Sinatra private life had one of its periodic flare-ups. Sinatra and Prowse were quoted as quarreling during one of their regular visits to Las Vegas, and Sinatra started to be seen with Dorothy Provine. But Prowse was still insisting at that stage, "I love him and I am going to marry him." Would she or wouldn't she? Onlookers began to feel that they had been here before, once or twice—or even thrice. It was probably during Sinatra's fortnight in February at the Sands Hotel that the Prowse trouble surfaced. But there might still be a month or even a year or more to run for this affair.

Meanwhile, Sinatra sang at a half-dozen benefit concerts, including those for the Martin Luther King Christian movement, given at New York's Carnegie Hall, and another for the Los Angeles Cedars of Lebanon Hospital. The charity work had been going strong for a long time and was beginning to increase.

Still closely connected with the Kennedy administration and John and Bobby personally, Sinatra also saw Monroe on several occasions that spring. When asked about her, he explained, "I took her out a few times so she wouldn't be cooped up in her hotel."

That same spring, he flew to Hawaii for the location work with Spencer Tracy on their new film *The Devil at Four O'clock*. Sinatra and Tracy got on well and had done so for years, as they were individualists, rebels, and unconventional stars. The scenes were shot around the Haleakala volcanic crater on Maui Island. The producers were Mervyn LeRoy and Fred Kohlmar.

"For me, this is another Maggio part—the part I had in *Eternity*." So said Sinatra about his role. His character was a cocky convict with a jaundiced eye on the world—a man who did not give a damn about anyone. Unfortunately, the film did not prove to be in the same class as *From Here to Eternity*. But any picture with Sinatra and Tracy must have been worth studying, if only for their interaction.

When he had finished filming in Hawaii, Sinatra fulfilled a long-standing engagement in Mexico City. This was really the inspiration for his amazing "people-to-people" program the following year. On this trip to Mexico, he did a show on behalf of the National Rehabilitation Institute to help the underprivileged in that country of widespread poverty. The generous gesture naturally created goodwill among the Mexicans and paved the path for his stay there in 1962.

Sinatra made a short stop in Britain, too, during a hectic 1961. He and Dean Martin flew over to make a single-scene guest appearance in the finale of the film being made at Shepperton Studios, *The Road to Hong Kong*. This starred the usual pair of Bing Crosby and Bob Hope, and the cameo spot was just one more nice gesture. In 1960, he had done something similar for the film *Pepe,* about a beautiful white stallion. While over in Britain, Sinatra finalized the arrangements for Pye to distribute Reprise Records in Britain. The first titles to be released, in September 1961, were three singles by Sinatra, Davis, and Toni Williams, respectively. The two songs chosen by Sinatra were the upbeat "Granada" and "The Curse of an Aching Heart." His last record for Capitol Records was also dated that same month and bore the slightly symbolic title *Point of No Return.*

With the launching of Reprise Records, 1961 marked yet another upgrade year for Sinatra. Among the first releases were numbers by Nancy Sinatra. She was already developing into a stylish singer, even before those boots! Then with the American release of Sinatra's first Reprise album, it was a case of *Ring-a-Ding-Ding.*

With Reprise, his own company, Sinatra seemed still happier and freer than ever. It was no accident that he launched the label with this title, for it established a clarion call that he meant to maintain. Its conductor, Johnny Mandel, was one of the best young jazz-based arrangers and had played under Jimmy Dorsey and Count Basie. Several of the soloists, too, were real jazz musicians. In this way, Sinatra spiced his Reprise albums with swing settings. And he was developing that vocal inflection of singing like a strong, mellow horn, bringing improvisation and individuality to some of the straightest songs such as "Let's Face the Music and Dance." Lyric liberties, too, were not unknown and were becoming more common, but always as a starting point. He was a prime fanatic in favor of the work of the lyricists he helped to fame—and fortune. Perhaps occasionally—it may be somewhat sacrilegious to say—he sometimes blurred the spirit of a song, proving that even Sinatra was not perfect.

For the title song of *Ring-a-Ding-Ding,* Sinatra had gotten Cahn and Van Heusen to write a bright melody and light lyric with phrases like "captivating creature." And to add a dash-and-splash of fun to the whole thing, "The Coffee Song" had a whole percolator-full of freshly brewed lyrics. As Ralph J. Gleason said of this record, "He is the living proof that quality has a place in the mass society. And in some mystical way, perhaps, his success with quality is a reaffirmation of the basic, positive good of life itself."

The final two weeks of 1961 were spent at the Sands Hotel, followed a week later by the remarkable three-day recording period for the forthcoming *Sinatra and Strings.* I will come to this later when it was released in Britain. Again, only one week after completing this landmark album, Sinatra was in Sydney for a group of concerts—and then home in time for Christmas. The Sinatras remained a civilized family and Sinatra and friends called on Nancy senior, where the children completed the family group. They had all long accepted Sinatra's personal lifestyle, even if Nancy might really never get over their parting.

CHAPTER NINE

A VERY GOOD YEAR

1962

Frank Sinatra turned forty-six in 1962. This year would eclipse everything he had done to date. Of all the preceding two decades since he had catapulted to idoldom in 1942, this year would prove to be the richest—in real terms—and probably the most rewarding of Sinatra's life. The New Year started auspiciously. He proposed to Juliet Prowse and she accepted. But now read on!

Back to business and another marathon album session in January for *All Alone*. Then a mere ninety-six hours later, straight into the start of the memorable thriller *The Manchurian Candidate*. And meanwhile, the period remake of the Rudyard Kipling classic *Gunga Din* came out. This was called *Sergeants 3* and turned out to be a real romp and a flagrant vehicle for Sinatra, Dean Martin, Peter Lawford, Sammy Davis Jr., and Joey Bishop—the Rat Pack, the Clan, call them what you like.

During 1962 he also conquered the world—all for children's charities. It took some planning. Even before this universal project, he was carrying out the old proverb about charity beginning at home. For in early February, Sinatra acted as host to 2,500 orphans and handicapped children at the great Capitol Theater in New York. The occasion was the special showing of the film *Sergeants 3* in aid of the children.

While Sinatra was busy there and elsewhere, Prowse wended her way back to South Africa to tell her parents about her engagement.

She talked to the press in terms of a family of two or three children. But only three weeks later came a surprising statement in Hollywood, issued jointly by Prowse and Sinatra. They had decided to call off their marriage plans. Through Charles Moses for Sinatra's Essex Productions, they announced that "a conflict of career interests has led us to make this decision jointly. We both feel it is better to make it now rather than later." The press read that as indicating Prowse's unwillingness to give up her promising career.

A month elapsed before Sinatra was next spotted in Hollywood escorting a lady. And the unpredictable—or predictable—Sinatra did not let down his reputation for the unconventional. Who was the woman he was escorting? Ava Gardner! Perhaps this could be taken to show that he did not like to sever himself from his past. Of course, it was a byword that he was always on the closest terms with his children, seeing them as often as he could when in California or elsewhere. And he never lost touch with Nancy, whom he referred to around this era as "the mother of my children." Incidentally, one day the previous year, while on a visit to Britain, he phoned her in Hollywood. They had a call spanning twenty minutes in time and 6,000 miles in space.

A week after completing an album for Reprise arranged by Neal Hefti, *Sinatra and Swingin' Brass,* he started his world tour for children. On 16 April, it was announced in England that Princess Margaret and the Earl of Snowdon would attend a midnight matinee to be given by Sinatra at the Royal Festival Hall, London, on 1 June. The show would benefit the Invalid Children's Aid Association, of which the princess was president.

Sinatra started his 35,000-mile trip, which was nothing less than a world charity concert tour in aid of sick and underprivileged children. As he left on this people-to-people experience, Sinatra told reporters, "You might say I have always been rushed in the past. Now I am slowing down." It did not really look like that, though. Nine countries and three continents in two months!

That same day, too, by coincidence came an item announcing that there was a new pack in Hollywood known as the Mink Pack. The qualifications to be a member were to have a million dollars or more. Among those mentioned as qualifying were such stars as Lucille Ball, Elvis Presley, Cary Grant, Rosalind Russell, Jimmy Durante, and, naturally, Sinatra.

He had not asked to be included in this ostentatious-sounding group, but it was just as well that he qualified, since Sinatra would be meeting every cent of the expenses of this tour from his own pocket. He set himself a target of $1 million to hand over to the various children's charities en route. And what a route. Nothing like it had ever been conceived prior to this. It all began in April.

For part of the trip, Sinatra and his team flew in his newly completed Martin aircraft. Built in Los Angeles, the jet could carry fifteen passengers. Sinatra had taken a close interest in its interior design and layout, specifying what he wanted. The result included a "nightclub room" with a miniature electric piano, a tape recorder, a hi-fi setup, and, inevitably, a circular bar. There was also a dining area and a bedroom, while an electric moon and stars shone on the ceiling!

The aircraft was fully laden for the flight. Sinatra's team comprised a band of six handpicked players who accompanied him at every concert he gave throughout the entire two months; a liaison man; a publicity woman; still and film photographers; a sound engineer and assistants; his catering friends from Hollywood; Gloria and Mike Romanoff; and the two pilots. In all, the passenger list contained fifteen people, not including Sinatra.

They were scheduled to visit Mexico, Japan, Hong Kong, Greece, Italy, Israel, Spain, Britain, and Monaco. The cine and sound technicians went along to take film and tapes of many of the memorable scenes on the tour, which Sinatra intended to sell to television networks afterward for fees to be donated to still more charities. This was quite apart from the actual charities in the countries concerned. Sinatra summed up the idea behind the whole mission in this straightforward way: "As an overprivileged adult, I'd like to help underprivileged children."

The first stop was Mexico. Sinatra appeared at the International Theater, Mexico City, where an audience of 5,000 heard him sing for three-quarters of an hour, having paid $12 each for tickets. They cheered him for five minutes before he started the show. Then he went into such numbers as "I Get a Kick out of You." The instrumentalists accompanying him were all top-drawer session players. They were Bill Miller, piano and leader of the group; Al Viola, guitar; Emil Richards, vibraphone; Ralph Penna, bass; Harry Klee, alto sax, flute, and clarinet; and Irv Cottler, drums. The charity to benefit by the proceeds from this huge audience was the same as the one Sinatra helped in previous years, the Mexican Rehabilitation Center.

The next stop was Tokyo, Japan. Sinatra saw the fantastic art forms of the neon signs traced in the night sky of the capital city. Those strange vertical hieroglyphics blinking out their messages to the multitudes below. Only seventeen years earlier, this had been the capital of an enemy empire. Now, the people of Tokyo honored Sinatra by giving him the key to their city. He was the first nonmilitary person to receive such recognition. He gave three concerts in Tokyo: two full-priced ones and a special, less expensive show for those who could not afford the others. The theme of the underprivileged of all ages was obviously in his mind, children and adults alike.

Over a thousand people crushed into the smart Mikado Restaurant in the heart of the city to hear the full-priced shows. The cover charge per person was then about $12. He was an astounding success. The article he had written in the *London Daily Sketch* about American music being international was proving perfectly true. Sinatra engendered more goodwill than a dozen political missions could ever accomplish.

Remembering the people who could not afford the Mikado prices, he then gave his third show in the Hibiya Park outdoor theater. The audience consisted of 7,000 young Japanese enthusiasts who went wild for him. The sum total of the three Tokyo concerts came to 9 million yen or $28,000. The proceeds were shared between a number of the city's orphanages and children's homes. The Japanese, in fact, named an orphanage after him in thanks for his help.

Sinatra somehow fit in special shows for American servicemen in Korea and Okinawa, where he was made to feel right back home. The sight of Tokyo and Okinawa could hardly help but prompt memories of World War II and the bloody battles in the Pacific.

Now, Sinatra was singing to Yanks and Japs alike and helping to promote peace: to heal.

The next stop was Hong Kong. Years after his concerts there, its residents still talked of Sinatra and those three days—26, 27, and 28 April—he spent there in that teeming metropolis. The locals nicknamed him the "Thin Monkey." Sinatra took it as intended: in affection.

He saw some of the great poverty in Hong Kong, that over-crowded island outpost. And all the time, fresh families were escaping from the Chinese Republic to its apparent sanctuary. Times did not change much in the ensuing four decades, with refugees coming from Vietnam and elsewhere. Despite it all—the extremes of riches and poverty—people were philosophical in their Oriental fashion. A hundred handicapped children sang to Sinatra and wove a garland of exotic flowers for him. In return, he gave them the money that would help them toward a fuller, happier life. The high prices for the charity concerts at the city hall ensured that he would achieve his target. These profits went to the Society for the Relief of Disabled Children, the Boys' and Girls' Clubs Association, and OMS St. Simon Home for Fishermen's Widows and Children.

While he was flying halfway across the world to Israel—one of his favorite nations—the unprecedented rush for tickets to the four scheduled London concerts began and ended. Needless to say, all 10,000 tickets were sold before they had even been printed. A stream of inquiries started in the personal columns of the national newspapers, offering up to 50 pounds ($120) for each seat. That was a lot of money in the England of the 1960s.

The following short saga recounts how I got my two tickets to see and hear Sinatra for the first time. I found out the name of the ticket agency that was supposed to be handling the bookings, but as it had about a half-dozen London addresses and branches, it was anyone's guess where spare tickets might be on sale. This was before the days of advance mailing lists and other slightly more civilized arrangements. Easier perhaps, but duller, like the world?

I heard the date when inquiries would be first considered. So, getting up an hour earlier than usual that morning, I set off for London and chose the branch of the agency nearest to the center of the West End and the theater district. I waited outside from 8:30 to 9:30 A.M. When it eventually opened, the manager at once disclaimed any knowledge of booking for the concerts. In fact, many tickets were being allocated through the charity organizations for which the shows were to be given. It looked like it was becoming a typical British mix-up.

The switchboards of all branches of the ticket agency started to get jammed from exactly 9:30 on that morning. There were hundreds of callers. The manager of this particular branch told me that the best thing to do would probably be to go around to Harold Davison, which was the concert promoter in connection with the Sinatra appearances. The time was then 9:40. At the Regent Street offices of Harold Davison, I was pleasantly told that the company was not handling the tickets and that I would be lucky to get any through the "usual channels." Then I was told, almost as an afterthought, that "the Variety Club of Great Britain is organizing the second concert, at the Odeon Theatre, Leicester Square, at midnight on 2 June. Why not try there? You might just stand a chance."

Several other people had already arrived at the Davison offices from the original ticket agency, so I started walking faster, and then running, to Wardour Street, home of the Variety Club. I arrived at 9:50. The offices opened at ten o'clock. I was actually the first one there, closely followed by six others. And then more.

As the offices opened, the phones started ringing and went on at intervals of ten to fifteen seconds for the next hour. That was a measure of the magnetism of Sinatra. After a wait of some time, while the wonderful Variety Club prepared to cope with this siege by telephone and personal callers, I was asked for my name and address. These details were entered fairly. The Variety Club naturally had the first choice of tickets, but there might be a few left over. It was tantalizing, yet that was how it had to be left.

I got my two tickets—the very first to be allocated to a member of the public for any of the Sinatra concerts! Quite a minor miracle. The tickets cost six guineas ($15) each. But that was not too much to pay for charity. Nor for what might be the experience of a lifetime. Applications for the total 10,000 seats eventually exceeded 250,000. Before leaving this short story of how I acquired these tickets, I would like to say thank you to Harold Davison personally, and to his organization, for enabling me to see Sinatra on each one of his subsequent visits to Britain—and indirectly this time, too. Even getting those later tickets was never easy and I had become a regular visitor to the Davison premises on the corner of New Bond Street and Conduit Street, in Mayfair.

But back to Sinatra's tour. He stayed in Israel for nine days, from 2–10 May. Here, he was happy. He always supported Jewish causes and he proved to be "the perfect diplomat," as S. B. Britt described him in the June 1962 souvenir edition of Britain's Frank Sinatra Appreciation Society. Sinatra visited Jerusalem, Beersheba, Haifa, and Tel Aviv, where he watched the Independence Week parade. While there, he met Prime Minister David Ben-Gurion.

In Nazareth, he received the keys and freedom of that historic place. And a special school was named after him: the Frank Sinatra International Friendship Youth House. He advocated and promoted fellowship between Jewish and Arab children, and perhaps this will belatedly bear fruit in the future. He sang at seven concerts in Israel—nearly one a day from first to last. Sinatra then felt that his voice needed a rest.

He took a week off and visited the historic island of Rhodes. It is really unnecessary to say "historic," as everywhere at this stage of the tour could be called so. At Rhodes, he saw Lindos before the tourist rush and looking more as it must have seemed when St. Paul preached there. The break included some days on a yacht sailing around Rhodes. Then it was on to Greece.

I suppose I know Greece and the Greek Islands better than any other country outside Britain: Athens, Piraeus, Cape Sounion, the Epidaurus amphitheater in the Peloponnese, Mycenae and the beehive tomb, Nauplion, and on to the southern extremities. And then there are the Islands of the Gods . . .

I wonder what Sinatra thought of it all. When I went to a symphony concert years later at the Herod Atticus Amphitheater, I did not know that this had been the venue for Sinatra's two Athens appearances. They must have been magical evenings below the Parthenon—floodlit on the Acropolis. The capacity crowd apparently received the familiar overpowering impact.

After brief breaks in Milan and Nice, Sinatra sang in Rome in aid
of the Boys' Town of Italy Association, one of the many charities
close to his heart. A couple of concerts in Milan were followed by a
wonderful Spanish welcome in Madrid. The London dates were
getting nearer now. Remember that at this stage of my sheltered life
I had not yet seen Sinatra in the flesh!

On 30 May, Heathrow officials received a message in the middle
of the night that the Martin aircraft would be arriving at dawn.
Throughout Europe, it had been a battle to beat the press and so
preserve not only privacy but time to rest. By touching down at
dawn, he did that and was whisked off to the Savoy Hotel. He was
pretty worn out and went straight to bed.

By teatime on 31 May, Sinatra was up and out walking in the traditional shopping area of Old Bond Street. He was dressed in sober
gray trousers and a dark blazer. And on the blazer was a badge with
the emblem J.D., a square whiskey bottle, golf clubs, and six balls.
The initials, of course, stood for Jack Daniels, the American
whiskey distiller. Sinatra and his entourage dined at a Chinese
restaurant in the depths of London's Soho. He also made a quick
move into a Savoy suite overlooking the Thames and the Royal Festival Hall. This would be the scene of the next night's concert. Excitement grew hourly!

During the day of 1 June, Sinatra went out to Northwood in
Middlesex, to visit the Sunshine Home for Blind Babies. This was
one of the homes administered by the Sunshine Fund, one of the
charities to benefit from his two concerts at the Gaumont Theatre,
Hammersmith, over the forthcoming weekend. They were the last
pair of his four shows. At Northwood, Sinatra was visibly moved by
the children there.

So at last the midnight matinee came. The Royal Festival Hall
gleamed with light, glowed with anticipation. It was Sinatra's first
of many memorable shows there, in this spectacular contemporary
setting. The concert had been sponsored by Princess Margaret and
naturally there were royal guests present—including the Earl of
Snowdon. Nelson Riddle was also there to witness the Sinatra triumph. So were Judy Garland, Douglas Fairbanks Jr., Dirk Bogarde, Shirley Bassey, Lord Montagu, the Duke and Duchess of Bedford, and many more celebrities.

At 1:00 A.M., Sinatra opened with "Goody Goody."

At 2:40, Sinatra closed with "Come Fly with Me."

Twenty-nine songs later. Nearly one hundred minutes. The only break had been a cup of tea with honey and a cigarette. He sang "Moonlight in Vermont," "All the Way," "The Lady Is a Tramp," and "Autumn Leaves," the last accompanied by just a flute and guitar. The Invalid Children's Aid Association and the Variety Club of Great Britain benefited. So did the audience. London had neither seen nor heard anything like it. Sinatra had an ovation lasting long after he had left the stage. The Variety Club bestowed its Gold Heart on him for his work.

By 3:30 Sinatra was in the celebrated River Room at the Savoy for a party in his honor. The whole night was a tremendous success— even by his standards.

He went to bed soon after dawn, slept for a few hours, and then took a helicopter down to Alton in Hampshire to see a friend of his, Robin Douglas-Home, who was recovering from an operation. Douglas-Home was a journalist who had written about Sinatra and his art. The thought of Sinatra in the still-sleepy little country township seemed somehow incongruous. It had been the home of Jane Austen—not a lady one would readily connect with the life and times of Frank Sinatra!

But there was nothing incongruous about Sinatra's appearance that night at the Odeon Theatre before 2,200 people—including me. Earlier, I had been to my niece Genevieve's wedding. And now Sinatra. It seemed almost too much.

Many of the audience had already watched the recording of the previous night's show televised by ITV that evening. From their television sets, they started out for the Odeon. As midnight neared, the crowds were already closing Leicester Square to traffic. Tickets were changing hands at ten times their printed price. Beyond the glittering foyer, the scene of so many later royal film premieres, the theater slowly filled. The clock on the wall at the back of the stalls pointed to midnight and 2 June ended as the show began. Johnny Dankworth and Cleo Laine had the job of preceding Sinatra. I admire them a lot, but somehow I could not concentrate on their music. The intermission came at a quarter to one. Finally, as the clock showed exactly 1:00 A.M. the huge curtains opened—and there he was! Only twenty yards away. An ocean of an ovation. It was the start of a long succession of my seeing Sinatra live that lasted exactly thirty-one years to the final Dortmund date.

He opened with "Goody Goody" and then rounded off this opening number with the cheeky reference to the tickets, "And I hope you're satisfied that you got yours!"

His genius generated a tremendous tension. Smiling and suntanned, the young-middle-aged Sinatra sang and 2,200 people listened rapt, silent. The ending of each song was followed with a sudden storm of appreciation. Then his fingers snapped or hands molded into some shape appropriate to the line of the lyric; he skidded through twenty-seven numbers, scarcely pausing for breath. Certainly no one heard him take one all night long. That was always one of his vocal features—threading whole lines on the seamless legato of breathing taken utterly inaudibly. His underwater swimming training paid off.

He brought out the poignancy and the poetry of "The Second Time Around"; the jazz imagery of "You're Nobody Till Somebody Loves You"; the absolution of "All the Way"; the bluster, bravado, and bravura of "Chicago"; the isolation of "One for My Baby"; the swingy chuckles in "The Lady Is a Tramp"; and the nostalgia of "Nancy." Standing or sitting, swinging or sighing, he held the theater for one hundred minutes. At 2:40 it was over, with "London by Night" still haunting us all—we who would never be quite the same again. We had become hooked and I am still addicted four decades later. For the record, Sinatra sang on that night:

"Goody Goody"	*"They Can't Take That Away from Me"*
"Imagination"	*"London by Night"*
"At Long Last Love"	*"You Make Me Feel So Young"*
"Moonlight in Vermont"	*"Come Fly with Me"*
"Day In–Day Out"	*"Nancy"*
"I've Got You under My Skin"	*"The Lady Is a Tramp"*
"I Get a Kick out of You"	*"A Foggy Day"*
"The Second Time Around"	*"Ol' Man River"*

"Too Marvelous for Words"   *"I Could Have Danced All Night"*

"My Funny Valentine"   *"Night and Day"*

"In the Still of the Night"   *"One for My Baby"*

"My Blue Heaven"   *"Chicago"*

"April in Paris"   *"All the Way"*

"You're Nobody Till Somebody Loves You"

Just pause and ponder on these songs and a singer who could imbue them with such an original imprint. The next night he did it all again. At the Gaumont Hammersmith there were no seats available for Mr. and Mrs. Armstrong-Jones, but Lord Snowdon's father and his wife finally sat in the wings and watched the show. She voiced the feelings of the whole audience when she said afterward, "It was wonderful. We've been looking forward to this for weeks. Sinatra's quite fantastic." It was his third concert in forty-eight hours.

Sinatra flew out of London for a week to appear at the Paris Lido and the Olympia Music Hall. He faced the same scenes as in London —and he was awarded the Gold Medal of Paris. Then he flew on to Monaco for his final charity show of the worldwide tour. On a perfect Mediterranean night, he sang at the Red Cross Ball held in the Monte Carlo Sporting Club. And there he sang to Grace Kelly, who had once called him "the perfect companion in a movie."

Back in London again on 12 June, Sinatra had with him Eddie Fisher, Tony Curtis, and Richard Condon, the author of the book *The Manchurian Candidate.* This had just been made into the film starring Sinatra and Laurence Harvey. It was the one that at the time took brainwashing one degree further than ever before—and in the process provided both male leads with golden-edged acting chances. When it opened soon afterward, the critics called it one of the most exciting films of the year, which it was. Compelling, spell-binding, hypnotic.

Apart from arranging a sneak preview of the film in London, Sinatra really returned to make the first LP he had ever recorded outside the United States. This was *Great Songs from Great Britain,* arranged and conducted by the Canadian Robert Farnon. The album was produced by Alan A. Freeman and Tony Hatch.

From 12–14 June, Sinatra spent three successive evenings in the recording studio at Bayswater, London, cutting the ten sides of this album of British ballads. From the first moment, the seventy-two-hour spell could be termed "extraordinary." As Sinatra entered the studio on that first evening, the whole orchestra of forty musicians rose in a burst of applause.

It became obvious after only a few minutes that Sinatra was the man in control. He spotted a wrong note among the second violins, amended the tempi, explained the crescendos and diminuendos that he thought should be made, and even gave the bar number once when he thought the tape might have to be spliced. He was the ultimate professional, thinking of a dozen things at once, yet producing a vocal standard as impeccable as ever.

The remarkable aspect of these British sessions was his blend of ruthless concentration and lighthearted self-mockery. The range of one song was causing him some profound thought. Halfway through the first take, he broke off while actually on the climactic line and emerged from the recording booth waving his arms for the orchestra to stop. To the studio in general he announced, "I can't even talk in that key!"

Then, as the clock pointed to 9:25 P.M., Sinatra drank a cup of coffee, exchanged a few friendly words with Farnon, and then went back to work. This time he did a perfect take and emerged from the booth beaming and commenting, "See what you get when you keep good hours and live a clean life!"

The contrast to this surface flippancy came during the actual take and the playback following it. While he was singing, Sinatra lived with the sentiments of the lyric and melody—eyes closed, body swaying, oblivious of those around him. Even when sentiments might not have been the most profound or sincere. Yet, he made them seem so. And when the take was fed back through the loudspeakers, he stood alone in the middle of the studio floor, listening and straining for the slightest deviation from his inbred standards. It was then that he looked like the isolated figure people sometimes imagine him.

This pattern of all-out concentration on the song in hand, alternating with the humor that arose out of extreme candor about his own ability, ran through all three evenings. When he heard the cascading ripples of the brass section in "Garden in the Rain" for the first time, he laughed in appreciation of the arrangement. When a doubt arose about which of two takes to accept for "A Nightingale Sang in Berkeley Square," he said sensitively, "Keep the second one—because the trombone solo was excellent." Shades of his years with Tommy Dorsey.

Of course, he included "London by Night," which had closed the concert at the Odeon. Another immortal number on the record was "We'll Meet Again," forever associated with Vera Lynn and World War II. Although the album was made and sold solely in Britain, Sinatra fans in America have heard it over the intervening years. For daughter Nancy, her favorite of the ten was "A Nightingale Sang in Berkeley Square."

During that week of the recording, Princess Alexandra called on Sinatra at the Savoy Hotel and talked to him about his world tour and his records. As she left, she was seen to be carrying an armful of LPs—a gift from Sinatra. And before returning home, Sinatra took some friends to the Italian restaurant in Soho called Trattoria Terrazza. The bill for nineteen people in 1962 was $80. Sinatra made a point of leaving a $50 tip. The reported phone bill for his group at the Savoy was over $3,000!

On 17 June, Britain became a duller place when the Sinatra team left Heathrow, with Sinatra flying out complete with a typical English umbrella! Although he would never be mistaken for a city gent.

Several things emerged from the global tour. First, Sinatra said, "I found out a lot of things I didn't know before." Second, Sinatra, his films, and his records were all banned from Arab countries because of his alleged pro-Israel propaganda during his visit to that state. Third, he made over $1 million for charity. The expenses for the whole tour totaled $150,000, all of which was covered by Sinatra himself. One last personal memory of the tour for me came when an official of the Variety Club of Great Britain appeared in the middle of the Odeon concert. The man presented Sinatra with a trophy specially inscribed in appreciation of his "magnificent efforts" in the area of charity. The end of the tour marked the end of merely one more chapter in the Sinatra story.

CHAPTER TEN

RING-A-DING-DING

1962-1963

It was no accident that Frank Sinatra launched the label of Reprise Records with *Ring-a-Ding-Ding*. This really established a tone he meant to maintain. We are still in 1962, in the wake of that world tour. For Sinatra, the year seemed to possess an iota of extra magic. On the sleeve of *Sinatra Swings* we get a glimpse of another side of him—Frankie the golfer—and we know he swam strongly, too.

Then to his third album. Sinatra looked back in admiration to launch *I Remember Tommy*. He naturally went at once to Sy Oliver to arrange a dozen of the old numbers associated with the halcyon days of Tommy Dorsey, who had helped him. They started with that hard-to-sing signature tune "I'm Getting Sentimental over You." Not all the numbers were slow, however, and Sinatra swung "Imagination" and "Without a Song" on the first side. Then from the perfectly phrased "There Are Such Things"—with its "faithful optimism," as our own beloved Benny Green put it—to "East of the Sun." Sounding slightly tipsy and yet dead in tune, Sinatra rendered the final lines three times.

On the other side, he created a Frankism in "I'll Be Seeing You," varying a phrase like "morning light" to "early bright." "It's Always You" took us straight back to the wartime era of Dorsey and Glenn Miller, while Sinatra somehow got away with the innocence of "Polka Dots and Moonbeams" through sheer sincerity. He even managed to make it sound poetic.

Sinatra himself was keen on this album, probably partly for sentimental and nostalgic reasons, but the wider acclaim was reserved for his next Reprise offering: *Sinatra and Strings*. This must rank as one of the best LPs he ever made, and the credit could be shared with the arranger Don Costa. Why apologize for dwelling in some detail on it? When composer Harold Arlen heard Sinatra erupting with intensity into that final "shine" of "Come Rain Come Shine," his first reaction was characteristic. He asked, "Who's the arranger?"

In each one of the ten songs, the instrumental framed the singing so artistically, set the mood so sensitively, and accented Sinatra's vocal line so sympathetically. The whole conception and execution were clearly committed and heartfelt. A classical parallel could be when a conductor surrounds a soloist in a concerto with orchestral sound yet leaves the individual player space to breathe and express the solo line. Together, they create a unique unity. So it was with Costa and Sinatra. And the classical allusion is apt, too, for much of the accompaniment is in fact reminiscent of concerto quality.

The songs selected were the kind that Duke Ellington always so eloquently expressed as "beyond category"—by Arlen, Cole Porter, Jerome Kern, Richard Rodgers, and Hoagy Carmichael. And to them all Sinatra brought a vibrant awareness, a newness. "Night and Day," for instance, sounded quite different from his recording on *A Swingin' Affair*. It was this capacity to develop and change his visualization of a song through the years and decades that remained one of his talents. This time the numbers were more than ever yearning, haunting. Frankie had lived a little longer.

Sinatra could modify his mood at will. From high emotion in "Night and Day," he slipped into the slightly more naive gear as a dewy-eyed innocent in "Misty" and "It Might as Well Be Spring." But on the first side of the record it was "Stardust" that drew most gasps and comments. The Costa strings, horns, and harp led into the verse about the "meadows" of one's heart. But the chorus never came. This was the first and last time that the Carmichael classic had ever been heard or recorded minus the chorus. The evocative effect achieved was to concentrate the musical and lyrical mind on all the neglected nuances of the verse. Behind it all, too, we wondered if Sinatra was chuckling to himself as he imagined listeners waiting for the familiar refrain to start.

The pacing of the five songs on the other side was worthy of a symphonic structure. After the lighter touch of "It Might as Well Be Spring" came the heavier "Prisoner of Love." Then lightness once more with "That's All," leading up to the climax of the whole record, "All or Nothing at All." Twenty-three years had separated this from the original tentative if promising recording with Harry James. Now, it was more pronounced. Sinatra sang "Yesterday" by Kern with new yearning. "Make like Brahms," Sinatra used to say to Nelson Riddle when discussing an arrangement. In this final number, we could imagine him asking Costa to "make like Sibelius." The arrangement is certainly sheer Jean Sibelius, with those ice-swept, high-rising chords. It reminded me immediately of Helsinki and the individualism of Finland.

One might imagine that Sinatra spent most of his time making records. He didn't. That summer he sang at his own Cal-Neva Lodge for a full week, and then appeared again with Dean Martin in September. The same month he was back at the Sands Hotel, Las Vegas, which became his second home over the years.

Shooting also started on the film *Come Blow Your Horn*. Sinatra costarred with Barbara Rush and the actor he had befriended in illness, Lee J. Cobb. *Variety* later called his performance "jaunty" and "rackish." Sinatra sang the title tune by Sammy Cahn and Jimmy Van Heusen—a hit when it came out to synchronize with the film.

Still the same year of 1962, October saw the American premiere of *The Manchurian Candidate*. Set during the Korean War, this was an acting test piece. Sinatra passed it. The *New Yorker* summed up the performances like this, "The acting is all of a high order, and Sinatra, in his usual uncanny fashion, is simply terrific." The cast included Laurence Harvey, Janet Leigh, Angela Lansbury, and James Cagney. It was Sinatra's most serious role since *The Man with the Golden Arm*.

Toward the end of the year, the American magazine *Melody Maker* ran a competition to find out the favorite LPs of the year of over one hundred writers on popular music records. The result was rather astonishing. The winner was predictably the sound track score to the film of *West Side Story*. Then came the following:

Second: *Sinatra and Swingin' Brass*

Third: *I Remember Tommy*

Fourth: *Sinatra and Strings*

What a tribute by the press en masse to a man who was "washed up" in 1952 according to that same fickle press.

Let us take 1962 to its logical end. Perhaps the press liked *Sinatra and Swingin' Brass* because it had that string of ten "babies" in "Don'cha Go 'Way Mad." Or possibly it had belatedly appreciated that Sinatra had long ago taken the advice of the lyrics of another number on the album, "Pick Yourself Up."

Sinatra could be satisfied with this year. The world tour had helped hundreds of poor children. His name was among the Oscar nominations for Best Actor in *The Manchurian Candidate*. And for the thirteenth time in a couple of decades, the readers of *Downbeat* magazine voted him their number-one Male Singer of the Year. This was in an era already embracing rock and roll and about to accommodate the Beatles. Meanwhile, Sinatra went his own way as singer, actor, producer, benefactor, businessman, conversationalist, painter, and father. Twenty years of fame so far. Could it continue like that? We know the answer, but this was the swinging 1960s and anything might happen. He had fallen out of favor once. Another New Year—1963—opened with his parents' fiftieth wedding anniversary. He was there.

CHAPTER ELEVEN

FROM VEGAS AND THE CLAN
TO CARNEGIE HALL
1963-1969

Frank Sinatra, Sammy Davis Jr., and Dean Martin were together for three weeks. Where else but the Sands Hotel in Las Vegas? The formula would be repeated in the future. Then within a week, Sinatra was recording a major album, *The Concert Sinatra,* the first of his many Reprise K series. My favorite: "I Have Dreamed," which he later featured in London at the Royal Festival Hall with Grace Kelly present. Nelson Riddle's name made its debut on this record; for contractual reasons elsewhere, he had not been allowed to be credited sooner than this. Later in 1963, Sinatra actually disposed of two-thirds of his interest in Reprise to the entertainment empire of Warner Brothers. He also joined the management board of this legendary Hollywood organization. The deal was dated and settled during August.

Come Blow Your Horn was finished and shown. The lighthearted frolic offered Sinatra a huge hit with that title song, aided by Sammy Cahn's snappy lyrics. *Variety*'s epithet of "jaunty" applied to Sinatra's portrayal was how many people liked him best, rather than in more soulful, love-lost roles on record. But life is not one long ball—not even for Sinatra. He balanced the light and the heavy: the facets were really music, comedy, and drama.

Never a week went by without Sinatra being engaged in some creative activity. Take April and May. He acted as host at the annual Oscars ceremony; made an album, *Sinatra's Sinatra,* in two days; and sang in a charity concert at Carnegie Hall in New York. Two of the

141

"beyond category" numbers on the album were "All the Way" and "I've Got You under My Skin." How many hundreds of times did he sing these throughout his life?

And another rhetorical question now. Why did he make films like *Four for Texas*? This film included Sinatra, Martin, Anita Ekberg, and Ursula Andress, a formidable quartet of sex symbols. For reasons best known to themselves and to Warner Brothers, these four worthies were teamed in the period Western. Little more need be added. I suppose it gave employment to a number of film technicians, but why waste resources and talent on this kind of enterprise? The happy denouement to the film was Sinatra and Martin marrying their respective girlfriends in a double wedding. The end. Sinatra seemed to spend his time in a rather gaudy scarlet jacket of the 1870s.

Sinatra flew to Palm Springs during the filming of this epic to be present at the premiere of *Come Blow Your Horn,* and that summer he also fitted in a cameo spot in *The List of Adrian Messenger.* Then he was back at the Sands for a fortnight with Davis and Martin. He also had to appear before a Nevada gaming commission in connection with some of his "alleged" contacts in the nightclub world. Some people chose to consider that he was "guilty by association," as Nancy Sinatra put it in her very fair book on her father. These accusations remained with him over the years, but it is fruitless and futile to spend space and time on them now. Sinatra knew thousands of people, privately and publicly. Why would he have needed the underworld?

A unique affair happened in September over on the East Coast. New Yorkers saw two Sinatras singing there at separate events. Sinatra Sr. was at Carnegie Hall for a charity concert on behalf of Martin Luther King's religious conferences. Frank Sinatra Jr. sang for the first time in New York at the Americana Hotel. He was only nineteen. Sinatra gave his verdict on his son, "Better than me at that age!" That was in September. Everyone now knows the momentous event shortly to befall the United States. But in October all remained normal. Sinatra sang with Lena Horne at Carnegie Hall. Then he and the Rat Pack hit Chicago to start the negotiations for filming *Robin and the Seven Hoods.* Sinatra, Davis, and Martin would be joined in the film by Peter Falk, Barbara Rush, and even Bing Crosby. And the film would at least be notable for one thing if little else: Sinatra sang "My Kind of Town." They began filming in Chicago. It was November 1963 . . .

Sinatra loved John F. Kennedy. And he had helped him win the U.S. presidency. On 22 November, the fateful day when Kennedy was assassinated, Sinatra and the others had nearly completed *Robin and the Seven Hoods.* He was back in Burbank, California, on one of the very last scenes of the film. They finished it that day and Sinatra hurried away to Palm Springs. He saw no one for several days. Kennedy had been one of his heroes.

But life went on, as it has a habit of doing after even unbearable events like the death of Kennedy. But America felt diminished in an indefinable way. There would never be another Kennedy. Even subsequent revelations about his private life did not change people's feelings much.

Then out of the blue came a Sinatra family crisis as sudden as it was unimaginable. Sinatra's son was kidnapped. Just sixteen days after the Kennedy killing, and four days before Sinatra's forty-eighth birthday, Sinatra Jr. was abducted at gunpoint from a club at Lake Tahoe where he was due to sing later that evening with the Tommy Dorsey Band. After a nightmare three days, Sinatra was able to arrange for the safe release of his son. The ransom was $240,000, which was later recovered. The story had a happy ending, but it could so easily have been otherwise. The minds of many older Americans went back to Charles Lindbergh. The whole family learned a lot from the ordeal, though the various winter journeys by air and road plus the emotional strain had a physical effect on Sinatra Sr. The prospect of possible death also changed Sinatra Jr., as it would anyone. The guilty kidnappers were caught and convicted. The Sinatra family became even closer than ever.

In the midst of all this turmoil and despite the reviews, *Four for Texas* had its general release and did good pre-Christmas and post-holidey business. Hard on its heels ran *Robin and the Seven Hoods,* the one that was being wrapped up as Kennedy died. All-singing, all-shooting, all-dancing, all-action in 1920s Chicago. It was a film, as I said, saved by the showstopper "My Kind of Town." The mob-

ster city certainly inspired a kind of brio in the title of the
Cahn–Van Heusen song. And they all made a sound track album
to immortalize a story that perhaps scarcely deserved such dignifi-
cation. But that was Sinatra and I suppose on balance, who would
have had him otherwise?

None but the Brave. Sinatra not only starred in this film, but also
produced and directed it. Clint Walker and Tommy Sands
costarred and the shooting took place partly on location in the Pacific. The story was plausible. An indictment of war, it zoomed in
on a small group of Japanese and American servicemen stranded on
one of those myriad, microscopic Pacific islands. When one of the
Japanese is wounded in the leg during a skirmish, a truce is called
and the two enemy groups actually fraternize. The Japanese soldier's leg needs amputation and Sinatra orders the American chief
pharmacist's mate to carry out the operation. This is the closest the
groups get to a permanent truce, for then an American destroyer
eventually arrives on the scene. Inevitably, the balance is broken,
fighting breaks out again, and the entire Japanese group is killed.
The *Citizen News* called Sinatra's direction "most impressive."

A sidelight to this film was that on 10 May 1964 Sinatra was
nearly drowned while swimming to the rescue of executive producer Howard Koch's wife, Ruth. The notorious Pacific undertow
might well have claimed the lives of both Ruth Koch and Sinatra.
Luckily it did not.

Interspersed among many recording sessions in 1964, Sinatra fit in
more charity appearances. In July, he was present at the dedication
of the Frank Sinatra International Youth Center for Arab and Jewish children. He had been instrumental in raising funds for the center and was gratified to be at the dedication ceremony in Tel Aviv.

After an actual holiday in September, he continued chalking up
classic songs on record and then returned as if magnetized to the
Sands. He was backed by Count Basie under the musically charismatic arranger-conductor Quincy Jones. A much quoted statement
from around his forty-ninth birthday is, "You gotta love living,
baby. Dying's a pain in the ass." Then a fortnight singing in Miami
followed by a further "fix" at the Sands! Life-enhancing but a bit
exhausting, too.

"His usual uncannily confident self"—this was how the celebrated *New Yorker* magazine described Sinatra's next film role, *Marriage on the Rocks,* when it was released later. Friends and relations starred with him in this tale of marriage, divorce, and remarriage: Deborah Kerr, Dean Martin, Cesar Romero, Hermione Baddeley, and Nancy Sinatra. Needless to say, she played Sinatra's daughter. Cynics might point out quite legitimately that it was actually while filming *Marriage on the Rocks* that Tommy Sands left Nancy—never to return.

The number of albums gradually grew: *The Days of Wine and Roses, It Might as Well Be Swing,* and *September of My Years.* The last one was reckoned as one of his finest and featured "It Was a Very Good Year." *September of My Years* marked more than a quarter-century of recordings and received a Grammy Award—the record-industry equivalent of an Oscar.

Among all this frenetic activity, he had somehow filmed *Von Ryan's Express.* This wartime adventure was set in Italy and evinced some strong and subtle acting from Sinatra. *Life* magazine said that the role called for "nuances that Sinatra has rarely had to express before." Unlike many of his films, it had an unhappy ending—he was killed in the accomplishment of his mission. There had been misgivings about this climax, but it brought home to audiences the realities of war and so was not just exciting escapism. The quality of his performance was compared to that in *From Here to Eternity* and gave rise to speculation about another Oscar, or at least a nomination.

In the summer of 1965, Sinatra met Mia Farrow. He was then forty-nine, she was twenty. Thereafter for a while, Mia, Nancy, and daughter Tina could all be seen in the audience at Sinatra's shows. And as a cameo of an archetypal Sinatra day, how was this one? The Fourth of July 1965. The setting was the Newport Jazz Festival, Rhode Island. Sinatra joined with Count Basie again to make a joint appearance at the famous midsummer festival.

Sinatra arrived by helicopter—how else? He and Basie sang and played a "knock-'em-dead set" (acknowledgments to Nancy) and in return got a typically fiery American reception from fans, older and younger alike. Then Sinatra left by helicopter just as swiftly as he had landed.

My postscript thoughts on this colorful scene. The Americans are a race of great enthusiasms and spontaneous reactions. I find this one of their endearing and innocent traits. They are also, of course, "simplistic" and oversentimental, but perhaps qualities always carry counterparts—or do I mean counterpoints?

The rest of July comprised concerts at Long Island, Detroit, and Chicago. Then he flew home to Hollywood. His two daughters watched while he immortalized his handprints and footprints at Grauman's Chinese Theater. In August, he took a cruise with Farrow and others off the U.S. East Coast. Farrow looked rather waif-like and Sinatra debonair in his skipper's naval cap. The press was never far away from them on their several ports of call. Farrow had been writing poetry for Sinatra. One of their calls was on the Kennedy family's home at Hyannis Port. This was followed almost immediately by Sinatra filming the nautical *Assault on a Queen*.

Two television programs made history in November 1965. On 16 November, a sixty-minute documentary presented by Walter Cronkite was called *Sinatra: An American Original*. Then a week later on 24 November followed the first of his many television shows. This was entitled *Frank Sinatra: A Man and His Music*. Add this facet to Sinatra's nonstop career and you get the prototype of all his subsequent television spectaculars. The NBC telecast was on Thanksgiving eve.

Without quoting all the numbers he sang, suffice it to say he opened with the obligatory "I've Got You under My Skin" and closed with "Put Your Dreams Away." Looking at the tape in retrospect now, he still seems absurdly young, even though he was verging on fifty. Other standards were "Nancy," "It Was a Very Good Year," "Come Fly with Me," and "I've Got the World on a String." He did.

In the course of the hour, Sinatra reviewed his career and the program won Edison, Emmy, and Peabody awards for general excellence. He celebrated the success of the show and his birthday with one of his legendary parties, held at the Beverly Wilshire Hotel in Hollywood. Perhaps one of the surprising things about 12 December 1965 was this short fact tucked away amid all the hyperbole of the reports. The party was given by Sinatra's first wife, Nancy.

What a really remarkable woman. Everyone was there. And that same month, Nancy junior's record *Boots* became number one on the American hit parade.

Back to Sinatra. Films, records, television, and some sort of private life. Sinatra always seemed best when at his personal happiest, too. Hence another happy-go-lucky year of 1966. His movie of the year was one of his own setups: a Sinatra Enterprises–Seven Arts Productions film. It was released by Paramount Pictures. The title, of course, was *Assault on a Queen.* The plot: simply to hijack the liner *Queen Mary.* Sardonic, masculine, and sympathetic were the trio of adjectives he collected from the *Hollywood Reporter* for his work in it. (Here, too, we just glance at a trio of cameo parts in three films around then: *The List of Adrian Messenger* [already mentioned], *Cast a Giant Shadow,* and *The Oscar.* In the last one he played himself.)

His song of the year was unquestionably "Strangers in the Night." He cut the title number on 11 April and within a couple of months the single was up there at number one. Then on 11 and 16 May he added nine songs in these sessions to compose the *Strangers in the Night* album, including a fresh interpretation of "All or Nothing at All." Riddle made the arrangements for this collection, which was destined to be a top album for seventy-three weeks. Yes, seventy-three.

"Strangers in the Night" went on to achieve success elsewhere in the world. In Britain, for instance, it emulated the American popularity by being Top of the Pops, too. And that was in the full-flood era of the Beatles. This represented quite an extradimensional triumph for a fifty-year-old "band singer." After that, he sang the number hundreds of times and owned up, rather tongue in cheek, to hating it on one occasion. We all took that with a slug of Jack Daniels.

The pace never slackened for long. Sinatra was a restless and inquiring soul. Still the same year. Still the same story. Reprise Records released the first "live" LP he had ever done. This turned out to be a thrilling double album, *Sinatra at the Sands.* The audience added a certain atmosphere. June in California meant taping the second of his annual television specials: *Frank Sinatra: A Man and His Music, Part II.* As this was not shown until December; we will wait until then to reveal the guest star he had with him.

Although we in Britain had to wait from 1962 to 1970 for his next live concerts, Sinatra came to London briefly around Independence Day to start yet another film, *The Naked Runner*. Then intermingling the public and private personae, his engagement to Farrow became known. Just five days later, after a record short while being affianced, they were married back in the United States. Richard Attenborough was one of the guests at the wedding. The cropped-hair, childlike Mia wore a diaphanous dress. Another five days and the couple was on the French Riviera, afloat and ashore. So the highly individual and petite actress became the third Mrs. Sinatra. She was the daughter of another film star, Maureen O'Sullivan, whom I had always admired from afar. Would this marriage last? Who could tell, but the odds were not in their favor. They acquired a house in Bel Air but also lived in the Palm Springs place for part of the time. When Sinatra was not globe-galloping or in Las Vegas, he did in fact appear in Las Vegas, with Mia shown off to the audience! A typical charity show in Las Vegas that November was for the Danny Thomas St. Jude's Children's Research Center.

Meanwhile, *Strangers in the Night* won a Grammy Award as the Best Single Record of 1966. And on 7 December America watched the television show with his special guest: Nancy. The show was a revelation—not only musically, but also in design, costume, and production generally. The conductor's baton was shared by Riddle and Gordon Jenkins, two of Sinatra's perennial favorites. From the moment he launched into "Fly Me to the Moon," it was clear that it would be a high-grade program. "Moonlight in Vermont" sounded virtually perfect in its expressiveness and control.

It was just as well that Sinatra was in top form, because otherwise Nancy might have stolen the show. She nearly did anyway! Appearing in dazzling pink, she gave a poignant account of "Bang Bang," she swung through "On Broadway," and she joined her father for "Yes, Sir, That's My Baby," "Downtown," and "These Boots Are Made for Walkin'." Nancy was already the accomplished professional to have been expected with such a surname. And they clearly adored each other. A final thought: she rendered "Bang Bang" so sincerely that one felt she must have associated its theme with the Tommy Sands breakup. The lyrics fitted as if tailored to her account of the real-life schism in their marriage. Still young, Nancy had learned about life—from family and personal experience.

The Naked Runner came out in the summer of 1967. It portrayed Sinatra in the camouflage of a gray raincoat and as an American businessman living in London who gets mixed up in East-West espionage. His performance produced a review by the *Hollywood Reporter* stating, "Sinatra has honed his laconic, hip veneer to the point of maximum credibility." This spy thriller was again a Sinatra Enterprises production, released this time by Warner Brothers. He now had an intimate tie with Warner's on both films and records.

After the anonymous raincoat character of *The Naked Runner* came quite a change of image. Enter Tony Rome, private detective, in the film by the same name. People picked up the point that perhaps what appealed to Sinatra about Rome was the detective's apparent similarity to some of Sinatra's own characteristics. With the setting of Miami and the girl Jill St. John, the film could not have proved too arduous to make. Also in the cast was the Hollywood faithful Richard Conte. Being in Miami, Rome was given the setting of living on a boat. How many detectives have had similar living quarters since this picture?

Going "fast forward" a little, the film turned out to be such a success that its producers persuaded Sinatra to "play it again"—this time with the adornment of Raquel Welch. It was the formula rather as before. The *Los Angeles Times* said, "Frank Sinatra has got him down perfectly." The film was called *Lady in Cement*. While diving for treasure off the Florida coast, Rome finds instead the corpse of a naked girl with her feet embedded in cement. He takes it from there.

Sinatra was spending a lot of time in Florida one way and another. February 1967 marked a fortnight run in Miami Beach, followed by a further one in April, while actually filming. June brought an appearance at a rally for Israel in the vast arena of the Hollywood Bowl. I always connect this venue with the famous scene in *A Star Is Born* in which Fredric March makes a drunken spectacle of himself. Summer and a seven-city tour in twice the number of days. They were all over the eastern United States. The strain of being on the road must have told on Sinatra occasionally, because a little later he had to miss two or three shows back at the Sands due to exhaustion.

Despite this tiredness, he bounced back rapidly and by October had started shooting *The Detective* on location in New York City. He was a member of the New York Police Department. The film was notable for several things—the theme of the main crime touched on homosexuality and the leading lady was the attractive and intelligent Lee Remick. What a combination—Remick and Sinatra. But it was a serious film about serious police principles. His performance was quoted as effective "interior acting"—the best kind.

Back to singing. Sinatra was branching out with backings by Buddy Rich, Sergio Mendes, and Brazil '66. And he met, and fell for the music of, Antonio Carlos Jobim. The resulting album was remarkable for its musicality and quietness. He did a duet with Nancy called "Somethin' Stupid," which clocked up another massive single hit. Nancy was becoming a star in her own talented right.

On 22 November 1967, there came the announcement of a separation between Frank and Mia, to be followed the next summer by divorce—actually on Victory over Japan Day 1968. Later, Farrow referred to their time together, "I think that for us, our ages finally mattered. We had a great amount of love between us, but we lacked understanding in everyday life, as well as of the major deeper themes. Today he is still a part of me."

Just before the separation became public property, Sinatra's third television special was transmitted. It seemed to become a yearly feature. This had the unwieldy title *A Man and His Music + Ella + Jobim*. Jobim, of course, introduced the world to the bossa nova—or vice versa. The program played five numbers by Sinatra, followed by Ella Fitzgerald, followed by medleys with each guest in turn. My favorites: "Day In–Day Out," "What Now My Love," "The Girl from Ipanema," and "At Long Last Love." Riddle had the baton.

On his fifty-second birthday, Sinatra was busy working—with Duke Ellington this time. They recorded the album *Francis A and Edward K*—the initials standing for their middle names. The album took precisely two days to create. One of the things about Sinatra's life is that the songs are part of all our lives, at least for those of us above a certain age. "Indian Summer," for instance, takes me straight back to a Kay Kyser recording during World War II. Duke Ellington summed up the sessions, "Elegant record, Francis."

Among all the recording "first times" at this period, before and after it, was Sinatra's cooperation with orchestral arrangers often new to his record scene: Neal Hefti, Johnny Mandel, Quincy Jones, Eumir Deodato, Marty Paich, Claus Ogerman, and those continuing legends of Don Costa and Riddle. Throw in Count Basie and now Duke Ellington, too, plus Jobim.

And he had vocal collaboration with a starry string of names like Bing Crosby, Rosemary Clooney, Keely Smith, Dean Martin, Sammy Davis Jr., and not forgetting Nancy herself. Reprise Records was the label for her striding success. And Reprise was handling other artists outside the Sinatra ambit: Tiny Tim, Jimi Hendrix, the Kinks, Kenny Rogers, the First Edition, and a group rejoicing in the name of the Electric Prunes. I suppose the Electric Currants would have been too obvious! Nancy also had her own television show—*Movin' with Nancy*—during the latter 1960s and insisted on Sinatra appearing, too. Did Sinatra ever rest, one wondered? In "Somethin' Stupid," they sang nose to nose!

Confirming Sinatra's insatiable drive for work—and play—could be cited that spring of 1968. As already touched on, while filming *Lady in Cement* around Miami, he was singing each night at the Fontainebleau there—one of his favorite venues. Nancy went to see him there, as after his marriage breakup both he and Mia had adjustments to make. Ironically, in Nancy's marvelous book, *Frank Sinatra: An American Legend,* there is a photo relevant to the Farrow time of Mia sitting in a small boat in the Palm Springs swimming pool—looking eternally childlike with her short hair.

Also in 1968 was another presidential election. The Democratic nomination had not yet been decided when Bobby Kennedy was assassinated in June. Hubert Humphrey received Sinatra's support, and Sinatra raised funds for him at five venues over the summer.

Flashing back two or three years, *Sinatra: An American Original* had been transmitted as a CBS News special. This took the form of doyen interviewer Walter Cronkite talking to Sinatra on various topics to do with music and world events. Sinatra was always interested in politics and people—probably in the reverse order. Part of that show had included a look at Sinatra at work inside a recording studio. Several people have written of their impressions covering such sessions. Following shortly is one that Hal Halverstadt wrote that fitted into the overall pattern of Sinatra's complex life. Always ready to try something new, without ever jettisoning the old, Sinatra made the courageous LP *Cycles* late in 1968.

He had a gratifying reward by seeing it ascend to the upper echelons in the American hit parade of album sales. The philosophy of *Cycles* was clear. It was modern and it reflected Sinatra at that moment. Included were songs by writers like Joni Mitchell and it reflected the cycles in both Sinatra's and everyone else's life. In short, it began to launch a more reflective, intellectual, and spiritual approach to the growing library or canon of Sinatra LPs. It marked the mood of the times—the revolutionary 1960s and especially 1968. And it matched his ever-changing existence.

Cycles was recorded in July and November 1968 with quite a Nashville flavor and took in some very recent numbers. Sinatra knew he was breaking less-trodden ground. The following is Halverstadt's version of one of those November sessions:

7.45 p.m. Into Studio One is poured the heavy cream of West Coast musicians. Also arranger-conductor Don Costa (energy-activated, with a Groucho Marx stalk and an insouciant smile that someday deserves to be rendered immortal on the wall of a high-class delicatessen), assorted engineers and record company personnel, approximately 25 visitors (stuffed into the booth and strung around the edge of the studio on near-to-collapsing chairs), and in the midst of it all, in the vortex, the man who told reporters that afternoon that he was giving up Los Angeles because of the smog (a medical clinic at UCLA had issued some hair-raising facts), and who now draped himself across the conductor's podium and announced to anyone: "I'm tired."

(A comment which elicited belly laughs from the boys in the band because, one, the session hadn't even begun, and two, Sinatra looked terrific in a body-tapered grey suit, red-and-white striped shirt, open at the collar, and a wine-colored paisley tie, knotted but loose. Except for the Cesar

Romero grey that had salted his hair, he was time standing still and the walking-talking image of his old record covers from Capitol days. The only things lacking were a lamp post, two lovers silhouetted and Peggy Lee, of Manana and the Vaselined lips, in the next rack. The eternal dangling cigarette was already on hand.)

At 8.00 the session rolls and so does Sinatra. Feeling his way through By the Time I Get to Phoenix as if it were newly written. Belying the lyric of *Cycles*. Capping Pretty Colors with a gritty dissonance, breaking into a beam-wide grin, and again flinging himself on the podium with: "Hey now, hey now, baby, what's Stan Kenton?"

The Countess Mara ties and dangling charm bracelets that once accessorized the sidelines of Sinatra sessions are no more. The spectators change with the times, and now there are turtlenecks and chunky chains with chunkier medallions and, on the distaff side—legs. Some very nice, some just okay, but all stretching out from a variety of minis, medium to micro. There is also a new wave of drop-in celebrities: a long blond actress (late arrival) in something like a navy-blue crepe gym suit topped with a blond mink chubby; the ineffable Tiny Tim (who in a sidelines conversation with Mr. Sinatra became so excited that, lacking a slip of paper on which to write some phone numbers, pulled up one pant leg and penciled them on his ankle); and (heads turning, eyebrows raised) Beatles George Harrison and his wife Patti, fresh from camera-waving and hand-shaking at a benefit showing of *Yellow Submarine*. (Also of note, the lone woman among the musicians, a perky, orange-haired mistress of the harp who whips up a mean glissando but, visually, would seem more at home as pastry lady in a college dormitory.)

And the reason for it all: Sinatra. Cranking up the world with a fine-and-dandy Moody River. Shifting tempo ever so slightly to make the second take of Little Green Apples the one. Acting the perfectionist and deciding to scrap a not-quite-right Wait by the Fire (even though the cover of this album had already gone to press, listing the song). Making it all the way to Nashville and back with Gentle on My Mind. And in the short space of three hours turning asbestos baffles and canned green bean walls into rosewood.

11 p.m. and the session is over. Sinatra raps with Harrison about the talents of American songwriters, bids all goodnight, and vanishes through a side door, followed by friends, assorted, and the long blond adjusting her chubby. It's cold for Los Angeles, and for once a fur looks right.

Later in November 1968, Sinatra's fourth television special was seen as usual. *Francis Albert Sinatra Does His Thing* had as guests Diahann Carroll and the "ultraslick" Fifth Dimension. It could not be overlooked that they were all African American artistes, so Sinatra could have been making a statement about civil rights and similar social and political themes prominent at the time.

He even referred to civil rights and the young in his script. As for the show itself, it was up to standard, but not one of my personally preferred spectaculars. The producers pointed out that it reflected the spirit of the time and Sinatra threw in the current title number from the *Cycles* album. Carroll sang with dramatic feeling "The Only Music That Makes Me Dance," while Sinatra acknowledged the flower-power generation musically with the Fifth Dimension numbers. Trendy but not quite vintage Sinatra!

So the philosophic *Cycles* had been launched. Sinatra would also later fall for the George Harrison classic "Something" and record it more than once. But for now the LPs rolled on. If *Cycles* was an album hit, then Sinatra's next single success eclipsed it. This was the sequence of how a legend was born. A French song was written. A Canadian singer, Paul Anka, came along. He wrote some English lyrics for it, with his own voice very much in mind. Enter Sinatra, who could scent a great number from a great distance. He took only the briefest time to see that this could also become his hit. The title was just inscribed in two monosyllables. Together they summed up his life: "My Way." The single leapt up the British charts and also the U.S. equivalent. Sinatra sang it from then on. It was always cataclysmic. Even as I write well into a new millennium, a new Sinatra CD has been released with "My Way" at the top of the list.

He actually made the single on 30 December 1968. It remained in the British hit list for over two years.

In January 1969, Frank sat for five days with his father, Martin, who slowly ebbed away. On 29 January, he buried Anthony Martin Sinatra. Now he had only his mother as a link with his beginnings back in New Jersey. As he had grown more mature, he had amassed enough sense to realize the depth of meaning of those early links in life.

Life was real—not a film script. The loss of Sinatra's father brought it home to him more than anything else could. But he bounced back. A bridge between his mourning self and normality was the album *A Man Alone*. True, it had been conceived while his father was alive, but the actual sessions came a month or two after his passing. The lyrics were by Rod McKuen, the poet with the husky voice whose songs sounded more poignant when sung by Sinatra.

Then it was business as usual again. He moved his affiliation at Las Vegas from the Sands Hotel to Caesar's Palace. Here, he sounded in form for a full fortnight. The rest of 1969 seemed to be a series of special dates. He sang at Houston in a celebrity show for the *Apollo 11* astronauts. They had actually heard his recording of "Fly Me to the Moon" while en route there, which must have kept them in touch with what they knew and loved back at home. Then also in August the three singing Sinatras were each appearing in Las Vegas at different venues: Sinatra at Caesar's, Sinatra Jr. at the Frontier, and Nancy at the International Hilton.

Amid his various dates on the road, he managed to record the *Watertown* album. This had been specially composed for him by Bob Gaudio of the Four Seasons group and indicated that he remained receptive to the best of newer music. But he never would countenance rock and roll or its varied successors—expressing himself forcibly on the subject, as we already know.

Television again in the fall. The three Sinatras came together in a special for Sinatra Jr., while Sinatra Sr.'s own annual was simply called *Sinatra*. Seventeen numbers in the usual fifty-one minutes. The differences this year were that he had no guest stars—and he introduced a selection of film clips from his Hollywood career. At least three numbers came from *Cycles* or *A Man Alone:* "Little Green Apples," "A Man Alone," and "Love's Been Good to Me." The rest were standards, with one or two fresh appearances. For instance, the opener was "For Once in My Life," "My Way," of course, and "Goin' out of My Head."

Nancy Sinatra said, "Because he had established scholarships for young musicians, UCLA showed its gratitude by making him an Honorary Alumnus." This was one of literally innumerable philanthropic gestures by Sinatra—and others followed over the next year. Needless to say, he was Top Male Vocalist for 1969 in the *Playboy* magazine poll.

But it had not been "a very good year" in a number of ways. And the same plot seemed to overrun the New Year of 1970. So instead of ending a chapter according to the calendar, we will go on to the end of this 1969 phase. In February 1970, Sinatra had to present himself in front of the New Jersey state committee that was at that time looking into organized crime. The outcome: the chairman said that he felt satisfied Sinatra had "cooperated fully" in responding to questions that had been posed to him several times in the past. These concerned the names of people he had met who were known members of the Mafia. Would that finally prove to be the end of the long-running story splashed by the press over so prolonged a period?

Now let us dispose of *Dirty Dingus Magee,* which he started filming a week later. Sinatra was a frontier rascal in the days of the U.S. Cavalry and the American Indians. The wanted poster offered a $10 reward for Magee! I had to pay rather more than that for seats to hear Sinatra in London in the spring of 1970.

CHAPTER TWELVE

LONDON AT MIDNIGHT
1970-1973

I was there—at Midnight with Sinatra in the Royal Festival Hall, London, on Thursday, 7 May 1970. This was a charity concert in "the gracious presence" of Princess Margaret, Countess of Snowdon, in aid of the National Society for the Prevention of Cruelty to Children (NSPCC). Margaret was the royal president of the NSPCC charity.

Actually, Sinatra did it on two successive nights. In retrospect, it has been claimed that these two shows represented the zenith of Sinatra's concert offerings. I can see the reasoning, while not agreeing with it. Anyway, I was there. That was all that mattered. This was how the night seemed to me then, and I do not think it has changed in memory more than three decades afterward.

"Weren't you lucky to get a ticket?" friends insisted on saying. "Fortunate, yes—but not lucky," I answered. Because I had put my name on that advance mailing list in 1962, straight after seeing him for the first time. Eight years earlier!

So this year it was to be at midnight—as before. By 11:00 P.M. the first furs of the celebrities were purring up to the riverside entrance of the Royal Festival Hall. It could so easily have been raining, but the sky was clear. It was a night tipped and tinged with magic. Mild for May. Pale amber lights of London. Hum of late traffic. The Festival Hall lights reflected in the Thames. The stars shone. So did the human stars: the Snowdons, of course, Michael Caine, Peter Sellers, Rosalind Russell, Richard Attenborough, and dozens of others.

Pick out a random handful: Brian Rix, Harry Secombe, the Bland-
fords, the Duke and Duchess of Bedford, the Ogilvies, Rupert Mur-
doch (the comedian), Tito Burns, Frankie Howerd, Bernard Del-
font (the impresario), Jimmy Young, Tony Blackburn, Barry Took,
Peter Cadbury, Barbara Windsor, Alan Freeman, Jimmy Tarbuck,
and hundreds more.

Heading his article on Sinatra in the golden program, the musical sage Benny Green wrote, "He can infuse his voice with the spirit
of laughter or sadness at will."

I drank a beer that I did not really want, just to pass the time.
Then came the climb to the seat. And it was a climb. By midnight
we were all there. The 136-page program contained just the ten
words directly relevant to the show: "Tonight's programme . . .
Count Basie and his orchestra . . . intermission . . . Frank Sinatra."
No one minded the cost of that program as it was all for charity.
This concert and the one on the next night raised over $100,000 for
children's charities.

I think it is worth quoting an open letter to Sinatra from the president and the two joint chairs of the NSPCC printed in the program. These three dignitaries were all, in fact, women. Camilla
Bowater (president), June Ogilvie, and Jane Westmorland (joint
chairs):

To Mr. Sinatra

We would like to thank you very much indeed for making this evening
possible and for your great generosity.

Your magnificent gesture has enabled the NSPCC to raise more money
on a single event than ever before, thus helping them to continue their work
of alleviating the unhappiness of countless children in this country. On behalf of these children and their families we repeat our tremendous thanks
to you.

Camilla Bowater
June Ogilvie
Jane Westmorland

As soon as Basie began, we knew we were in for a night never to
forget. His band was as precision drilled as ever. And the fortes
were really fortissimo. Half an hour. Well judged. Then the inter-

mission. I was at the back of the Grand Tier, but it didn't really matter. And since then I have seen Sinatra at closer quarters

Finally, at 1:00 A.M. a wandering spotlight settled on the famous left-hand entrance to the stage, the curtains there parted—and he stood for a second. Then, of course, the storm. At fifty-four years old, could he be as good as last time? Some people were really wondering. I felt fairly confident. I trusted him. And the reassuring answer came at once with the first number: "I've Got the World on a String." He still had it. He sounded better than before. More mature. We were hearing over thirty years' unique experience.

With each fresh introduction, a light ripple of recognition crinkled across the audience. A man behind me moaned in something akin to ecstasy! "I Get a Kick out of You," "At Long Last Love," and "Fly Me to the Moon." Eight swingers later and Sinatra brought the house down with "My Kind of Town."

Then he turned to the strings, some three dozen of them, and defined "ballad" with a cluster of slower numbers: "Autumn Leaves," "Yesterday," "If I Knew Then," "Lady Day." He even made "Try a Little Tenderness" sound like a masterpiece. Which it was for just a few brief bars of its life. I never thought I would react to "Ol' Man River," but along with everyone else, I did.

Scarcely seeming to be aware of the applause, he bounced into his next batch of standards, from "Moonlight in Vermont" to "I've Got You under My Skin." "The Lady Is a Tramp" stirred filmic memories. And who else but Sinatra would or could tackle an upbeat "Road to Mandalay" at 2:10 A.M.? His twenty-second nonstop number. With apologies to Rudyard Kipling. And who else could claim that he did it "My Way" and bring an entire audience to its feet for more than a mere ovation. Perhaps this was one of his peak points. Modestly, he acknowledged his right to this accolade—and then he was gone. No lingering farewells. No encores. And so right.

Now it was early in the morning, yet people were reluctant to relinquish this fragment of time torn from their workaday world. London by night had never seemed so wandlike, so gossamer-winglike. I caught a train toward home. At 3:30 A.M. I was as near as I could get. Six miles off with three hours to wait. I felt I could not simply sit in a railway waiting room. So instead I headed into the countryside and walked the six miles home. The air smelled earthy, heavy, yet heady. Into the dawn with the strange sensation that nothing could be the same again after those eighty minutes. At least, until the next time I tried to unravel the secret of Sinatra. Some people would understand how I felt; others would find me mad.

So much for me. The rest of the audience and the critics reacted very similarly according to information gleaned afterward. The first concert had been for the NSPCC. The second one was in aid of the Alexandra Day charity. Take just two typical quotes from the response of the British press. Kevin Henriques in the *Financial Times* wrote:

> Rare is the entertainer who brings royalty voluntarily and spontaneously to its feet, but Sinatra (the Christian name is now discarded as naturally as it is from Callas, Fonteyn or Heifetz) achieved that at 2.15 yesterday morning as the entire Festival Hall audience rose ecstatically to acclaim after 85 minutes of the most immaculate singing and entertaining one could be fortunate to hear . . . he left with the highly personal and meaningful My Way, and Sinatra's way, like that of every top-class professional artist, is to leave the multitude clamouring for more—which he did. Truly the Guv'nor.

The music press echoed this view. Ray Coleman wrote in the *Melody Maker*:

> There is no need to go along with the myth that Sinatra is a God to be worshipped and exalted. But to deny his unique talent for interpreting lyrics with a musician's ear would be spurious. The man has a magic—and it does not need qualifying with any reference to his 54 years. He's not just "good for his age." He's good . . . he interprets the words to his songs as if they really mean something, unlike hundreds of other ballad singers.

On 7 May 1970, Sinatra sang these twenty-three numbers:

"I've Got the World on a String"	*"My Way"*
"I Get a Kick out of You"	*"Road to Mandalay"*
"At Long Last Love"	*"The Lady Is a Tramp"*
"Don't Worry 'bout Me"	*"Please Be Kind"*
"Fly Me to the Moon"	*"I've Got You under My Skin"*

"On the Street of Dreams"	*"You Make Me Feel So Young"*
"Pennies from Heaven"	*"Angel Eyes"*
"My Kind of Town"	*"Moonlight in Vermont"*
"Autumn Leaves"	*"Ol' Man River"*
"Yesterday"	*"Lady Day"*
"Beautiful Girl"	*"Try a Little Tenderness"*

"If I Knew Then"

We are left with a lingering image of Sinatra in 1970—holding a mike in his right hand, forefinger of his left hand outstretched to stress some lyric line. Vocally reaching for the sky.

Sinatra achieved much more in 1970, but for his fans the shock waves would come the following year. Meanwhile, it was still spring and summer of 1970 back in the States.

And back to benefits. Along with his scores of performances in the name of charity over the years, Sinatra undertook a special one. He learned that Dan Mitrione, an American, had been kidnapped and killed in South America. Mitrione left a widow with nine children to raise in Richmond, Indiana. Sinatra went out of his way to organize a benefit show in the town's high school gymnasium. The performance comprised a rock group, Jerry Lewis, and Sinatra. This benefit raised more than $100,000 for the education of the Mitrione children. An amazing gesture. Sinatra was called a paradox. He was certainly that, but just for once we could call him a paragon. But he would not really have approved of that.

It was not as if this show were the sole charity event of his season. Soon after the London benefits came one for St. Jude's Children's Research Center, another for Villa Scalabrini at the Chicago Civic Opera House, on the following day yet another in the Hollywood Bowl for a Hispanic American charity, and then several more in support of his actor-friend Ronald Reagan, who was running as a Republican candidate for the governorship of California. Nothing to do with these charity shows, American radio stations were vying with one another to present the longest "Sinatrathon"—one actually reached almost three days and nights playing his records!

Mid-November brought Sinatra back to London for a two-show charity night. On 16 November, he participated in this rare one-night stand, once more at the Royal Festival Hall. The whole affair was entirely devoted to a charity cause and was known as "Night of Nights." The proceeds this time went to the United World Colleges project, an undertaking dear to the heart of Lord Louis Mountbatten, who had introduced both concerts to set the scene and the seal on yet another evening to savor. Princess Alexandra was at the earlier performance, while the second one was heard and seen by Prince Charles and Princess Anne.

The program was split between two legendary names: Bob Hope and Sinatra. Hope did his veteran stand-up act for the first half and had never been funnier—wisecracking as throwaway as ever. Then Grace Kelly strolled onto the stage to introduce Sinatra. She recounted that scene of years earlier, when she and Ava Gardner were in Africa filming and Sinatra had brought the Christmas cheer for all the company there. As she ended, Sinatra appeared and thanked her, with the quip after she left the stage, "What a press agent!" That was his way to brush aside all the compliments.

It was as good as it had been in May, except shorter. Sinatra sang only about a dozen numbers. I remember the standards naturally and also the innovations. Something was still quite a novelty, given the full Sinatra intensity. He also did "I Will Drink the Wine," by the young British composer Paul Ryan. Paul was the son of a good British friend of Sinatra's, the singer Marion Ryan. Sinatra was in top form, rounding off with an impassioned "I Have Dreamed" (leaving him out of breath), "My Kind of Town," and "My Way." The standing ovation was captured on tape by the BBC for subsequent television screening. It was well known that his reception by the British at the four concerts that year had thrilled him. But it was not a good omen that he sold the flat he owned in Grosvenor Square, London. This was apparently part of a general buying, selling, and building plan for the family's future. On his fifty-fifth birthday, Sinatra gave away Nancy to her new husband, Hugh Lambert. The Tommy Sands era was finally over.

The bombshell year of 1971. On 15 January, Sinatra was at the dedication of the Martin Anthony Sinatra Medical Education Center, named after his father. Sinatra had been responsible for the funds that created it.

Then a fortnight later he proved that he could not be accused of political partisanship or deserting the Democrats for the Republicans because he gave his considerable support to another old friend, Senator John Tunney—a staunch, undoubted, and undying Democrat!

Then the real shock came. Sinatra announced his forthcoming retirement from the music business, covering all aspects of his art—and for good. He said that he needed time for "reflection, reading, self-examination." Meanwhile, he still went on for a while. He received a special Academy Award in April: the Jean Hersholt Humanitarian Award for all his philanthropic endeavors, in both public and personal spheres.

The date fixed for Sinatra's two final shows was 13 June 1971. They were given in aid of the Motion Picture and Television Relief Fund, which was celebrating its fiftieth anniversary. The cast lists for the shows read like a roll of honor of the American entertainment industry: Sinatra, Sammy Davis Jr., Jack Lemmon, Jack Benny, Pearl Bailey, Barbara Streisand, and the Fifth Dimension, amid many others. The audience, too, was composed of show business people from all areas of the industry. The Sinatra farewell was made at both shows and was reported to have been an "extraordinarily moving experience." At that moment, Sinatra felt convinced that it would be a permanent decision. He had had enough. It seemed so. The end of an amazing career. But could it really be? Could he be facing "the final curtain"? Whatever else the night achieved, it raised $800,000 for the industry's relief fund.

So Sinatra took time to pause, reflect, relax, read, paint, and play golf. All those things he had done only briefly in between working and singing. From mid-1971 to the following two years plus, he did not make a single public appearance. That is a long spell to attenuate into a period of suspense in a life story such as this. And all the while we went on living, subconsciously aware that we could not count on seeing or hearing him again. Retirement seemed premature.

We will skim over the intervening months for everyone already knows that he did return. But what happened to him in that interim limbo? Senator Tunney read into the *Congressional Record* a glowing testimony to him; he received a Freud Award of the Century; he played charity golf matches; he supported Richard Nixon for some reason; the Friars Club gave Sinatra its highly prized Humanitarian Award; he accepted Israel's Medal of Valor in Los Angeles; and he was on the winning side when Nixon became president. It is true that Sinatra had actually sung at Madison Square Garden for the Italian American Civil Rights League—but he did not count that as infringing his retirement rule.

In 1973, he was showered with more awards. These were just a clutch of them: Man of the Year by the All American Collegiate Golf Association for his work toward scholarships; Man of the Year by the March of Dimes; and the Splendid American Award by the Thomas A. Dooley Foundation. Then in April he accepted Nixon's invitation to sing at the White House for the guest of honor there, Giulio Andreotti, the premier of Italy. Sinatra sang eleven numbers for this illustrious audience. It came to light at this time, too, that no fewer than 30,000 people from all over the world had written to Sinatra, pleading that he should reconsider his retirement. This mass expression of feeling must have influenced his thinking, nor could he have remained unmoved when given yet one more title, Entertainer of the Century, by the Songwriters of America. It was a small gesture by them in return for what Sinatra had done for their compositions over the decades.

Unable to cut himself off from the part of his life that had so dominated it, Sinatra took the first steps to edge back to the arena he had graced for thirty-five years. The first manifestation of his decision to return to public performance came with the news that he was back in the recording studio. The date was June 1973. The album was to be entitled *Ol' Blue Eyes Is Back*—or it would be when released later that year. The two years in the wilderness would soon be over. He would go on performing for a further twenty years.

CHAPTER THIRTEEN

OL' BLUE EYES IS BACK

1973-1981

So Ol' Blue Eyes was back—and to prove it, he was photographed smiling and wearing a light-colored sweater bearing the same legend. Gordon Jenkins and Don Costa were entrusted with the arrangements for the important album *Ol' Blue Eyes Is Back*. It had to be a success. Sinatra chose the songs most meticulously for his comeback and they possessed undeniable poignancy for the occasion. "You Will Be My Music" could so easily be read as a love letter to the public for its loyalty. So, too, could the great song "Let Me Try Again." No need to appeal for a second chance—he had one without the asking. We were all grateful to hear him back in the land of living entertainment.

The voice was still in consummate form, despite his mentioning adjectives like "rusty" in connection with it. "Send in the Clowns" he at once made his own, with an archetypal stamp. "Winners" was another winning number. "There Used to Be a Ballpark" was nostalgic but for the very right reasons. Conservationism, not only of places but people and ways of life. The mechanical age and mechanical amusements were taking over. Sinatra was no fool. He knew it more than most. And he was always for individuals. Real people, not people in the abstract or mass. It all added up to memorable music. The following is quoted from the liner notes by Stan Cornyn from the album (Cornyn was nominated for four Grammys for his liner notes for Frank Sinatra and won for *September of My Years* and *Sinatra at the Sands*):

"The first questions you had were what he'd be like. Would he be fat, maybe, and would you hate him for blowing what was—a couple of years back—a pretty fair exit?"

It was 106 degrees that day, 21 June 1973, and it was the hottest June day ever in Los Angeles. And the longest of the year.

Inside Goldwyn Studios, a scruffy demimovie lot that looks like it's hung around town only because nobody has come up with enough cash to level it and put up a good modern Zody's in its place, there remains good Sound Stage Seven. Thirty feet inside before you hit anything there are industrial walls. Their best feature is the "Fire Hose" sign.

He is maybe a little tanner.

He signs with his hands, which are placed at the top of the music stand, holding firm on the music stand, trying hard. In shirt sleeves, light blue, three buttons per cuff, little puffs at the shoulders.

He sings and it's the voice that brings it all back and you realize that not one—isn't it curious?—not one other voice so clear and clean in all the years has come along, not one other.

He is still, no contest, the best this world knows.

And tonight ol' blue eyes is back.

In the row of metal folding chairs lined up before ten-foot-high speakers sit guests, listening. Ed McMahon, who after one song says, "Let's have a drink on that one." Sinatra's secretary, Lillian, leans in to say that Sinatra had received 30,000 letters begging him to "at least make an album again." Other guests: white-haired expensive men in black suede loafers with gold tiger head buckles. They sit upright and appreciate the playback.

During playback, Sinatra concentrates, eyes shifting from chair to table top but not to any other eye, hearing only.

String men, violins and violas, who don't get called in to record as they once did, string men standing around the speakers now, listening, when a couple of years back they were out in the hall phoning their service.

And at the end of the playback, the white-haired expensive men stay sitting upright, applauding on their knees and saying, "Magnificent!"

A record executive whispers in anticipation, saying how he wants to "go on the road with this album and compare him to . . . to Lincoln."

But Sinatra is keeping it low key.

As if anticipating the questions and knowing there's no thunder roll of an answer to give if he's asked why he's doing this, he lays out the answer to everyone's most tiresome question and says, "I just figured I'd do some work. No fun trying to hit a golf ball at eight at night."

Gordon Jenkins asks, "Where did the baritone go?"

And the baritone appears and goes to his microphone, his music stand, his chair with the jacket over it, and sings again. . . .

Despite his trying to keep the evening offhand, despite the jokes, it's clear that he really, really wants this one. As he sings, it's easy for you to feel thankful; you can understand the words, for one thing. It's easy to feel pompous, too. Husbands there in the string section who'll later drive home and have to explain to their sleepy wives how it had been to spend three hours in the same room with . . . with Roosevelt maybe.

A man of no little confidence. He is, to his audience, as he sings, a real and enduring value, a firm handhold in a very slippery, very anonymous world.

Ol' blue eyes is back as the singer who'll still close his eyes when he's getting into it. This song is ending, the violin's last string echoing through the stage. Sinatra puts up his hand, so no one speaks. Egg shell city. And this, from a man of no little confidence, is to be The Take.

The engineer walks in and gets the evening's understatement award, "Gee, I hope we got that on tape." This comment relaxes all.

Another Sinatra song is recorded, for a world that still needs them. Sinatra walks again into the center of it all. "I figure," Sinatra says, "we got a record."—Stan Cornyn

At the end of it all, the shirt still looks crisp. So does Sinatra. Here's to the heroes. Those who move mountains. He was still a winner.

A television special bore the same name as the album and proclaimed that he was back in business. His sole guest was Gene Kelly, a friend from the good old film days. Gordon Jenkins called Sinatra "my favorite baritone." By the reaction to both the album and the television show, quite a few people shared his view. Sinatra realized that he was not forgotten. The show was recorded in September and was broadcast in November. For me, the two most moving numbers were "Send In the Clowns," sung sitting on a step at the edge of the sound stage, and the finale, of course, "You Will Be My Music." The star-studded audience, Elizabeth Taylor and all, rose in unison. He was definitely back!

The next eagerly awaited event was the first appearance in person after the two-year sabbatical. It came in January 1974. This took the substantial form of an eight-show week at Caesar's Palace, the scene of so many past triumphs. He had not sung there for five years. It was getting to be nearly that long since he had been back in Britain, too. While in Las Vegas, Sinatra gave away his Tina, his younger daughter, to Wes Farrell. She looked exquisite as a bride is always supposed to be on her wedding day. Then that same night Sinatra was back singing at Caesar's.

The schedule was filling up fast once more. A charity show raised $200,000 for a college gymnasium at a California university. Exactly a month later, he was about to tour on behalf of Variety Clubs International and then came the film *That's Entertainment,* copresented by Sinatra and others. Scenes from several of his own MGM musicals were included. The next news in real time was that Nancy had her first baby daughter, Angela Jennifer. Then for Sinatra it was back to Caesar's for an encore run, while Las Vegas bestowed on him the accolade of Man of the Year.

It was through the medium of records, concerts, and television that the reinvigorated singer returned to full-time performing— especially shows in concert halls, nightclubs, and outdoor arenas. Since his return, it was the live Sinatra who made most of the news. He played more in-person dates per period than during the previous decade. But television appearances became fewer than earlier. The series *A Man and His Music,* together with others in this medium, had been a significant aspect of those previous years. And now his films were rarer, too.

It was a measure of Sinatra's stature, as an entertainer and a man, that his comeback was something of a major triumph. It could so easily have been otherwise in the fickle world he inhabited. He continued to make albums, and after the *Ol' Blue Eyes Is Back* hit, he graciously acknowledged that the world had not stopped during that time. He then recorded *Some Nice Things I've Missed.* This was a collection of songs that were either on the agenda just before the sabbatical or had come out during that hiatus. The album mixed contemporary sounds across a wide spectrum, from the tender ballad "If" and the theme from *Summer of '42,* to "The Summer Knows," to the hard-racing and raunchy "Satisfy Me One More Time."

His life at this time seemed to revolve around a succession of starry concert dates—any one of which would satisfy a normal person as a major achievement for life. So, starting on Independence Day 1974, he made a circuit of the Far East. This comprised dates in Tokyo, where he was always received with almost surprising rapture by the Japanese at large, and a swinging show aboard the

USS *Midway*. The sailors gave him an avenue-of-honor salute as he boarded the ship bearing the name of the immortal World War II battle. Sinatra wore a naval-type cap and looked very much at ease. Which is more than can be said about his short stay in Australia! A furor between a public relations officer and Sinatra was blown out of proportion by the press there and almost provoked an international incident. The situation was retrieved partially, but the visit became scarred and marred as a result.

Sinatra had his two singer children with him during his shows in September—and even Nancy senior was present as well. Then after a charity concert for the Cedars-Sinai Medical Center, Sinatra embarked on one of the many highlight spells on the road. This was in October and the cold statistics read eight cities in thirteen days across the eastern United States. All of these had been sold out weeks in advance, and he got rave reviews. The tour turned out to be so successful that a second one had to be arranged by clamorous demand. These two record-breaking circuits demonstrated that the Sinatra name and magic remained as potent as ever.

One of these concerts was the now legendary hourlong spectacular at Madison Square Garden. It was autumn in New York. The famous sports palace was choked with "clamoring misty-eyed Sinatraphiles" who poured out their love for the singer originally from just across the river. The concert was telecast live as an ABC special: *Sinatra the Main Event: Madison Square Garden*. The show is still talked about by afficionados as the most exciting event of that season or many others since. And a quarter century or more is a long time in this age of instant electronic gratification. The album recorded and edited at the concert became a treasured possession of fans. Through listening to it, they could recapture and relive that night under the colossal canopy of a roof, with the arc lights firmly focused on one human being.

The concert took place on 13 October. The number of staff who worked on preparations for the live show totaled 350. The program was televised almost globally and scheduled to start at 9:00 P.M. The garden was crammed by 8:30 P.M. and Sinatra still had not even arrived! He rolled up calmly with a mere quarter hour or so to spare, with everyone else in a state of near panic. The stage had been

arranged as for a major boxing bout, with Sinatra as the main event.
Twenty thousand were there, plus a plethora of show-business
celebrities, such as Rex Harrison, Robert Redford, Carol Channing,
and the rest. But the abiding impression left by the whole hour was
that feeling of love. As the introductory voice said, "Sinatra comes
to the entire Western Hemisphere live."

From the moment of the emotional welcome, it was truly one of
the pinnacles of Sinatra's live shows. Some of the credit for the television production—and subsequent video of it—must go to the
photographic direction and editing, which picked out fans' reactions. These had a potent effect on viewers, just as Sinatra was having a similar effect on them at the instants of time. Woody Herman
conducted the orchestra, and the eleven numbers were as follows:
"The Lady Is a Tramp," "I Get a Kick out of You," "Let Me Try
Again," "Autumn in New York," "I've Got You under My Skin,"
"Leroy Brown," "Angel Eyes," "You Are the Sunshine of My Life,"
"The House I Live In," "My Kind of Town," and "My Way." The
last one was introduced by Sinatra as, "We will now do the national
anthem, but you need not rise!" At the end, everyone rose.

How do you follow that? With the rest of the eastern U.S. tour,
including New York City and Florida, and then Lake Tahoe for a
fortnight, and a return to the lake setting in February 1975. In the
spring, Sinatra made a seven-nation sortie to Europe, his first Continental tour in more than a decade. The venues were Paris, Vienna,
Munich, Frankfurt, London, Brussels, and Amsterdam. The two
concerts at the vast Royal Albert Hall in London were described as
"the musical and social events of the season." The total of 15,000
tickets shared by the two audiences was sold out within hours of going on sale. Requests by mail had come in that totaled 350,000 tickets! The few that went on the black market were sold by scalpers
for as much as $500. The audiences included the Princesses Mar-
garet and Anne and Sinatra's buddy from *High Society*, Grace
Kelly, now in her own high society. These shows marked Sinatra's
debut in the august Victorian hall and he took to it immediately.
We all reciprocated.

The concerts came toward the close of the tour. Britain was his
penultimate stop and he seemed to be blessed to be among English-

speaking people. One of the most interesting aspects of the Albert Hall shows was the repertoire chosen, more diverse than at previous British events. Composers and songs ranged in period and style from Matt Dennis ("Angel Eyes") to Stevie Wonder ("You Are the Sunshine of My Life"). The selection also embraced Stephen Sondheim ("Send In the Clowns"), David Gates ("If"), Bert Kaempfert ("Strangers in the Night"), and not forgetting the older masters Richard Rodgers and Lorenz Hart plus Jimmy Van Heusen and Johnny Burke. Which one received a roar above all others? "Strangers in the Night." Sinatra's last stop of the tour was in Monte Carlo for Grace Kelly's sake.

But all was not yet over for 1975 in Britain. For hardly had the last cheers swirled round the Royal Albert Hall upper gallery than the news broke that Sinatra would be returning to London in mid-November. The parting became easier to bear!

Meanwhile, two months after the European tour, Sinatra starred in a unique nightclub entertainment at Harrah's, Lake Tahoe. He appeared at the midnight show, while country-music star and composer John Denver sang at the dinner show. It was a "first" in nightclub bookings, and these seven days of back-to-back shows were completely sold out. This is actually an understatement. The switchboard at Harrah's was swamped with phone calls for reservations from would-be applicants. A staggering total of 672,412 requests came in not only from California and the rest of America but also from the rest of the world!

Continuing this schedule, Sinatra did a series of one-night stands, including slipping across the border into Canada. And then he helped to click up a record amount of money for muscular dystrophy aid. The story goes on. He had a wonderful two weeks with Count Basie and Ella Fitzgerald at the Uris Theater in New York City. It was the first time that the three names had appeared together and it shattered previous box-office records for a Broadway theater. A good number of gossip-column items came out around this time when Sinatra was seen at a prominent New York club with Jacqueline Kennedy.

The three stars went on from the Uris to Philadelphia, and Sinatra could not resist another week at Lake Tahoe. On the everlasting

charity front, the Frank Sinatra Child Care Unit was set up in
Memphis, Tennessee, as a result of money he had been instrumental in providing through benefits.

November brought the promised return to London for a six-
concert booking covering one week at the London Palladium. He
was joined there by a legendary figure of the jazz world, Sarah
Vaughan. They had the solid backing of Basie, too. They each had
their own segments of the show, as well as appearing together. The
formula worked well enough, although for me it represented his
least sensational session in Britain. The reason was simple: when
you want to see Sinatra, you do not want to share him on stage with
someone else—however good.

This was the pattern of the programs. He sang solos like "Where
or When," "I Believe I'm Gonna Love You," "Here's That Rainy
Day," "Leroy Brown," "My Kind of Town," "Send In the Clowns,"
"At Long Last Love," and "Violets for Your Furs." And to end
every evening, Vaughan returned to the stage, when each sang a
solo number as well as duetting on "The Song Is You," "They Can't
Take That Away from Me," and "The Lady Is a Tramp."

After London, Sinatra flew on to the Middle East, where he sang
in Iran for the first time. The Tehran concert was for the favorite
charity of Her Highness Farah Pahlavi, the wife of the shah of Iran.
The next stop was Israel for concerts whose proceeds helped the
Jerusalem Foundations program for Arab and Jewish families. This
illustrated his lifelong interest in conciliation between peoples,
however deep-seated their friction. A personal sidelight for Sinatra
was that throughout this trip, he had with him Spiro Agnew and a
new name among lady escorts: Barbara Marx. Then in a flash he
was sixty years old. Three weeks later, Sinatra returned to "My
Kind of Town," where he gave a special show at the Chicago Stadium on New Year's Eve. This had been the location of his first solo
starring appearance in the Windy City back in 1946. Nearly thirty
years on from then, he was back.

I cannot close 1975 without a glancing reference to the follow-up
album to *Ol' Blue Eyes Is Back. The Best of Ol' Blue Eyes* was a collection culled from some of his greatest recordings. Don Stone
called Sinatra's voice "a voice of total honesty and extraordinary

sensitivity." Here, Sinatra gave us a classic dozen including a sizzling and vibrant "I've Got You under My Skin," a rare up-tempo "All or Nothing at All," "Fly Me to the Moon," and "I Have Dreamed," with Nelson Riddle at his inspired best.

In 1976, he was voted Top Box Office Name of the Century by the Friars Club. Then he was performing at Caesar's Palace, Lake Tahoe, and Maytime and did more grinding around "on the road." But he seemed to love it. The month was rounded off with a four-day stopover in Philadelphia. Or not quite ended. The engagement was announced between Sinatra and Marx. They were married on 11 July 1976 and remained so for the following twenty-one years or more. Just a few of the guests, apart from family members, were Ronald Reagan, Kirk Douglas, Gregory Peck, and Agnew.

The year was also distinguished by more artistic achievement and by numerous honors for various humanitarian endeavors: Doctor of Humane Letters from the University of Nevada at Las Vegas and the Scopus Award of the American Friends of the Hebrew University of Israel, including the naming of the university's new structure, the Frank Sinatra International Student Center. In receiving the award, he joined such noted former recipients as Harry S. Truman, Chaim Weizmann, Israel's first president, Queen Elizabeth of Belgium, Albert Einstein, and philosopher Martin Buber.

Sinatra started to lose one or two of his friends from the world of American entertainment—and it upset him considerably. First Jack Benny had died and now toward the end of 1976 one of his really longtime platonic female friends, Rosalind Russell. I always recall her films with affection, linking her style with that of Myrna Loy. Russell was a lady with a sense of humor that remained with her throughout her life. And then came one of the greatest losses of Sinatra's whole life.

The date was 6 January 1977. Dolly Sinatra was then eighty-two years old. She was due to join Sinatra in Las Vegas, where he would open at Caesar's Palace. The plane took off from Los Angeles airport in bad weather, with a storm brewing. The flight reached Palm Springs at 5:00 P.M. with twenty minutes' flying time to Las Vegas. The plane became overdue. Two nights and two days passed. Family and friends traveled to Palm Springs to

wait for any news. Sinatra flew in a helicopter around the San
Bernardino Mountains searching for signs of the wreckage. Finally at nearly midnight on the third day the news came through.
The plane had been spotted. Friends Mickey Rudin and Jilly
Rizzo had been a wonderful help as usual. So had Sinatra's family. He needed them with him in the days following the crash. The
funeral was held on 12 January, and Sinatra's face on the occasion
showed all the signs of anguish that had marked it throughout the
previous week.

For a few weeks Sinatra abandoned all personal appearances and
singing sessions in the studio. Then he flew down to Barbados to be
with another of his old friends, Claudette Colbert, who lived on the
island. (It is strange how lives and places overlap. My niece
Genevieve was married to Tom Adams, one-time prime minister of
Barbados, and she also knew the legendary film star Colbert.)

The opening days of March saw Sinatra back in London for another stint at the Royal Albert Hall. The opening night was attended by Princesses Margaret and Anne—as usual—and was devoted to the benefit of the National Society for the Prevention of
Cruelty to Children. At the final two-concert evening on 5 March,
the atmosphere was high on emotion. This was the date when I actually touched him!! My wife, Joyce, and I were waiting for press
tickets in a corridor near the stage-door entrance to the Albert Hall.
Outside, a sudden upsurge of sound heralded his car. The next moment, Sinatra and two guards were moving past me. I was taken
aback. It was all utterly unexpected. All I could muster in the best
British tradition was a hurried "Good evening." But at least I had
brushed against him!

Briefly, I remember "Night and Day," updated with a disco-
slanted arrangement by guitarist Joe Beck; Barry Manilow's "Why
Don't You See the Show Again"; Bruce Johnston's magnetic "I Sing
the Songs"; and Cy Coleman and Michael Stewart's "I Love My
Wife." Nearly 50,000 people saw him that week. The seamless
legato survived. James Green of the *London Evening News* wrote:

> He looked good (as he should after three weeks' holiday) and took up posi-
> tion before 38 musicians. Then he moved continuously into the old routine.

. . . A singing storyteller proving that not only the phrasing, breathing, and timing remain unchanged, but that the golden pipes are little worse for wear. I have heard all his London concerts, and he is singing this time as well as in recent years. . . . Where the show really took off was when he lit a cigarette, tilted his head back at the lights, and went into his classic songs for swinging lovers.

In 1977, Reprise Records issued *Portrait of Sinatra: Forty Songs from the Life of a Man*. Here are five men's views of Sinatra the singer:

Bing Crosby: "*Frank is unique in many ways. He is the most magnetic performer we have. He can come out on a nightclub floor and hold an audience spellbound for an hour, or even an hour and forty-five minutes, by singing one great song after another. I don't know anybody else in show business capable of doing that.*"

Hoagy Carmichael: "*He is one of the finest phrasers of a song; he puts together the words and the music, each vowel sound with the right note, so that the song tells a story.*"

Frankie Valli: "*I don't think there is a singer alive who doesn't look at this majestic man and feel that they would like to create the impact and achieve the success that he has. You can only learn from people like that.*"

Nelson Riddle: "*In working out arrangements for Frank, I suppose I stuck to two main rules. First, find the peak of the song and build the whole arrangement to that peak, pacing it as he paces himself vocally. Second, when he's moving, get the hell out of the way; when he's doing nothing, move in fast and establish something. After all, what arranger in his right mind would try to fight against Sinatra's voice? Frank undoubtedly brought out my best work. He's stimulating to work with. You have to be right on mettle all the time. The man himself somehow draws everything out of you. He has the same effect on the boys in the band—they know he means business so they pull everything out. Frank and I both have, I think, the same musical aim. We know what we're each doing with a song, what we want the song to say.* "

Count Basie: "*He's just beautiful. To me, he is a pigeon-blood ruby— and that's the greatest ruby there is.*"

Let us dispose of the 1977 crop of benefit shows for the Friends of the Eisenhower Medical Center; for the Institute of Sports Medicine and Athletic Trauma; for the University of Nevada; for Jane Levintraub, Mother of the Year; for Villa Scalabrini at Las Vegas; and for Hubert Humphrey. In June, Sinatra was honored by the State of Israel with the bestowal of its Cultural Award in recognition of his humanitarian efforts and his generous support of Israel's economic, artistic, and cultural development.

A few months after the London week, he was welcomed back to television with his acclaimed ABC-TV special *Sinatra and Friends.* The latter included Tony Bennett (that great singing survivor), Natalie Cole, John Denver, Loretta Lynn, Dean Martin, Robert Merrill, and Leslie Uggams. It was a "singing special" and it dispensed with the often inane dialogue patter of musical variety shows, concentrating instead solely on singing.

They opened with that true classic "Where or When"; a Tony Bennett highlight was "One"; and Sinatra did "Night and Day" among others. One of those friends of many years, Martin, joined Sinatra for a series of club and concert engagements after the television show. It was the first time in many years that the pair had worked together on stage and not for fifteen years had Martin ventured out of the Las Vegas–Reno–Tahoe casino-club circuit.

On the longest day of the year, Sinatra started shooting his first television film. This was the three-hour *Contract on Cherry Street.* Shot on location in New York City, the film depicted Sinatra as a big-city detective inspector battling against a criminal gang. The detective's friend and fellow detective is killed in a shoot-out, and he takes matters into his own hands to try to trap the underworld leaders. The film was shown in the autumn of 1977 on American television and received critical as well as popular approval. This was almost Sinatra's final film.

Martin hosted a television "roast." This meant an evening to laud the Man of the Hour and to express their love for him. The event presented such stars as Gene Kelly, George Burns, Don Rickles, James Stewart, Flip Wilson, Milton Berle, Red Buttons, Rich Little, Peter Falk (Columbo), Redd Foxx, Jack Klugman, Lawanda Page, Ruth Buzzi, Telly Savalas, and Jilly Rizzo.

Sinatra accepted all the tributes with his legendary flair. It was all very American, rather lovable. It could hardly have happened in any other country. Frank and Barbara were clearly a happy couple and she seemed to be having an ideal effect on him. He was happy and still singing well, as he did when he had a stable emotional life. Yet, without the turbulent times, could he have interpreted some of those songs so uniquely?

Before leaving tributes, another one was the dedication of the Frank Sinatra International Student Center at the Mount Scopus campus of the Hebrew University of Jerusalem. As leading American and Israeli government and civic officials looked on, he dedicated the center housing facilities for thousands of students of the university. These students came from America, Australia, Canada, Africa, and Europe. The center stands at the heart of the campus, adjacent to the Harry S. Truman Research Institute of Archaeology, the Martin Buber Center for Adult Study, and the Albert Einstein Institute.

Through the winter of 1977–1978, Sinatra was still pushing himself and his voice for a man sixty-two years old. It came as a shock to learn that he had to abandon part of a week scheduled in Fort Lauderdale, Florida, due to a bad throat infection. On medical advice, he flew down to nearby Barbados for a weeklong spring holiday. After that time, he tended to get bored with a surfeit of inactivity. The Israel trip actually followed this break, and then he insisted on returning to Fort Lauderdale to honor his commitment to fans there. He was back in the harness again. Even though he did it in considerable comfort nowadays, the physical effort was always there.

That September brought him back to London for eight concerts at the Royal Festival Hall. Brian Case, writing then for the *New Musical Express,* offered as apt a definition of Sinatra as may be found anywhere:

> Less mannered than Bing, less limber than Torme, more upright than Martin, more multi-dimensional than Bennett, Como, Haynes, Eckstine and Greco, Sinatra is the greatest singer of the best popular songs of our century, not an accolade you get with Wheaties. You can dislike the image, the ambiance and genre, but if you can't clock the artistry you are Mutt and

Jeff. . . . Where he really came into his own was in the confessional The Gal
That Got Away. It Never Entered My Mind and Angel Eyes were spell-
binding performances: barstool, cigarette smoke, the pipes gravid with
pain. . . . The last one, You and Me, was a masterpiece: we wanted it all,
passion without pain.

I hope it will not be construed as too self-indulgent if I include my
own review of one of these 1978 shows at the Royal Festival Hall. In
covering this particular visit for *The Stage Newspaper* (London), I
fulfilled an ambition of seeing and hearing Sinatra, plus writing a
review of it. This was it, word for word:

The charismatic magic of Frank Sinatra makes him still the entertainer
supreme on any stage. It is an inner incandescence that can glow or blaze.
He becomes each song he sings. He assembles his whole being and projects
it to us complete. He defines our aspirations, articulates our emotions.

Sinatra has just concluded a conqueror's week at the Festival Hall, London. I have seen him on each of his visits here from 1962, and followed his
career since the 1940s. I have watched the mastery expand to its present maturity. Of course he is different from 10, 20, 30 years ago: we all are. Yet today an incredible quality is there, the phrasing, timing, inflection, control
and sheer living spirit. In short, he has never been better.

He sang 20-odd songs in 80 minutes. And while maintaining the mes-
merism, he has added a dimension in depth of acting, an extra expression in
his lyrics—dwelling over such phrases as "made some sense of it" in This
Time.

He imparts an almost personal testimony to Something by George Harrison; Ray Noble's I Hadn't Anyone Till You; Lonely Town by Bernstein;
the gentle Gershwin tune Someone to Watch over Me; and The Gal That
Got Away (Arlen/Gershwin). You and Me has the ingredients of an intelligent new hit and is on his forthcoming LP. Other new numbers, Remember by Elton John, and That's What God Looks Like to Me.

Sinatra is at his most irresistible when handling standards like At Long
Last Love and My Kind of Town. And he summons poignant power to the
Cabaret number Maybe This Time I'll Be Lucky. When he finally comes to
My Way, we are all aware that we have witnessed a performance by the
most exciting entertainer alive.

Remember that this week in London represented literally a couple of lines in the overall story of his life. It is so tempting just to recall every single date. For instance, the following month he was

singing in aid of the World Mercy Fund. Then back to the vault-like Radio City Music Hall for just over a week. In November, he had to skip the last performance of a short spell in Las Vegas. He was worn out but recovered rapidly. He made up for the missed night the next spring when he did a whole week in Las Vegas. He and Barbara went together whenever possible, and before this latter date they had taken a brief break back on their preferred island of Barbados.

Back at work, some singing dates were one-night stands, but more often the engagements ran for a week or so. As at Chicago, Philadelphia, Atlantic City, and Las Vegas, plus charity events like the one for the Juvenile Diabetes Foundation.

Throughout the summer of 1979, Sinatra was busy at recording sessions, working on the ambitious new project of *Trilogy*. This would be a three-LP album arranged by Billy May, Don Costa, and Gordon Jenkins. I will return to this shortly. Then in September he flew over to Egypt to sing under the stars beside the pyramids. The show yielded in excess of a half-million dollars for the Faith and Hope Rehabilitation Center.

More honors! A Humanitarian Award; International Man of the Year Award; Grand Ufficiale dell'Ordine al Merito della Repubblica Italiana, Italy; the Pied Piper Award from the American Society of Composers, Authors, and Publishers; and the Trustee Award from the National Academy of Recording Arts and Sciences. (I am indebted to Nancy Sinatra's book for these facts.) And a trio of benefits somehow squeezed in between all else for the World Mercy Fund, for the Memorial Sloan-Kettering Cancer Center, and for the presidential campaign cause of friend Ronald Reagan, even though he was a Republican! The cancer show raised over a million dollars.

Which brings us to 12 December 1979, Sinatra's sixty-fourth birthday. The occasion was also an excuse to celebrate his forty years in show business. A celebrity audience of around a thousand at Las Vegas saw the show staged in his honor. This was taped and transmitted on network television. Later, of course, it was released on video as number ten in the set of thirteen to celebrate his seventy-fifth birthday.

Before proceeding to the memorable evening itself, here is the text of the telegram that Sinatra received from President Jimmy Carter. The familiar Western Union insignia was in the left-hand corner and it read as follows:

> For those of us who remember a big voice on the radio coming out of a skinny kid from Hoboken, it seems incredible that Frank Sinatra could be celebrating his fortieth anniversary in show business. That most of that time was spent at the top of what, for most, is a mercurial business, is a tribute not only to your great talent but to your growth as an artist and your willingness to master new challenges.
>
> Although I heard you in person for the first time only last month, the sound of your voice has long been a part of my life—as it has for all Americans and for much of the rest of the world. Over the years you have given us all many memories on records and on film. When we recall the great events of our times or the important moments of our individual lives, it is always with the accompaniment of a song—sung your way. Rosalynn joins me in sending best wishes that your next forty years in show business will be as rewarding as these introductory years have been.
>
> Jimmy Carter

That set the scene for the Las Vegas show. Among the performers at Caesar's Palace were Sammy Davis Jr., Dean Martin, Dionne Warwick, Gene Kelly, Tony Bennett, Nancy Sinatra, Lucille Ball, Robert Merrill, and Paul Anka. Among the audience were Cary Grant, Glenn Ford, Orson Welles, Don Rickles, and Milton Berle. Bennett sang "New York, New York," "My Kind of Town," and "I Left My Heart in San Francisco"; Davis sang "The Lady Is a Tramp"; Anka sang "My Way"; and then, last of all, Sinatra came on to offer five numbers, carefully chosen to represent the forty years, though not necessarily from any particular era.

"This is a song that takes me back to the city where everything started for me." And then he launched into "New York, New York."

"It's a fraction hard for me to believe that what started out with Harry James in Times Square has lasted these forty years." That was the cue for "It Was a Very Good Year."

"It's right that I should look ahead as well as back tonight. I don't know how much of the next forty years I'll be given, but . . ." Followed by "The Best Is Yet to Come."

"I'd like to take a special moment to say how honored I am to be among a particular group of men and women here tonight. Because the written word is first and I refer to composers like Sammy Cahn and Jimmy Van Heusen, and conductors I have worked with—Jeff Alexander, Quincy Jones, Don Costa, Billy Falcone. They are my peers and I am honored to be among them. And now I'd like to turn the tables and say how I feel about all of you." And he sang "I've Got You under My Skin."

So to the finale and how Sinatra felt at that memorable moment; he sang "I've Got the World on a String."

What a night!

"New York, New York" reminds me of a special moment in the 1970s. One night I was walking down Broadway on the west side of the street, when the vibrant voice of Sinatra assailed me out of a record store. That was the first time I had heard the theme from "New York, New York," and I stood there on the sidewalk utterly transfixed. It marked one of those moments when a rare conjunction occurs in time, space, and sound. I shall always remember it. Just as I remember the many other occasions when Sinatra has touched me and my life—adding to it a dimension of the transcendental, the eternal, the magic.

How do you top that forty years' celebration show? In the case of Sinatra, by completing his recordings for *Trilogy*—past, present, and future—and also on New Year's Day 1980 by becoming campaign chairman for the National Multiple Sclerosis Society. And on top of that? An incredible five days in Rio de Janeiro, where he was seen live for the first time. The South Americans went wild on the opening four shows, and then for the final concert the venue was moved to the overwhelming Maracana stadium. The audience did not number 1,800 or 18,000, but rather 180,000! And then that June, Carnegie Hall was sold out for a fortnight of Sinatra. The august old building has now passed its century of existence, but this engagement is far and away its record in terms of sheer sales.

The triple-album *Trilogy* was finally released in the spring of 1980. His first new album for six or seven years, it was bold, brilliant, controversial, and challenging. And if for no other side than number three (album 2, side A), I think it would be worth the price. The five titles were "You and Me," "Just the Way You Are," "Something," "MacArthur Park," and "New York, New York." Sinatra at his most expressive and extreme. It was the future (album 3) segment of the three that caused controversial comments, but it was really full of imaginative music and sung most courageously.

Henry Kissinger handed him the Humanitarian Award of Variety Clubs International and among many summer dates was a special benefit in Los Angeles for St. Jude's Children's Research Center. The modest proceeds: $2 million. The organization presented a plaque to Sinatra: "To the legend and the man." Then he was off to Monaco for Grace Kelly and singing in support of muscular dystrophy.

He returned to London in September for two dates, the first at the Royal Festival Hall and the second at the Royal Albert Hall. I saw him three times altogether. My wife, Joyce, and I shared the first time. For the second, my daughter, Francesca, and I sat in the choir seats immediately behind the Festival Hall stage. We were closer to Sinatra than ever before. And we could appreciate the reaction of the audience—facing right in front of us. Francesca had never seen Sinatra before, so that added to my joy. I suppose this must rank as almost the most potent Sinatra show I have ever seen. When he ended with "New York, New York," I felt that nothing could follow such a day. But it did the following week at the Royal Albert Hall. The next morning Joyce and I flew off to Greece on holiday. It seemed somehow right to leave London while Sinatra was still there. A week or so later, we were lounging on a Greek island.

Sinatra was back in New York singing on behalf of Reagan, who was soon to be elected president. Sinatra sang on behalf of Reagan at a Boston benefit in November 1979, then another in February 1980, and then during his nomination at the Detroit convention. At a function two or three years later, Reagan said of Sinatra, "His love of country, his generosity for those less fortunate, make him one of our most remarkable and distinguished Americans."

One last word on the Mafia. I do not propose to dwell on the alleged link, but owing to the persistent stories, I will just repeat Nancy Sinatra quoting Pete Hamill in *New York Magazine* of April 1980: "He is the most investigated American performer since John Wilkes Booth, and although he has never been indicted or convicted of any Mob-connected crime, the connection is part of the legend." Then the return to Las Vegas—inevitably.

Earlier in 1980, Sinatra had made his first feature film for a decade—since *Dirty Dingus Magee*. This one was *The First Deadly Sin* and costarred yet another of his many leading ladies: Faye Dunaway. The combination proved as exciting as might have been anticipated. He had his favored role of detective, but in this story with a wife perhaps terminally ill. The couple produced some emotional moments. The film's premiere in New York was in aid of the worthy charity the Mother Cabrini Medical Center. More benefits that winter meant that large dollops of dollars went to the University of Nevada, St. Jude's Ranch (one of his longstanding charities), and yet another one, the Memorial Sloan-Kettering Cancer Center. Meanwhile, former film star Reagan had been duly elected and who else but Sinatra would be asked to take charge of the traditional inaugural gala. So stupendously successful was this event that forty-eight hours later Ronald and Nancy Reagan were entertaining Frank and Barbara in the White House. With children always in mind, Sinatra and Davis put on a concert in Atlanta to boost funds for investigating several murdered children there. The violent seam in America surfaced again when a man took a shot at Reagan. Sinatra flew straight to the capital to comfort Nancy. Happily, Reagan recovered and Sinatra later performed after a lunch held to honor Nancy in Washington. The two were on very friendly terms and Sinatra spent the weekend in the capital—including Independence Day and Nancy's birthday on 5 July.

Another first-time event for Sinatra came that summer when he visited the African resort of Sun City. A friend of mine, Dorothy Brooker, traveled hundreds of miles and for many hours to be there. The journey from her hometown of Durban to Sun City was no brief excursion. She assured me, however, that it had all been worth the effort—in 90 degrees Fahrenheit weather! Sinatra was making a political and ethical point in appearing there before white and ethnic groups. Quick trips to Buenos Aires and São Paulo were followed by a long booking at the Carnegie Hall with George Shearing, the legendary blind pianist.

The year's album was *Sinatra: She Shot Me Down*. The title number was, of course, the one Nancy had sung so convincingly on one of his earlier television shows. The album had a certain stamp to it, revealing the distillation of a lifetime's experience and emotion—and still those consummate consonants! If only some singers since Sinatra could enunciate. "Thanks for the Memory" was painted with fresh lyrics credited to Leo Robin and Ralph Rainger; "I Loved Her" confirmed that the art of the lyricist was alive; "She Was Boston, I Was Vegas" and "Bang Bang" could be taken as a gesture in Nancy's direction by an admiring and adoring father; and "The Gal That Got Away" evoked potent images of Judy Garland. So he somehow unerringly knitted together passages, people, and places from his life into yet another musical mosaic.

Sinatra: The Man and His Music was the name of the 1981 television special broadcast nationwide by NBC in November. Count Basie and his orchestra accompanied Sinatra in a distinguished transmission. The two men clearly loved one another—musically and platonically—so that the result was really foregone. Nothing to add, except that I have always felt that "Monday Morning Quarterback" has been much undervalued.

I remember that at this precise time I was writing about Sinatra and ended with the following: "He has enriched our existence, given us great joy. As long as Sinatra is still singing, our world is secure. But we are all mortal in the end. Somehow we will him to go on. But how much longer can he?"

Fortunately, the answer was, for a long time. Another dozen years anyway.

CHAPTER FOURTEEN

ON THE ROAD

1982-1998

I n 1982, Frank Sinatra was busier than ever. It would be impossibly repetitious to try to list all his activities. These are about one-tenth of them during that year! He sang with Luciano Pavarotti at Radio City Music Hall and took part in a television program to help the Polish people. This plea for freedom was seen and heard in over forty countries worldwide. Then came another Washington, D.C., appearance at the White House. He and Perry Como entertained at a dinner for the Italian president, who was in America on a state visit.

A clutch of benefits led into midsummer, when he presented "A Legendary Evening with Frank Sinatra" at the new Universal Amphitheater. With half of Hollywood in the audience, Sinatra raised a cool $1 million for charities. After this, he joined Nancy Sinatra for a week or so to form the opening run at the amphitheater.

That took him into August, when he and Barbara flew down to the Dominican Republic for the opening of the fabulous new Santa Domingo arena there. The event was billed as the Concert for the Americas and his supporting band bore another legendary name: Buddy Rich. The drummer did his unique brand of playing in some solo spots. The audience gave Sinatra a phenomenal reception and in return he offered them an hour and a half of vintage singing. It would be hard to choose from a score of numbers. I liked especially "The Gal That Got Away," coupled with "It Never Entered My Mind." Accompanied by Tony Mottola, he then paid his own tribute to Carlos Jobim with "Quiet Night of Quiet Stars." By then, he had introduced Barbara to the audience. A jaunty "I Won't Dance" led into "New York, New York" and a fireworks finale.

After a week's holiday in Europe with the Rainiers, Sinatra had a repeat engagement with Buddy Rich and Charlie Callas in New York for the World Mercy Fund. Callas had also been with Frank and Nancy at the Universal Amphitheater. During another long run at Carnegie Hall, Sinatra heard the news that Grace Kelly had died. It was a blow to him. The pattern of the year wove on: Caesar's Palace, Atlantic City, an American Cancer Fund show, and a weeklong break in Acapulco.

Sinatra always felt the death of a friend or relative very acutely. The latest loss in the New Year of 1983 was the distinguished arranger-conductor Don Costa. Sinatra's response was to write lovingly to Costa's daughter, to go on singing at Caesar's and Lake Tahoe, and perhaps most poignantly, to record one final Costa arrangement entitled "Here's to the Band."

A memorable forty-eight hours for Sinatra came at the end of February 1983. He was one of the stars performing in Los Angeles before Queen Elizabeth and the Duke of Edinburgh. And the next night he was one of their guests aboard the royal yacht *Britannia,* off the California coast. Ronald and Nancy Reagan were naturally among the others invited to dine with the royal couple.

Sinatra was still pursuing painting whenever he had time and needed the diversion it brought him. He had developed a modern abstract style and sold some of his paintings for a local charity near his Palm Springs home. And that spring, too, found him in the open air following another pastime: golf. This was one of a number of celebrity golf matches for charity he enjoyed. These activities were in no way instead of singing, but as well as. Witness dates in Washington, D.C., Atlantic City, New York, and Los Angeles.

Sinatra's final film was scarcely a starring role or vehicle. It was a cameo part in *Cannonball Run II* and he only took it to be with Dean Martin and Sammy Davis Jr., who were in the main parts. Sinatra was cast as the chairman, but I don't think a plot detail is necessary. It is typical of life that such a glittering film career should fizzle out on such an absurd note. That's life!

He had a rare four-week holiday on the French Riviera that summer, interrupting it only once, for a Red Cross charity concert in Monaco. But it was not the same atmosphere without Grace Kelly. Back in the States, a tribute to Sinatra by Variety Clubs International was for all his work over many years. Through his efforts, an entire wing had been added to the Seattle Children's Orthopedic Hospital. In December, he was given the award of the Kennedy Center Honor for Lifetime Achievement. All of his family was invited to the White House in Washington, D.C., for this special occasion. The relevant television show was transmitted from the Kennedy Center in Washington.

While writing this, I just happened to be reading a program of one of his shows and I decided on the spur of the moment to include the introduction as summing up Sinatra:

> There have always been two dominant sides to the complex being known the world over as Frank Sinatra. The public one is, of course, the better known. The singing star who almost alone raised popular music to new critical respectability, coupled with the flamboyant personality of one of the most charismatic stars in the world.
>
> The private one is only known in the most superficial aspects. Mr. Sinatra has always been a concerned citizen. And a generous one. But as best as one can, in this day of the global village, he has tried to keep this part of his life under wraps. Modesty is a word that one doesn't usually associate with Frank Sinatra. But it's one that fits him well to those who know him best.
>
> A recitation of some of his personal charitable endeavours would emphasise this fact. It's awesome. Mr. Sinatra has one motivating force when it comes to a charity—he must believe in the cause. Once he does, he devotes the same drive, energy and personal involvement to it that he does to his professional career.
>
> And if Frank Sinatra can easily be nicknamed "Mr. Humanitarian" for his private contributions, he can also be called "Mr. Show Business" for his professional ones. (This is reproduced courtesy of Theatregraphics, the compilers of the show's program.)

Into 1984 and more of the same: the trio of Sinatra, Davis, and Martin for charity in Los Angeles; and again with Pavarotti in New York; and tucked in almost as a postscript to the season—thirteen nights in New York. At sixty-eight-and a-half years old.

With his marital life on an even keel, Sinatra poured all his extra energy into work. Which he did. Apart from the hundreds of live dates, one of the results this year was a new album created with Quincy Jones: *L.A. Is My Lady.* The title number became a hit and Sinatra swung youthfully in others like "Mack the Knife." Both of these stayed in his concert repertoire for a long time hence. Then in between some support for the Reagans in the forthcoming election, he hopped over to London for six shows.

I heard him twice. On the last night, the huge, horseshoe-shaped hall sparkled with the firework-like flashes of a thousand cameras. Perhaps he blazed a bit less, glowed a little more. But so what? Once he would have sung five fast opening numbers. Now, there were two.

We heard "L.A. Is My Lady" for the first time. He wove melodic embroidery around "Pennies from Heaven." "Luck Be a Lady Tonight" was dispatched with panache. And then his gracious tribute to the many musicians who have shared the Sinatra magic: "Here's to the Band," the Don Costa arrangement. He had mellowed with the years, too. "These Foolish Things" marked a triumph of technique over slightly shortened breath. "New York, New York," those opening bars boomed out again. And the years peeled away as Sinatra mustered all his mastery. An almost perfunctory "Strangers in the Night." "Mack the Knife" reminded us again of the swinging Sinatra who had been a crucial part of our individual lives for however long we had heard him sing. The night ended. The story went on. As it did after literally hundreds of such nights.

While in Europe, Sinatra flew over to Paris and was heard at the Moulin Rouge—shades of Henri de Toulouse-Lautrec. Then on to Vienna—shades of Johann Strauss. The show took place for children's charities and Sinatra picked up the Medal of Honor for Science and Art First Class—the country's top award for a civilian.

Just a selection of whistle-stops that fall and winter: Las Vegas, Chicago, Los Angeles, and New York City (for cerebral palsy). Sinatra was still supporting Reagan and January 1985 brought another Republican inauguration gala. In April, Sinatra was in Japan. Three Tokyo arena concerts were followed by a fourth at a hotel in the capital.

The arena event was later issued as the last in that thirteen-video set for his seventy-fifth birthday five years hence. The Japanese audiences were enthusiastic but better mannered than more vociferous ones elsewhere in the world. But their appreciation could be sensed. Local musicians augmented Sinatra's basic players who invariably traveled with him. And he gave the locals a sincere bravo once or twice. Sinatra was in his seventieth year. No diminution in his powers yet. Sixty-eight minutes of nonstop songs—eighteen in all. "Mack the Knife" had extra lyrics to include Ella Fitzgerald, Bobby Darin, and "Ol' Blue Eyes"—"ain't gonna add nothing new!" At the end, Sinatra had a message in neon across the arena to the effect that eleven years was too long a time to wait to visit such a country and people. He always did his best to bridge every sort of barrier between different countries and cultures. One more date in the Far East was at Hong Kong, the British outpost in its final decades as part of the old empire.

After a long struggle with cancer, Nancy's husband, Hugh, eventually succumbed on 18 August 1985. Frank had been his usual strong self throughout the prolonged ordeal, helping both Hugh and Nancy in any way he could. Frank had known Hugh Lambert before Nancy met him. After Hugh died, Frank and Tina coped with all the arrangements and bound together the three generations—himself, his daughters, and Nancy's children.

It was a measure of Sinatra's resilience that a week or so after all this, he was back singing at two extensive engagements. Four more friends died: Nelson Riddle, Yul Brynner, Orson Welles, and Morton Downey. And amid many more dates, he fit in a charity show for Barbara Sinatra's Children's Center in Palm Springs. To celebrate Sinatra's seventieth birthday in December 1985, EMI released the twenty-album boxed set *Sinatra: The Capitol Years,* with 200-plus numbers! By March 1986, Sinatra had reached number four in the British record charts with "New York, New York." Then on 16 March, too, in the city that never sleeps, he presented Sinatra VI, the sixth concert at Radio City Music Hall in aid of the Memorial Sloan-Kettering Cancer Center. The fund was benefited by the astounding amount of $12 million from these six concerts.

Through 1984–1986, Sinatra went on supporting Reagan. Once again it was the usual fund-raisers from New Jersey to Dallas, and then in January 1985 he sang at the inaugural gala and White House reception. In 1985, he received the Medal of Freedom from Reagan and then in September he sang in support of Nancy Reagan's antidrug campaign benefit. February 1986 saw him celebrating Reagan's seventy-fifth birthday, again at the White House.

Later that year Sinatra was at the opening of the Barbara Sinatra Children's Center at Eisenhower Medical Center. She said, "Frank is our biggest fund-raiser." Barbara herself received a special show when Sinatra and Liza Minnelli joined in the Friars Tribute to her for all the charity work she had undertaken over the years. She and Frank seemed to be a harmonious couple.

From 1986 to 1994, Sinatra undertook what can only be termed an incredible quantity of concerts "on the road." In 1986, for instance, they totaled fifty-eight separate shows. Clearly, I cannot list all of them here. Wedged in among this widespread travel, Gregory Peck gave him the Coachella Valley Humanitarian Award and Sinatra gave his services in song for Mexicans who had suffered from recent earthquake tremors.

While fulfilling a week in Atlantic City, Sinatra had acute pain in his abdomen. He was forced to cancel shows and fly to the Eisenhower Medical Center, Palm Springs, where he was operated on for what transpired to be diverticulitis. He returned to another date, perhaps too soon. But by mid-December he was well enough to participate in the special event celebrating the centenary of Carnegie Hall. Need we wonder what he chose to sing there?

In April 1987, he was back on the road, as if the surgery had never happened. He was officially quoted as feeling "positively fine." He felt on familiar territory before audiences in Las Vegas, Chicago, and Boston. In May, he received the Life Achievement Award from the Los Angeles Chapter of the National Association for the Advancement of Colored People. Then in June he flew to Italy, where he gave six shows, in Palermo, Bari, Rome, Genoa, and Santa Margarita. It rained in Verona at the famous opera amphitheater! Sinatra's father had been born in Palermo, his mother in Genoa, so in a way it was a pilgrimage to his family roots, which were always strong.

September meant conquering Carnegie Hall all over again. He said, "I'm having a fantastic time performing. I'm feeling better than ever. I'm exhilarated." Then on 9 January 1988, he crossed the Pacific to revisit Australia after a long absence. A crowd of some 40,000 people crammed into the Sanctuary Cove, Sydney. "You Will Be My Music," he sang to them. All former acrimony was forgotten on both sides.

In March, Sinatra, Martin, and Davis launched a tour together at Oakland, California. Martin had to cry off early in the circuit of a score of cities, due to his health. But Sinatra and Davis went on with the show—to Houston, Phoenix, Atlanta, Miami, Philadelphia, Boston, Buffalo, Kansas City, Denver. Liza Minnelli joined them to tour as the Ultimate Event. Interspersed were tribute shows to Barbara Sinatra and to George H. W. Bush! At the former of these, Minnelli shared the bill with Sinatra and of course they sang "New York, New York"—where they were.

Catching up on the number of those Sinatra engagements. We left them at fifty-eight in 1986; in 1987 they reached seventy-eight; and in 1988 just over one hundred. So instead of slowing down, he was doing more and more!

When appearing with such stars as Davis and Minnelli, Sinatra did not automatically dominate the shows. Take a typical night or two on The Ultimate Event circuit. The dates: 30 November to 4 December 1988. The place: the Fox Theater, Detroit. Davis sang his heart out in "Music of the Night" from *Phantom of the Opera;* Minnelli brought the whole house to its feet with her intensely imaged "Cabaret." Then Sinatra strolled on. Wisely not trying to upstage them, he took "Where or When" in a pensive, philosophic mode before floating slightly bemused through his other classics. The final medley was, as the show's video later described it, "a testament to these living legends."

In 1989, he returned to Japan, as promised or implied, after a mere four years' lapse this time. He sang in Osaka and Tokyo. A long haul down the Pacific took him back to the southeastern coastline of Australia and Melbourne and then to Sydney. Finally, on his way back he made a two-show stopover at Honolulu.

Pausing only for breath in the States, he headed east across the Atlantic to Holland, Sweden, Norway, Finland, England, France, the Netherlands, West Germany, Austria, and Ireland. In France, Jacques Chirac presented him with the Great Plate of the Bimillenary of Paris. That was one he had never accepted hitherto! That November, Sinatra took part in a television program for the sixtieth year of Sammy Davis Jr. in show business. The beneficiary of receipts from the show was the United Negro College Fund. Appearances in 1989: sixty-three. Six months later, Davis died—one more loss to Sinatra. He was coming to realize that this seemed to be an inescapable side effect of getting older oneself and surviving.

Now it looked like the last time in London. It was billed as "A Summer Affair" at the vast new London Arena in the much bombed (during World War II) East End of the capital. The dates were from 4–8 July 1990. I remember it clearly more than a decade later. The setting was unusual—with the arena built right alongside the docks and backwaters of the Thames. And also I decided not to go. Joyce had been ill all that year and was awaiting a serious operation. She insisted that I should not miss the show, which I ultimately didn't, but I felt guilty at leaving her even for a few hours. Frank Warren presented the five concerts. Sinatra was as superb as ever. For a change, let me just add a note about two of the items in the program. It revealed that he had acquired a radio station in Casa Grande, Arizona. The call letters were KFAS and he said, "I'm looking forward to personal involvement in the station. Perhaps KFAS will play a tune or two of my music once in a while." And the second news item: Sinatra's Sugo da Tavola—sauce for the table—would soon be in select locations throughout America! At home, when word got out that "Frank's cooking tonight," friends called and dropped by. "I love to watch our guests enjoy the meal. . . . that's the real joy of cooking," said Sinatra.

After the show, I recall strolling across a footbridge spanning two banks of a waterway near the London Arena. The reflected moon wobbled in the waters of the Thames. From there it was a mundane bus ride to the nearest underground station. Back to earth. Looking at the other passengers in the tube sitting opposite me, I felt a strange sense of having been lucky to experience something they had missed. Pretentious of me, probably. Then I phoned home to check that Joyce was all right. She was and still is.

Before and after that London week, Sinatra had sung in Stockholm, Sweden, and Glasgow, Scotland. At the latter, he filled the vastness of the Ibrox Park football stadium. Back in the States, the Sinatra sauces went nationwide in three flavors: tomato basil with parmesan cheese, Milano-style marinara, and marinara with mushrooms.

Joyce nearly died in 1990, but by the end of the year she was recuperating though still rather weak. She was quite determined to be fully restored to health by 1991, because that was the year of Sinatra's Jubilee Tour. It started in September at the vibrant Spanish city of Barcelona. The schedule looked punishing, but Sinatra seemed to relish and revel in it. That was the first of the twelve-stop circuit on 16 September. There followed a hectic fortnight before we saw him. This was his European route: Amiens, Belgium (19 September); Milan, Italy (21 September); Montecatina, Italy (23 September); Rome, Italy (24 September); Pompeii, Italy (26 September); Oslo, Norway (28 September); Malmö, Sweden (1 October); and then Paris, France (3 October).

Pompeii and Sinatra. How I wish I had been there! The incomparable sweep of the Bay of Naples makes a magical setting for any event, with the ancient city of Naples at the northwestern end, the splendor of Sorrento to the southeast, the Mediterranean on the southwest, and Mount Vesuvius to the northeast.

I remember Pompeii in three-dimensional terms—both in space and time. Four dimensions, really. With the sea as a backcloth one way and the volcano the other, there could never have been more dramatic drapery for the art of Sinatra. And what would the inhabitants of Pompeii have thought and felt in A.D. 79? We shall never know, as we can never transcend time. All we can do is imagine the night Sinatra sang there; imagine the crowds walking the narrow Roman roads of Pompeii; imagine Sinatra standing amid those same stones that had had been there for 2,000 years . . .

But back to Paris. It was yet another of those bejeweled and bewitched nights at the Palais des Congrès. The first half of the show featured that pleasant pair, Steve Lawrence and Eydie Gorme. Sinatra formed the top of the pyramid of three stars. The Parisians warmed to Sinatra quite quickly, but it was interesting to observe the different opening ovation. It was comparatively restrained compared to most English-speaking nations. In fact, one or two French couples looked at us with a quizzical gaze as we cheered his entrance! I do not have a listing of the songs he sang, but the seventy-five-year-old was still in command. The magic had a Parisian touch to it, and afterward we walked back to an archetypal French hotel off the Champs-Élysées. The Arc de Triomphe was floodlit. So were we! Not April but October in Paris . . . Sinatra left the French capital the next day heading for the last three cities in his tour: Frankfurt, Germany (5 October); The Hague, Netherlands (7 October); and finally three shows in Dublin, Ireland (9–11 October). He was already part way home as his plane took off due westward from one of his favorite countries.

That month saw the publication of the book entitled *A Man and His Art: Frank Sinatra*. This was introduced by his daughter, Tina, and featured his paintings. In her words, art was "another window to his soul." Then in 1992 we saw Sinatra for the final time in Britain. Among audiences were Prime Minister John Major, Gregory Peck, and me! I seem to remember replying in print to a carping criticism that had infuriated me in some newspaper. I pointed out that 50,000 people had seen Sinatra at the Royal Albert Hall and this critic had been the only person finding fault.

That same fall, Tina had turned her hand and talents to producing the formidable television program *Sinatra*. It was a dramatized series with Sinatra portrayed by the young actor Philip Casnoff.

Sinatra spent a lot of 1992 still on the road—entirely in the United States. Then 1993 opened with the next loss of life—that supreme lyricist Sammy Cahn. So strongly did Sinatra feel about the words of each song that he was bound to be affected by the death of a friend like Cahn, who had been so integral a part of Sinatra's singing life.

And then in 1993 Sinatra set out on what proved to be his last appearances in Europe. The first one was in Göteborg, Sweden, on 29 May. There ensued five concerts in Germany: Dortmund (31 May), Hamburg (2 June), Berlin (3 June), Stuttgart (5 June), and Cologne (6 June). It's interesting to note that this final one fell on the anniversary of D-Day.

The first of these German concerts was the one I covered for *The Stage Newspaper* (London). I do not apologize for repeating the review's last line, "Meanwhile, the man and the legend live on."

In retrospect, I suppose I knew we should never see him again. Now as I write, I happen to be exactly the same age as Sinatra was in 1993—seventy-seven. How he did what he did, I have no idea.

In October the *Duets* album appeared—to be hailed by the press and public alike. The novelty here, of course, was that Sinatra's voice was heard alongside a dozen or more famous singers of the time in the form of duets. I cannot say I was mad on the idea, but I suppose Sinatra in any form was better than none at all. Or was it? Certainly the arrangements embraced the vocal score perfectly, but I am still not convinced. I heard it for the first time aboard the cruise liner *Royal Princess,* where I was lecturing at the time. The cruise director knew I loved Sinatra's voice and put it on as a surprise late one night. That certainly gave it a magic touch.

"The Voice Is Eternal" proclaimed the liner notes headline of *Duets.* For the record, I ought to list the thirteen titles and artists: "The Lady Is a Tramp," with Luther Vandross; "What Now My Love," with Aretha Franklin; "I've Got a Crush on You," with Barbara Streisand; "Summer Wind," with Julio Iglesias; "Come Rain or Shine," with Gloria Estefan; "New York, New York," with Tony Bennett; "They Can't Take That Away from Me," with Natalie Cole; "You Make Me Feel So Young," with Charles Aznavour; "Guess I'll Hang My Tears Out to Dry" and "In the Wee Small Hours of the Morning," with Carly Simon; "Witchcraft," with Anita Baker; "I've Got You under My Skin," with Bono; and "All the Way" and "One for My Baby," with Kenny G. That was in October. By November, it had risen to be the number-one album in America. Having sold over a million copies, *Duets* was partly responsible for Sinatra receiving the Legend Award for lifetime achievement at the 1994 Grammy Awards.

Four days after this event, Sinatra had a two-date engagement at the Mosque in Richmond, Virginia. During the second of these evenings, he collapsed on the stage. This proved to be only a temporary setback, though possibly a precursor to events later in the year. Later that same month of March, he was in fine form again in a trio of states: Oklahoma, Illinois, and Nebraska. He went on through the year. Nancy junior was in Chicago to see him for the last time, when he had a triumph that outshone previous occasions there—especially when he went into "My Kind of Town."

That was October 1994. The next month *Duets II* came out. It was the same formula as the first album and featured these fourteen tracks: "For Once in My Life," with Gladys Knight and Stevie Wonder; "Come Fly with Me," with Luis Miguel; "Bewitched," with Patti Labelle; "The Best Is Yet to Come," with Jon Secada; "Moonlight in Vermont," with Linda Ronstadt; "Fly Me to the Moon," with Antonio Carlos Jobim; "Luck Be a Lady," with Chrissie Hyndi; "A Foggy Day," with Willie Nelson; "Where or When," with Steve Lawrence and Eydie Gorme; "Embraceable You," with Lena Horne; "Mack the Knife," with Jimmy Buffett; "How Do You Keep the Music Playing" and "My Funny Valentine," with Lorrie Morgan; "My Kind of Town," with Frank Sinatra Jr.; and "The House I Live In," with Neil Diamond.

How do you keep the music playing? This was always a poignant number when sung by Sinatra. Now at this moment in his life it became more than that. It transcended the title of a song to become a question in the real life of the singer. Sinatra's final pair of concerts took place on 19 and 20 December 1994 in the Fukuoka Dome, Japan. He was seventy-nine years old.

Let us dispose of the statistics for those final eight or nine years on the road. He was seventy years old when we start counting in 1986. These were the number of concerts each year: 1986—58; 1987—78; 1988—100+; 1989—66; 1990—67; 1991—73; 1992—85; 1993—85; and 1994—67.

They added up to an astounding 680 or so.

Although Japan marked the virtual end of his live shows, he did in fact perform one last time before an invited audience at Palm Springs. He was still in superb form, as confirmed by everyone there. The last song was "The Best Is Yet to Come."

That was in February 1995, about the same time that Frank and Barbara moved from Palm Springs to be nearer to their multitude of friends in the Hollywood–Los Angeles environs. Sinatra had always loved Palm Springs—ever since 1954. Now they divided their time between their Malibu Beach home and the other one in a Beverly Hills setting. Sinatra's actual last appearance on any stage came in the month of his eightieth birthday at the Shrine Auditorium. Then in 1997 he received the U.S. Congressional Gold Medal—the very pinnacle of American civilian awards. In January 1998, Nancy was deputized by him to receive the American Music Award of Merit on his behalf.

Frank Sinatra turned eighty-two in December 1997. On 14 May 1998, he was in the Cedars-Sinai Medical Center suffering from an acute heart attack. He died at 10:50 that night. Bill Clinton's envoy presented a Stars and Stripes flag "on behalf of a grateful nation."

And now, throughout the world, the man, the music, and the legend live on. Frank Sinatra, "May you live to be a hundred—and may the last voice you hear be mine."

APPENDIX

SINATRA SONGS, SINGLES, ALBUMS, FILMS, AND SHOWS

SONGS

"Adelaide"

"All of Me"

"All or Nothing at All"

"All the Things You Are"

"All the Way"

"Angel Eyes"

"Anything Goes"

"April in Paris"

"April Played the Fiddle"

"Around the World"

"As Long as There's Music"

"At Long Last Love"

"Autumn in New York"

"Autumn Leaves"

"Bali Ha'i"

"Bang Bang"

"Beautiful Girl"

"Begin the Beguine"

"Bess"

"The Best Is Yet to Come"

"Bewitched"

"Bewitched, Bothered, and Bewildered"

"Bim Bam Baby"

"The Birth of the Blues"

"Black Eyes"

"Blue Skies"

"Brooklyn Bridge"

"Castle Rock"

"C'est Magnifique"

"The Charm of You"

"Cheek to Cheek"

"Chicago"

"Ciribiribin"

"The Coffee Song"

"Come Blow Your Horn"

"Come Dance with Me"

"Come Fly with Me"

"Come Out Come Out Wherever You Are"

"Come Rain or Come Shine"

"Come up to My Place"

"The Continental"

"Count on Me"

"The Curse of an Aching Heart"

"Dancing in the Park"

"Day by Day"

"Day In–Day Out"

"Deep Night"

"Don'cha Go 'Way Mad"

"Don't Worry 'bout Me"

"Downtown"

"East of the Sun"

"Embraceable You"

"Ever Homeward"

"Every Day of My Life"

"Farewell to Love"

"A Fine Romance"

"Fly Me to the Moon"

"A Foggy Day"

"Fools Rush In"

"For Once in My Life"

"From This Moment On"

"The Gal That Got Away"

"Get Happy"

"The Girl from Ipanema"

"Goin' out of My Head"

"A Good Man Is Hard to Find"

"Goodnight Irene"

"Goody Goody"

"Granada"

"Guess I'll Hang My Tears Out to Dry"

"Guys and Dolls"

"Here's That Rainy Day"

"Here's to the Band"

"Hipster Exuberance"

"Home Sick That's All"

"The House I Live In"

"How about You?"

"How Deep Is the Ocean?"

"How Do You Keep the Music Playing"

"I Begged Her"

"I Believe"

"I Believe I'm Gonna Love You"

"I Concentrate on You"

"I Could Have Danced All Night"

"I Couldn't Sleep a Wink
Last Night"

"I Could Write a Book"

"I Cried for You"

"I Didn't Know What Time It
Was"

"I'd Know You Anywhere"

"If"

"I Fall in Love Too Easily"

"If I Could Be with You"

"If I Knew Then"

"If I Steal a Kiss"

"If I Was a Bell"

"I Get Along without You
Very Well"

"I Get a Kick out of You"

"I Guess I'll Have to Dream
the Rest"

"I Hadn't Anyone Till You"

"I Have Dreamed"

"I Haven't Time to Be a
Millionaire"

"I Hear a Rhapsody"

"I'll Be Around"

"I'll Be Seeing You"

"I'll Follow My Secret Heart"

"I'll Never Smile Again"

"I Loved Her"

"I Love My Wife"

"I Love Paris"

"I'm a Fool to Want You"

"Imagination"

"I'm Getting Sentimental
over You"

"I'm Gonna Sit Right Down and
Write Myself a Letter"

"Indian Summer"

"In the Still of the Night"

"In the Wee Small Hours
of the Morning"

"I Saw You First"

"I Sing the Songs"

"It Happened in Monterey"

"It Might as Well Be Spring"

"It Never Entered My Mind"

"It's All Right with Me"

"It's All up to You"

"It's a Lovely Day
Tomorrow"

"It's Always You"

"It's Fate Baby It's Fate"

"It's Nice to Go Trav'ling"

"It Started All Over Again"

"It's the Same Old Dream"

"It Was a Very Good Year"

"I've Got a Crush on You"

"I've Got the World on
a String"

"I've Got You under
My Skin"

"I Won't Dance"

"Just One of Those Things"

"Just the Way You Are"

"Kisses and Tears"

"La ci darem la mano"

"Lady Day"

"The Lady Is a Tramp"

"L.A. Is My Lady"

"The Lamplighter's
Serenade"

"The Last Dance"

"Laura"

"Learnin' the Blues"

"Leroy Brown"

"Let Me Try Again"

"Let's Do It"

"Let's Face the Music
and Dance"

"Let's Take an Old-Fashioned
Walk"

"Little Green Apples"

"A Little Learnin' Is a
Dangerous Thing"

"London by Night"

"Lonely Town"

"Lonesome Man Blues"

"Lonesome Road"

"Love and Marriage"

"Love Is Here to Stay"

"Love Is the Tender Trap"

"A Lovely Way to Spend an
Evening"

"Love Means Love"

"Lover"

"Love's Been Good to Me"

"Luck Be a Lady Tonight"

"MacArthur Park"

"Mack the Knife"

"Makin' Whoopee"

"A Man Alone"

"Maybe This Time I'll Be Lucky"

"Mind If I Make Love to You?"

"Misty"

"Montmartre"

"Moonlight in Vermont"

"The Music Stopped"

"My Blue Heaven"

"My Funny Valentine"

"My Heart Stood Still"

"My Kind of Town"

"My Way"

"Nancy"

"The Nearness of You"

"New Romance"

"New York, New York"

"Night and Day"

"A Nightingale Sang in
Berkeley Square"

"The Night We Called It a Day"

"No One Ever Tells You"

"Not as a Stranger"

"O'Brien to Ryan to Goldberg"

"Oh Look at Me Now"

"Old Devil Moon"

"The Oldest Established . . ."

"Ol' Man River"

"One for My Baby"

"One Love"

"On the Street of Dreams"

"On the Town"

"Our Love Affair"

"Over the Rainbow"

"Peachtree Street"

"Pennies from Heaven"

"Pick Yourself Up"

"Please Be Kind"

"Polka Dots and Moonbeams"

"Prisoner of Love"

"Put Your Dreams Away"

"Quiet Night of Quiet Stars"

"The Right Girl for You"

"Road to Mandalay"

"Satisfy Me One More Time"

"Saturday Night Is the Loneliest
Night of the Week"

"The Second Time Around"

"Send In the Clowns"

"Señorita"

"September in the Rain"

"Shake Down the Stars"

"She's Funny That Way"

"She Was Boston, I Was Vegas"

"Should I"

"Siesta"

"The Sky Fell Down"

"Soliloquy from Carousel"

"Some Enchanted Evening"

"Someone to Watch over Me"

"Some Other Time"

"Something"

"Somethin' Stupid"

"The Song Is You"

*"The Song's Gotta Come
from the Heart"*

"Stardust"

"Stella by Starlight"

"Stormy Weather"

"Strangers in the Night"

"Strictly U.S.A."

"Sue Me"

"The Summer Knows"

"Summer of '42"

"Summer Wind"

"Sweet Louise"

"Take a Chance"

"Taking a Chance on Love"

"Tea for Two"

"The Tender Trap"

"Thanks for the Memory"

"That Old Black Magic"

"That's All"

*"That's What God Looks
Like to Me"*

"There Are Such Things"

"There's a Small Hotel"

"There Used to Be a Ballpark"

*"These Boots Are Made
for Walkin'"*

"These Foolish Things"

*"They Can't Take That Away
from Me"*

*"The Things We Did
Last Summer"*

"This Love of Mine"

"This Time"

"Three Coins in the Fountain"

"Time after Time"

"Too Marvelous for Words"

"Too Romantic"

"Trade Winds"

"Try a Little Tenderness"

"Violets for Your Furs"

"The Way You Look Tonight"

"We Hate to Leave"

"Well Did You Evah?"

"We'll Meet Again"

"What Do I Care for a Dame?"

"What Makes the Sun Set?"

"What Now My Love?"

"What's Wrong with Me?"

"When You're Smiling"

"Where Does Love Begin?"

"Where or When"

"White Christmas"

"Who Wants to Be a Millionaire?"

"Why Don't You See the
Show Again"

"Will Drink the Wine"

"Winners"

"Witchcraft"

"Without a Song"

"Wrap Your Troubles in Dreams"

"Yes Indeedy"

"Yes, Sir, That's My Baby"

"Yesterday"

"You and Me"

"You Are the Sunshine
of My Life"

"You Belong in a Love Song"

"You Do Something to Me"

"You Go to My Head"

"You'll Never Know"

"You Make Me Feel So Young"

"You My Love"

"Young at Heart"

"Young Lovers"

"You're a Sweetheart"

"You're Awful"

"You're Nobody Till Somebody
Loves You"

"You're Sensational"

"You Will Be My Music"

ALBUMS/SINGLES

All Alone

The Best of Ol' Blue Eyes

Cannonball Run II

Close to You

Come Dance with Me

Come Fly with Me

The Concert Sinatra

Cycles

Daybreak

The Days of Wine and Roses

Duets

Duets II

Francis A and Edward K

Great Songs from Great Britain

I Have Dreamed

I Remember Tommy

It Might as Well Be Swing

*A Jolly Christmas with
Frank Sinatra*

L.A. Is My Lady

A Man Alone

Nancy

Nice 'n' Easy

No One Cares

Ol' Blue Eyes Is Back

Only the Lonely

Our Love

Point of No Return

*Portrait of Sinatra: Forty Songs
from the Life of a Man*

Ring-a-Ding-Ding

September of My Years

Sinatra: The Capitol Years

Sinatra: She Shot Me Down

Sinatra and Strings

Sinatra and Swingin' Brass

Sinatra at the Sands

Sinatra Plus

Sinatra's Sinatra

Sinatra Swings

*Some Nice Things I've
Missed*

Songs for Swingin' Lovers

Songs for Young Lovers

Stardust

Strangers in the Night

Street of Dreams

Swing Easy

A Swingin' Affair

Swingin' Session

This Is Sinatra

This Is Sinatra II

Trilogy

Watertown

Wee Small Hours

Where Are You?

*Why Try to Change
Me Now?*

Without a Song

Young at Heart

FILMS

Anchors Aweigh (1945)

Around the World in 80 Days (1956)

Assault on a Queen (1966)

Can-Can (1960)

Cannonball Run II (1983)

Cast a Giant Shadow (1966)

Come Blow Your Horn (1963)

Contract on Cherry Street (1977)

The Detective (1968)

The Devil at Four O'clock (1961)

Dirty Dingus Magee (1970)

Double Dynamite (1951)

The First Deadly Sin (1980)

Four for Texas (1964)

From Here to Eternity (1953)

Guys and Dolls (1955)

Higher and Higher (1943)

High Society (1956)

A Hole in the Head (1959)

The House I Live In (1945)

It Happened in Brooklyn (1947)

Johnny Concho (1956)

The Joker Is Wild (1957)

Kings Go Forth (1958)

The Kissing Bandit (1948)

Lady in Cement (1968)

Las Vegas Nights (1941)

The List of Adrian Messenger (1963)

The Manchurian Candidate (1962)

The Man with the Golden Arm (1955)

Marriage on the Rocks (1965)

Meet Danny Wilson (1951)

Meet Me in Las Vegas (1956)

The Miracle of the Bells (1948)

The Naked Runner (1967)

Never So Few (1959)

None But the Brave (1965)

Not as a Stranger (1955)

Ocean's Eleven (1960)

On the Town (1949)

The Oscar (1966)

Pal Joey (1957)

Pepe (1960)

The Pride and the Passion (1957)

Reveille with Beverly (1943)

The Road to Hong Kong (1962)

Robin and the Seven Hoods (1964)

Sergeants 3 (1962)

Ship Ahoy (1942)

Some Came Running (1958)

Step Lively (1944)

Suddenly (1954)

Take Me Out to the Ball Game/Everybody's Cheering (1949)

The Tender Trap (1955)

That's Entertainment (1974)

Till the Clouds Roll By (1946)

Tony Rome (1967)

Von Ryan's Express (1965)

Young at Heart (1955)

TELEVISION SHOWS

Francis Albert Sinatra Does His Thing (1968)

Frank Sinatra: A Man and His Music (1965)

Frank Sinatra: A Man and His Music Part II (1967)

The Frank Sinatra Show (1950+)

A Man and His Music

A Man and His Music + Ella + Jobim (1967)

Ol' Blue Eyes Is Back (1973)

Sinatra

Sinatra: An American Original (1965)

Sinatra: The Main Event— Madison Square Garden (1974)

Sinatra: The Man and His Music (1981)

Sinatra and Friends

RADIO SHOWS

The Frank Sinatra Show

Your Hit Parade

BIOGRAPHICAL INDEX

FILMOGRAPHICAL INDEX

ABOUT THE AUTHOR

John Frayn Turner was born in Portsmouth, England, and served in the British Royal Navy during the 1940s. He is the internationally known author of twenty-seven books and has been closely associated with all the arts. He was managing editor of five prestigious arts magazines—*Art and Artists, Dance and Dancers, Films and Filming, Music and Musicians*, and *Plays and Players*. Turner was also a critic for *The Stage Newspaper*, London, and a music reviewer for many years.

Author of several books relating to aviation, Turner has had personal associations with aviation for many years. While closely connected with the Royal Air Force as a senior information officer, he made numerous test flights of new aircraft; flew at twice the speed of sound as long ago as 1963; and accompanied the famous RAF Red Arrows aerobatic team.